English in Today's Research World: A Writing Guide

A sequel to *Academic Writing for Graduate Students*
and an advanced text mainly designed for
junior scholars and graduate students
who are not native speakers of English.

John M. Swales and Christine B. Feak

Illustrations by Vivian Scott Hixson

MICHIGAN SERIES IN ENGLISH FOR
ACADEMIC & PROFESSIONAL PURPOSES

Series Editors John M. Swales and Carolyn G. Madden

Ann Arbor
THE UNIVERSITY OF MICHIGAN PRESS

Acknowledgments

The production of this volume has been a multiyear enterprise. In the process, we would like to acknowledge the many people who have made notable contributions. First, we would like to thank all the participants in ELI 520 and 600 over the years (now well into three figures) who have often made incisive comments on the draft materials. We would especially like to thank all those who have been willing to allow their own writings to be used as illustrative materials, whether under their own names or under pseudonyms. We are also grateful to the following former students of the Program in Linguistics for various kinds of assistance, Margaret Luebs and Betty Samraj, and to two current students, Yu-Ying Chang and Stephanie Lindemann. We are particularly indebted to Yu-Ying for her careful and incisive reading of the prefinal manuscript. We are also most appreciative of the efforts made by Chia-Ho Hua from ELI 520, who took valuable time away from his own research work to reformat his poster so that it could be included in this book. The contribution of Deanna Poos deserves special acknowledgment. Deanna spent countless hours painstakingly checking our final revisions against the suggestions made by our copy editor. Her attention to detail without a doubt reduced our stress level during the final weeks of working on this volume. We have also appreciated the support and encouragement of our colleagues at the English Language Institute, Elizabeth Axelson, Carolyn Madden, Susan Reinhart, and Julia Salehzadeh, and that of Kelly Sippell of the University of Michigan Press.

Further afield, we would like to acknowledge the feedback we have received from the following: Diane Belcher and Alan Hirvela of the Ohio State University; Joy Reid of the University of Wyoming; Davide Giannoni of the University of Brescia, Italy; Christine Räisänen of the Chalmers Institute in Gothenberg, Sweden; Anna Mauranen, now of the University of Tampere, Finland; and particularly from David Wilson of the University of Jyväskyla, also in Finland. We would also like to thank those who have allowed us to present and discuss, either individually or together, draft versions of some of the materials contained in this book: the Horace H. Rackham School of Graduate Studies at the University of Michigan, the English Department at Central Michigan University, the University Language Centre at the University of Jyväskyla, and those who were responsible for organizing the following conferences: The ESL Reading-Writing Connections conference at Ohio State in July 1998; the Latin-American conference of university foreign language teachers in Mendoza, Argentina, in April 1999; and the LSP Forum '99 in Prague in September 1999.

Finally, on a more personal level, John would like to express his deep appreciation for the sustaining support of Vi Benner during the long gestation of this volume and for again cheerfully putting up with the messy process of writing a rather complex textbook in a small house. Chris is indebted to Glen, Karl, and Angie for enduring her late nights and countless pasta "dinners." Their love, encouragement, and support have made it possible for her to carry out this and countless other projects.

JMS & CBF
Ann Arbor
June 2000

Remarks to Our Fellow Instructors

We are aware that advanced EAP courses for NNS doctoral students and faculty are slowly being introduced in more and more research universities across the world. As far as we know, most of these courses are being taught by experienced English/ESP specialists or applied linguists with an interest in academic discourse. As a result, we have included a fair amount of illustrative material that easily falls within the "comfort zone" of such specialists. We know, however, from feedback we have received on *Academic Writing for Graduate Students* (*AWG*) that this approach is not without its critics; in particular, there have been some complaints about the amount of applied linguistics material in the *AWG* units devoted to Critiques and Constructing a Research Paper. We hope in this volume to have reached a reasonable compromise between the content expertise of instructors and that of their students. And here we would like to emphasize that our experience has mostly been with classes that attract participants from a very wide range of graduate degree programs. Of course, instructors of disciplinary-specific courses have particular responsibilities to make sure that the general materials offered here are supplemented— and hopefully challenged and corrected—by those drawn from the specific discipline.

Since it is often believed that courses designed for homogeneous groups are intrinsically "better" than general EAP ones, we would like to offer some counterevidence to this belief. We actually prefer that heterogeneity! There are several reasons for this preference. First, since the students are drawn from across the university, they are not directly competing with each other; second, they know that arguments about the accuracy or up-to-dateness of the disciplinary content will have little relevance to the class as a whole. Third, students have an opportunity to compare their own academic experiences and expectations with those of other individuals whom they might not otherwise meet because they come from very different departments. These exchanges can be most enlightening. But most importantly, all participants soon come to realize that what they have most in common is a concern with language, with discourse, and with rhetoric. In our view, these benefits more than counteract the possible disadvantages.

In *English in Today's Research World* (ETRW), we basically employ a genre-based approach with a strong focus on rhetorical consciousness-raising. Indeed, we go further than we did in *AWG* by asking users of this book to conduct mini-analyses of the language and discourse in their fields and to share their findings with others. We introduce research findings about research English wherever appropriate, and again we are "up front" about areas of uncertainty, ignorance, or conflicting findings. It is our experience that our participants react better to such expressions of honesty than to a more stridently prescriptive approach, since these hesitancies seem to accord more closely with their own attitudes about research, scholarship, knowledge, and knowledge claims.

Because we anticipate that most instructors using this book will have considerable expertise in EAP, we only offer the occasional "teaching hint." Certainly, we prefer to think of our fellow practitioners at this level of teaching as being our professional equals. If this book is used as a class text, it would be our fervent hope that the instructor can also find time to see his or her students on an individual basis, if not every week at least a couple of times a month. Class participants are typically engaged in individual writing projects for which they welcome discussion, advice, and suggestions for emendation. Finally, we welcome comments and feedback, most easily addressed to cfeak@umich.edu and jmswales@umich.edu.

Contents

Language Focus Sections

Introduction

This volume is in many ways a follow-up volume to our 1994 textbook *Academic Writing for Graduate Students* (*AWG*), also published by the University of Michigan Press. The *AWG* text, while by no means perfect, has been generally well received by reviewers, instructors, and students, and in the years since publication, we have often been asked for "more." In one sense then, this book is our response to those requests. However, *English in Today's Research World* (*ETRW*) is also an outcome of our experiences with teaching the two most advanced writing courses at the University of Michigan's English Language Institute, ELI 520 (Research Paper Writing) and ELI 600 (Thesis and Dissertation Writing). These courses were initially developed by John a decade ago, but more recently Chris has become increasingly involved in them.

In *ETRW*, then, we essentially continue where we left off in *AWG*. For example, the final activity in the earlier book concerned the writing of Conference Abstracts. In the new volume, the Conference Abstract forms the topic of the first substantive unit (Unit Two). However, there are also some important differences between the two textbooks. Here, attention to more purely linguistic aspects of research English (grammar and vocabulary) has been somewhat reduced, even though 16 Language Focus subsections have been included. This reduction, along with positive reactions from many native speakers of English, has persuaded us that a volume of this kind can, if used judiciously, also be helpful to graduate students who have English as their first language or who are bilingual or bidialectal. For this reason the gloss on the title page reads that this is "an advanced text *mainly* designed for junior scholars and graduate students who are not native speakers of English."

Another difference from *AWG* is that we have dispensed with a separate *Commentary* volume. Since we believe that a greater proportion of users of *English in Today's Research World* will be using it for self-study or individual reference than has been the case with *AWG*, we have provided Notes and Comments (including some "answers") at the end of each unit. Entries such as "(See Note X)" will refer to bibliographic information or to

1

further explanations and/or suggested answers. Users will also come across in the notes the occasional appearance of "Teaching Hints" that, as might be expected, are directed toward classroom instructors.

ETRW is primarily a book about American written research English. In focusing on this variety, we do not want to imply that this targeted discourse is necessarily superior to research writing in other languages such as German, Japanese, or Mandarin or indeed to other anglophone varieties such as British or Australian English. Rather, this focus has been determined by the fact that American English has a dominating position in today's research worlds. In a 1995 survey by W. Wayt Gibbs in *Scientific American* (August, 92–99), it was calculated that about 31 percent of the world's research papers in major journals came from the United States. Japan was a distant second with 8 percent. (See Unit One, Section 1.3 for further discussion of this data.)

We have been able to make some use in preparing these materials of recent developments in corpus linguistics, that is, computerized databases of texts upon which word or phrase searches can be run. We are grateful to Professor Ken Hyland of the City University of Hong Kong for making available to us his corpus of 80 research articles drawn from 10 disciplines. If readers of this volume are interested in spoken academic and research English, they are encouraged to visit the Michigan Corpus of Academic Spoken English (MICASE) Web site at http://www.hti.umich.edu/micase/.

The book is organized in the following manner. After an opening orientation unit entitled "The Positioning of the Research Writer," the remaining units focus on the main types of text that researchers and scholars need to construct. Units Two and Three deal with the Conference Abstract and the Conference Poster, respectively. The next two deal in some detail with the many complexities surrounding the construction of a successful Literature Review. Unit Six then moves on to some salient sections of the Dissertation itself. The final two units switch attention to texts that are not themselves part of a research process product but contribute to it indirectly. Unit Seven covers written communications "in support of the research process," and the final unit is concerned with those communications that operate "in support of a research career." As readers may have realized, we have not given any direct attention to the genre of grant proposals. This is one genre that is already well covered by existing texts, the one most likely to be handled in workshops and seminars, and the one most likely to be supported by technical writers and editors.

Unit One
The Positioning
of the Research Writer

"All right, so it's depressing, obscure, and unreadable. The real question is, will they accept it as a dissertation proposal?"

This opening unit is different from the others since it does not focus on a particular type of text. Instead, we try to "situate" the user of this book as a researcher (or potential researcher). More than anything, this unit provides a set of preliminary activities designed to help you reflect upon sociological, cultural, and rhetorical aspects of research writing. Overall, we are primarily concerned with the "positioning" of the research writer—the means by which he or she creates in writing a credible image as a competent member of the chosen discipline. The unit is divided into two parts. The three sections of Part A are best worked through at the outset. The three sections of Part B can be picked up whenever it seems most appropriate.

The layout of the unit is as follows.

Part A

Part B

Part A

1.1 Writing Processes:
How Effective Are Your Writing Strategies?

We now have a fairly substantial literature describing which non-native speaker (NNS) strategies and attitudes for tackling academic English writing tasks are effective and which are less effective. These conclusions are often supported by individual comments and observations from NNS students and their instructors and advisors. Needless to say, exceptional individuals can successfully "break the rules."

Task One

Here are 10 possible strategies. If you use a particular strategy a lot, score it as 2; if you use that strategy a fair amount, score it as 1; if you don't use it at all or only rarely, score it as 0. Place your scores in the spaces provided.

___ 1. Translating or making use of (human) translators

___ 2. Spending a lot of time on research and then at a much later stage planning to quickly "write it up" from your notes, data sources, or outlines

___ 3. Paying attention to "role-model" papers in your discipline, noticing in particular such matters as how the papers are organized, how phrases are used, and where and why examples or illustrations are provided

___ 4. Having a mentor (either native or non-native speaker) who "knows the ropes" and who can anticipate how a particular piece of research might be received by a particular set of reviewers—and who can thus advise on which journal or conference a piece might be submitted to and why

___ 5. Relying on native-speaker friends (who are not researchers) to help you with phraseology

___ 6. Developing a sense of the anticipated audience, particularly with regard to what needs to be said and what does not

___ 7. Recognizing the need for some stylistic variation and acquiring the linguistic resources to achieve this

___ 8. Constructing an appropriate author "persona," so that the individual statement maker (or makers in co-authored papers) comes across as a member of the disciplinary community

___ 9. Engaging in judicious co-authorship but without becoming dependent on others for the writing of all the "hard parts"

___ 10. Believing that "fixing up the surface" (i.e., getting the small grammar points correct, like use of articles) is essentially all that is required

Self-evaluation

Six strategies (3, 4, 6, 7, 8, and 9) are thought to be good strategies (although some, like 4 and 9, are not always easy to put into effect). These are your positive scores. Put your positive total in the first box below (the maximum will be 12).

Positive Strategy Score

Negative Strategy Score

Four strategies (1, 2, 5, and 10) are thought in most cases to do more harm than good, especially in the long term. These are your negative scores; place their total in the second box above. Subtract their total from the positive total in the first space above and place the result in the box below.

Final Score

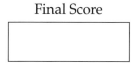

The maximum score is 12: wide use of the six "good" strategies and no use of the four "less good" ones. How did you do?

Any score of 8 or above suggests that you have a good sense of what research writing in English involves and that you are probably on the way to achieving the goal of a fluid and mature style in research English.

Any score of 5 and below suggests that you may be at present rather hesitant about research writing in English. Such a score might suggest that

a. you may be hesitant (perhaps for good reason) about your ability to become an expert writer of research English; and/or

b. you might be too dependent on others; and/or

c. your approach to writing may be too "instrumental"; that is, you think it is just a matter of fixing the surface errors.

What is your reaction to the following excerpt from an interview with Stephen Jay Gould, a paleontologist and author admired for his eloquent writing style?

> **Q:** What does writing do for you?
>
> **A:** It's the best way to organize thoughts and to try and put things in as perfect and as elegant a way as you can. A lot of scientists hate writing. Most scientists love being in the lab and doing the work and when the work is done, they are finished. Writing is a chore. It's something they have to do to get the work out. They do it with resentment. But conceptually to them it is not part of the creative

process. I don't look at it that way at all. When I get the results, I can't wait to write them up. That's the synthesis. It's the exploration of the consequences and the meaning. (See Note 1.)

Task Two

Reflect upon these questions. Send an e-mail response, if possible, to your instructor, be prepared to explain in class, or write a comment in a writing journal, if you are keeping one.

a. What is at least one other strategy that you use?

b. Which of the strategies that you don't use would you most like to develop? And how might you go about developing it?

c. Do you think the six positive strategies listed above apply equally well to all fields? How might they vary in importance for

1. a physicist?
2. a historian?
3. a researcher in public health?
4. an economist?

Which of them is most crucial in your own field?

(See Note 2.)

1.2 Written Products:
Genres, Genre Networks, and Genre Plans

In Section 1.1 we had a first look at research writing processes; in this section we have a first look at research writing (and speaking) products. The category most commonly used today to identify these products is that of *genre* (originally a French word meaning *type*). A genre is a recognized type of communicative event. In today's research world, common genres are a research paper, a grant proposal, an application letter, or a conference paper. As you can see, genres can be written (e.g., a class handout), spoken (e.g., a press interview), or both (e.g., a lecture with a lot of board work). More discussion of the concept of genre is given in Note 3.

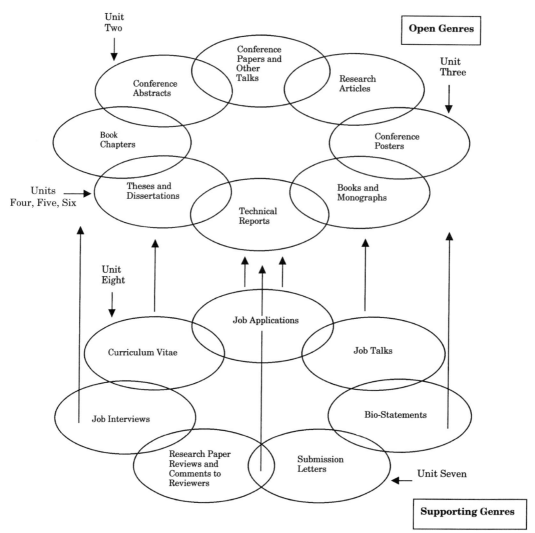

Fig. 1

Genres of importance to the research world form networks. In figure 1, the first network provides a representative sample of "open" genres. By this we mean genres that are public, often published, and easily visible or audible and that typically appear on a researcher's CV. Below this you will see a network of what we call "supporting" genres; that is to say, genres that operate to support or assist an academic or research career. Traditionally, this second class of genres had largely remained "hidden" or "closed" (apart perhaps from grant proposals) and was not in the public domain. Today, more information on help with these genres is

becoming available, especially through the Web, but some of these supporting genres can pose particular problems for junior researchers.

Task Three

The dual network outlined in figure 1 necessarily provides a highly
generalized picture and one perhaps not so well suited to a beginning
researcher. How would you want to modify or simplify the figure to suit
your circumstances? Are there additional genres that you might want to
add? (See Note 4.)

During the final years of your graduate study and the beginning of
your research career you will likely be involved in the production of
many genres—seminar talks, a dissertation, research papers, or grant proposals, for example. Of course, the length of time to produce these genres
will vary quite a lot. A dissertation can take years, while writing a letter of
recommendation for a student might take only an hour or two. Gauging
the amount of time you need to complete important writing or speaking
tasks and knowing your deadlines can help you successfully complete
them. One way to get a handle on what lies ahead is to prepare a genre
planner—a diagram or an outline of work to be completed over the
course of a year. This can provide a useful road map for your academic
future and also help you prepare for what will be ahead of you.

Task Four

Look over the two sample genre planners in figures 2 and 3, the first from
a graduate student in film and the second by a postdoctoral fellow in
electrical engineering. With a partner, if possible, answer the questions
that follow.

1. Do you think they have planned their time well?
2. How do their academic lives over 12 months compare with yours (and
   your partner's)?
3. Plan B from the postdoc strikes us as very ambitious and may perhaps
   be more an example of wishful thinking than of realistic goals. What
   do you think?

January Complete research for film presentation; prepare the talk	**July** Research in Spain; begin film paper on fictional modes of representing reality in Spain
February Present film talk to departmental audience	**August** Write up report on summer research
March Prepare summer research grant proposal	**September** Prepare grant proposal for "Spanish-speaking cultures" film series
Begin research for Kentucky conference paper in June	Revise Chapter One; revise film paper
April Begin and (hopefully) finish writing first chapter of dissertation	**October** Begin writing second chapter of dissertation
May Write prospectus for dissertation	**November** Prepare abstract for NYU film conference; revise film paper
June No major writing; focus on research	**December** Revise Chapter Two of dissertation

Fig. 2. Genre planner A (graduate student in film)

Task Five

Prepare a genre planner to cover your next 12 months.

1.3 "Research Writer Positioning": Different Approaches to the Same Data

In table 1.1 you will find some data on where research articles come from, in terms of countries of origin. We believe that these figures should be intrinsically interesting for users of this book. However, we also use this data to make a different point. The three very different commentaries that follow the table are designed to show that academic writers have a large number of options even when faced with the task of discussing basic quantitative information. The approach adopted and how well it is expressed in words are part of that "research writer positioning" (RWP) that we have already mentioned.

FALL		SPRING		SUMMER	
September	Prepare status report on laser fabrication for advisor Prepare short talk on new mask design for group Give talk at group meeting	January	Prepare MBE[b] poster for EE[c] department conference Research	May	Prepare talks for summer professional development workshops Prepare outlines and handouts for workshops Research
October	Prepare abstract for IEEE[a] conference (in March) based on research group presentation Group meeting to discuss abstract	February	Prepare presentation for IEEE conference Revise poster and submit poster abstract to Applied Physics Conference	June	Workshop presentations first two weeks Research
November	Begin writing up results of work on three-terminal laser for submission to *Applied Physics Letters* Continue analyzing results	March	IEEE conference presentation Revise *Applied Physics Letters* article—if not rejected Work with advisor on NSF grant proposal	July	Workshop presentations first two weeks Poster presentation last week Prepare my part of annual research report for group
December	Finish draft of *Applied Physics Letters* article and submit	April	Finish NSF proposal by the 30th Research	August	Vacation first two weeks Update CV[d]

[a] Institute for Electronic and Electrical Engineers
[b] Molecular beam epitaxy
[c] Electrical engineering
[d] See Unit Eight.

Fig. 3. Genre planner B (postdoctoral fellow in electrical engineering)

TABLE 1.1.   Share of Mainstream Journal Articles

Country	% of Total	Country	% of Total
U.S.	30.817	China	1.339
Japan	8.244	Israel	1.074
U.K.	7.924	Belgium	1.059
Germany	7.184	Denmark	0.962
France	5.653	Poland	0.913
Canada	4.302	Finland	0.793
Russia	4.092	Austria	0.652
Italy	3.394	Brazil	0.646
Netherlands	2.283	Ukraine	0.578
Australia	2.152	Norway	0.569
Spain	2.028	South Korea	0.546
Sweden	1.841	New Zealand	0.426
India	1.643	South Africa	0.415
Switzerland	1.640	Greece	0.411

Source: Adapted from "Lost science in the Third World," by W. Wayt Gibbs, *Scientific American,* August 1995, 92.

Task Six

Examine table 1.1, which is based on the 1994 Science Citation Index. Then read the three commentaries (sentence numbers have been added for ease of reference) and answer the questions that follow. (See Note 5.)

Text A

[1]The percentages are derived from the papers published in 1994 by approximately 3,300 scientific journals included in the Science Citation Index (SCI). [2]The 28 countries listed are those countries that produced more than 0.4% of the world's total output. [3]It is significant that a number of countries with large university systems still fall below the 0.4% cut-off point. [4]These include Mexico, Egypt, Turkey, Nigeria, and Venezuela. [5]Overall, the dominating position of the U.S. is striking, with 30% of the total output of scientific research papers. [6]None of the next group (Japan, U.K., Germany, and France) reaches double figures. [7]The world's two most populous countries, India and China, rank 13th and 15th respectively. [8]It seems clear from the table that scientific productivity is probably even more unevenly distributed around the world than average per capita income.

Text B

[1]The figures in the table are based on the small percentage of the world's scientific journals that is indexed by the SCI. [2]This commercial database, which is located in Philadelphia, is strongly biased toward English-language journals and those which are located in the most advanced countries in the Northern Hemisphere, because the SCI's selection criteria emphasize such factors as citational impact and regularity of publication. [3]The percentages illustrated in the table, therefore, do not reflect the quality and quantity of the scientific research being carried out internationally. [4]Telling evidence of this can be seen in the low rankings and low percentages given for India (13th, 1.6% of the total) and China (15th, 1.3% of the total), even though both these countries are known for their strong research traditions, especially in theoretical areas.

Text C

[1]The percentages given in table 1.1 are open to two different interpretations. [2]At first sight they would seem to indicate that the U.S. has an overwhelmingly dominating position in terms of research productivity as measured by publications in mainstream journals. [3]However, a somewhat different perspective emerges when we consider research article production in relation to national populations. [4]As a Finnish researcher, working in a country with a total population of only about five million, I can note that the percentage for Finland is only about 0.8. [5]However, the population of the U.S. is about fifty times larger than that of Finland, and a simple calculation shows that in terms of journal article production *per capita*, Finland is actually more productive than the U.S.

In Unit Four of *AWG* we offered a number of suggestions for data commentaries. Assess each text in terms of those suggestions. In each case, "grade" each text as "very good" (✓) or "could be improved" (✓–). Work with a partner if possible.

1. Use suitable *locating phrases* ("As shown in Table 5") as and when necessary.

   Text A ___   Text B ___   Text C ___

2. Concentrate on the key or most interesting results.

   Text A ___   Text B ___   Text C ___

3. "Round" very precise figures. (In this case, do not write "30.817" but "30.8" or "nearly 31%.")

Text A ___　　　　　Text B ___　　　　　Text C ___

4. Open with general comments; close, if necessary, by pointing out problems with the data set.

Text A ___　　　　　Text B ___　　　　　Text C ___

5. Do not read too much into the data and make claims that are hard to justify.

Text A ___　　　　　Text B ___　　　　　Text C ___

6. Write enough commentary to demonstrate that you have interesting things to say; do not write so much that you bore your audience.

Text A ___　　　　　Text B ___　　　　　Text C ___

7. How would you briefly characterize the approach (and RWP) of each text?

8. Which text would you prefer to have written and why?

(See Note 6.)

Task Seven

Do one of the following.

a. Write a new commentary for table 1.1. Feel free to use parts of Texts A, B, or C as seems appropriate, adding any further commentary that you wish.

b. Write a commentary on the following two charts. (*Science*, as you may know, is the leading U.S. interdisciplinary scientific journal.)

(See Note 7.)

Articles Accepted by Science

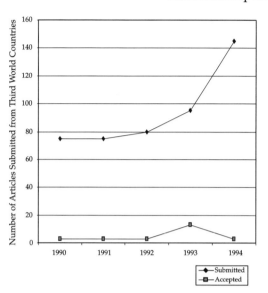

Fig. 4. Articles submitted from Third World countries and acceptances. (Data from "Lost science in the Third World," by W. Wayt Gibbs, *Scientific American* [August 1995]: 92–99.)

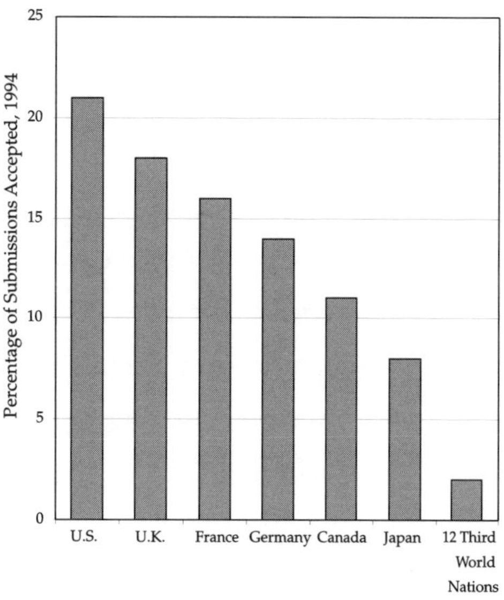

Fig. 5. The percentage of articles accepted by *Science* in 1994. (Data from "Lost science in the Third World," by W. Wayt Gibbs, *Scientific American* [August 1995]: 92–99.)

Part B

1.4 Where Do You Stand?
Cross-cultural Differences in Research Languages

In recent years, there has been considerable research interest in tracing similarities and differences in research languages. (See Note 8.) Because of the dominating position of academic English and because of the wish of many people to acquire this variety of the language, the great majority of studies to date have compared some other academic language with the English one. These languages include Arabic, Chinese, Finnish, French, German, Japanese, Korean, Malay, Polish, Spanish, and Swedish. Simplifying somewhat, the overall conclusions point in one basic direction: research English, especially American research English, has a number of features that place it toward one end of a number of continua. These features are listed below.

American academic English, in comparison to other research languages, has been said to

___ 1. be more explicit about its structure and purposes

___ 2. be less tolerant of asides or digressions

___ 3. use fairly short sentences with less complicated grammar

___ 4. have stricter conventions for subsections and their titles

___ 5. be more loaded with citations

___ 6. rely more on recent citations

___ 7. have longer paragraphs in terms of number of words

___ 8. point more explicitly to "gaps" or "weaknesses" in the previous research

___ 9. use more sentence connectors (words like *however*)

___ 10. place the responsibility for clarity and understanding on the writer rather than the reader

Task Eight

Reflect upon your own first academic language. Place a check mark (✓) before those items in the preceding list that reflect differences between academic writing in your native language and American academic English. If you do not think a particular difference holds for your language, do not check it.

Are there other differences that you think ought to be mentioned?

If you are writing for an American audience how much do you think you need to adapt to an American style? Do you think you need to fully "Americanize" your writing, or can you preserve something of your own academic culture in your academic writing? (See Note 9.)

1.5 Investigating Style:
Informal Elements in Academic Writing

A fully formal research writing style was standard in most disciplines until fairly recently. This style was associated with objectivity, the experimental method, and the disappearance of the researcher from the text. For example, in 1934 Albert Einstein wrote that there was no place for *I* in scientific writing. (See Note 10.) Although this style continues to predominate in certain fields, in others the need for strict formality has been relaxed. This formal academic style has a number of typical features: the avoidance of the first and second person pronouns *I* and *you*, of contractions such as *isn't*, and of colloquial expressions such as *pretty nice*. This style favors the use of the passive and of vocabulary of Latin, Greek, or French origin, choosing, for example, *eliminate* over *get rid of*.

Chang and Swales (1999) investigated the occurrence of certain "informal" elements in research articles from three fields: statistics (science), linguistics (social science), and philosophy (arts and humanities). (See Note 11.) Ten recent articles were selected from each field for analysis. Among the features they investigated in the main texts of the 30 articles (i.e., notes and footnotes were excluded) were the following.

1. The use of imperatives ("Now consider this case.")
2. The use of *I / my / me*
3. Sentences beginning with *but*
4. Sentences beginning with *and*
5. Direct questions ("Is that correct?")
6. Verb contractions (*won't, isn't*)

As you may have guessed, such uses are often frowned on in style guides for academic and research writing. Now take a look at table 1.2, which presents a brief summary of the researchers' results.

TABLE 1.2.   Occurrences of Six Informal Elements in 30 Research Articles

Element	Number of Occurrences	Average per Paper	Number of Authors Using Element
Imperatives	639	21.3	30
I / my / me	1,020	34.0	23
Initial *but*	349	11.6	23
Initial *and*	137	4.6	17
Direct questions	224	7.5	17
Verb contractions	92	3.1	11

Source: Adapted from Yu-Ying Chang and John M. Swales, "Informal elements in English academic writing: Threats or opportunities for advanced non-native speakers?" in *Writing: Texts, processes, and practices*, edited by C. N. Candlin and K. Hyland (London: Longman, 1999).

Further Notes

1. All writers used one or more imperatives, but the philosophers used the least.

2. All the philosophers and all but one of the linguists used *I / my / me,* but only 4 out of 10 statisticians did.

3. There was only 1 sentence beginning with *and* in the 10 statistics papers, but there were 120 such sentences in philosophy!

4. None of the statisticians used verb contractions.

Task Nine

Take a photocopy of what you consider to be a good but typical paper from your own specialized area and highlight or underline all occurrences of the six informal elements that you find. However, exclude all material from your analysis that is quoted from other authors or comes from interviews, speeches, or transcripts. Count and tabulate your findings. (You may need to count some bits of language more than once; e.g., "But let me explain" would count as an initial *but,* as an imperative, and as a first person singular use.) Then list and count the number of each different verb you found in the imperative (if any). If you are in a class, e-mail your instructor your findings.

The purpose of this task is to train your attention on the stylistic characteristics of writing in your own field. In effect, it asks you to skim for language rather than for content. Technically, the outcome of this process is known as *rhetorical consciousness-raising.*

In general, how does your field compare to those in table 1.2 and in the Further Notes? What explanations for any differences occur to you?

Which of these elements would you feel comfortable using yourself?

Have you come across or been told other prescriptive rules such as "never start a sentence with *however* as the first word," or "never use *which* to introduce a defining or restrictive relative clause"? Do you think such rules have validity? Have you been told things about academic writing in your own native language that wouldn't work in English?

(See Note 12.)

Chang and Swales (1999) went on to investigate how a number of international graduate students and visiting scholars reacted to the "opportunities" provided by such informal elements. With one exception, a Thai doctoral student in architecture writing a very "humanistic" dissertation, the informants thought having these options somewhat available was in fact more of a problem than a solution. In essence, they argued that developing a consistent formal style was hard enough. They did not want to have to decide whether using *I* was "natural" or "egocentric," or whether using an imperative was "crisp and concise" or "bossy," or when it might be appropriate to begin a sentence with *and*. However, subtle pressure to adopt a new informal way of writing might be stronger in some areas than in others. For example, this pressure may arise for qualitative research in education but not for quantitative research.

Task Ten

Below are some comments from the informants. From your perspective, decide whether you agree or disagree and why. Then, if possible, discuss your reactions with a partner.

Imperatives

1. In reference to figures (e.g., See Table 1), it is commonly used. Otherwise, I think it is uncommon. I often use it only in references, never in the full text. I feel it is risky to use it in text. (Visiting medical scholar from Japan)

I / My / Me

2. One good thing of having co-authors is that I can use *we* as many times as I want. (Korean Ph.D. student in psychology)

3. Only usable for senior scholars (Chinese Ph.D. student in chemistry)

Initial *and* and *but*

4. If I used these, my advisor would edit them out! (Chinese Ph.D. student in science)

5. Although I am not sure it is grammatically correct, since many authors use it effectively, I feel it is quite tempting to follow. (Thai Ph.D. student in architecture)

Direct Questions

6. I don't think so. . . . I think the literature in my field is very, very formal, very old-style, nothing elaborated. (Thai Ph.D. student in engineering)

7. I have never used it. However, I would like to try using it because the impact is strong. (Visiting medical scholar from Japan)

8. Although direct question is sometimes avoided, it can give a strong message. (Master's student in urban planning from Korea)

1.6 Academic Names, Autobiography, and Bio-data

We close this opening unit with a few reflections on and observations about the names we use on the title pages of our manuscripts or when we appear in print and on how we describe ourselves. (The CV is discussed in Unit Eight.)

1. Some academic names are much more common than others. There were 23 participants in John's research paper writing class for fall 1999. He looked their last names up in the 1998 Social Science Citation Index. For five of the class there were more than one hundred author names listed (Lee, Wu, Liu, Chang, and Huang). Eight others reached double figures (Zhou, Tsai, Shin, Sim, Nam, Saeto, Zeng, Sakamoto). A further four produced single figures (Luong, Swales, Masuda, Kitajima), and the final six names were unlisted (Chairatananon, Klangsin, Putthividya, Quartey, Tsuneta, Yook).

   Comments? Why not look your last name up in an appropriate index (SCI, SSCI, MEDLINE, etc.)? How many authors with your last name are already there? Are there people with the same initials as well?

2. Although "John" and "Christine" are common given names, by lucky accident neither of us has a common family name.

   Chris has been able to keep her full academic name (Christine B. Feak) throughout her writing and speaking career. However, her master's thesis from Cornell was written by a certain "Christine A. Beer Feak." As you may have guessed, Beer was her maiden name.

   Until about 1987, John's authorship name was "John Swales"; thereafter it has been "John M. Swales." There were, in fact, two reasons for this change. One was simply a wish to adopt standard U.S.

practice soon after he moved to America. The other had to do with the Social Science Citation Index. When he began to appear in this publication, which uses initials, not first names, he noticed some confusion between himself and another "J. Swales," apparently a medical psychologist. So he added the "M."

Although changing one's academic name by adding a middle initial "solves" one problem, it causes another bibliographic one, especially for published scholars. What might this be? (See Note 13.)

3. Some people, especially in North America, have two forms of their name. One they use in all social and educational contexts, but another one is just for publications (and usually for CVs and presentations). John has a friend who is a professor in the School of Art. She is universally known as "Sherry Smith," but her official academic name is "Sherril A. Smith." A Korean-American doctoral student in linguistics at Michigan was always known as "Sunny Hyon," but the name on her dissertation is "Sung-hee Hyon." What are the advantages and disadvantages of this?

    Academic names are typically more formal than individuals' everyday names or their nicknames. But not always. A well-known researcher in our field is always known in person and in print as "Tony Dudley-Evans," never "Anthony." Another is always known as "Liz Hamp-Lyons," never "Elizabeth."

Do you know of any other similar counter-examples?

4. Some people have names that are very long (such as names of Sanskrit origin in Thailand or in parts of India), have many parts (Islamic names such as Mohammed Abdulla Al-Kikhya Al-Sennari), are hard to spell (Theresa Rohlck), or are hard for anglophones to pronounce. (Indeed there is a long tradition in the United States of immigrants changing their names.) Further, a number of Asians choose to adopt an English name or at least an anglicized version of their first name. Some years ago there was a Chinese economics student in the dissertation writing class who was always known as Hsin. When he obtained an assistant professor position at another university, he changed his name to Gene. It looks as though a new academic life can mean a new academic name.

Do you have opinions about such simplifications or anglicizations? (See Note 14.)

5. The name problem, at least in the West, can be even more complicated for women, especially for those who change their marital status during their academic careers. Consider this extract.

> But the journals are littered with the names women have used and discarded: M. F. Whiteman eventually disclosed her gender and became Marcia Farr Whiteman; this was apparently a precursor to the dropping of Mr. Whiteman, and she has now long been known as Marcia Farr. The person I met in 1980 as Fran Hinofotis became Frances Butler Hinofotis, and has since become Frances Butler. Similarly, Joan Eisterhold became Joan Carson Eisterhold and then . . . Joan Carson. These are all stories of men met, loved, and lost or left behind. (Reprinted from *English for Specific Purposes,* 16, L. Hamp-Lyons, "More thoughts on academic naming practices, 73–74, [1997], with permission from Elsevier Science)

Are name changes as a result of one's marital status a problem only for the English-speaking world? Do women ever change names in your culture?

So what is your confirmed academic name?

Task Eleven

Now that you have a confirmed academic name, you can put it to use in one of those short bio-data statements that might accompany a grant application or journal article. But before you do, take a look at the following draft bio-data statement for a travel grant application written by one of our students. What advice might you give her before she starts the second draft? A CV (see Unit Eight) will accompany the application.

> As an undergraduate student in botany at the University of Illinois I developed a keen interest in the study of the systematics and biogeography of the tropical plant family Malpighiaceae and had the opportunity to work in Dr. Lindquist's lab. My laboratory experience gave me a taste of what it would be like to be a botanist, and after one year as an assistant at the University Botany Field Station I began my graduate program at the University of Michigan. Since starting the program I have been a teaching assistant for Introduction to Botany during the fall and winter terms. For two summers, under the guidance of Dr. Gupta, I have continued my research on the tropical plant family Malpighiaceae, the results

of which Dr. Gupta and I are presenting in the form of a poster for presentation at the 10th Annual Conference on Biological Diversity. In addition to this presentation, Dr. Gupta and I are also working on a paper based on our research, which we hope will eventually be published. Recently I have become more interested in historic aspects of systematic botany, particularly the development of classification systems in Linnean and pre-Linnean periods, an interest that I plan to link to my work on Malpighiaceae. I am now in my third year and will be finishing my required coursework this semester. (223 words)

Task Twelve

Write your own 200 to 250-word bio-statement.

Task Thirteen

We are often asked to provide as part of a conference program or as part of an article a short 50-word bio-statement. A colleague comes to you and says, "I have to write one of those short bio-data statements; please help me." You reply, "Well, remind me of what I need to know." This is the response.

> As you know my name is Dushy or Dushyanthi Gunesekara, and I come from Sri Lanka, where I have a lectureship at Colombo University. I took a leave of absence to come to this university to do a Ph.D. in history because they gave me a teaching assistantship. I've been here for three years now, and my main research is on the origins of ethnic conflict in my country, particularly during the British colonial occupation of what was then Ceylon. I work mostly with Bill Johnson, who is a leading authority on the recent history of the subcontinent. We have an article coming out next year in the *Journal of Oriental History,* and it's this journal that wants the bio-data. That'll be my first quote-unquote real publication, although I have had several pieces in local journals such as the *Sri Lanka Historical Gazette.* I have got a travel grant to go to London next year to do archival research. I am fluent in both Sinhala and Tamil.
>
> Is this the kind of thing you want?

Highlight the parts of this account that you would keep. What further questions would you want to ask?

Task Fourteen

Look at this statement written by a former student and answer the questions that follow. It is written in the appropriate style but is not perfect in other ways.

> Y. S. Lee is currently a GSRA in the Department of Mechanical Engineering and working on the mechanical behaviors of spot welding. He received his BS in mechanics from Beijing University and MS from the Chinese Academy of Sciences. His major research interests are solid mechanics and spot welding. (48 words)

1. Lee began his statement with what he is currently doing, but there are some major information gaps. Can you find them? How can they be corrected?

2. Notice also that Lee uses the word *currently*. Let's assume this bio-data will be attached to a published paper. Considering that there may be a time lag between the time of submission and time of publication (during which time he may actually finish his degree), do you think this is a good strategy?

3. Rather than beginning with where he is now, Lee could have started by describing his educational history. What are the possible advantages or disadvantages of this type of beginning?

4. What are the advantages of stating several research interests as opposed to perhaps only one?

5. Here are some other kinds of information that our students have included in their bio-data statements. Which of these should be included? And in what circumstances?

Names of journals you have published in
Special fellowships or funding
Names of well-known people in the field you have collaborated with

Can you think of other kinds of information that you might include? (See Note 15.)

Now here is a revised version of Lee's bio-data statement. What changes have been made?

> Y. S. Lee received his master's degree from the Chinese Academy of Sciences in 2000. He is a graduate research assistant in mechanical engineering at the University of Michigan. His major research interests include solid mechanics and spot welding, the latter of which is the focus of his forthcoming Ph.D. (50 words)

Now write your own bio-data summary (or rewrite that of Ms. Gunesekara). But before actually writing your own bio-data statement, read through a few of them in journals in your field. What kind of information is typically included? How is it organized?

1.7 Notes and Comments for Unit One

"Welcome to the notes. There is quite a lot going on here, and you won't want to miss it." (See Unit Four, Note 2.) Here we provide possible answers to those tasks that are more closed ended, references and citations as needed, further remarks on the linguistic characteristics of research English, and a few other miscellaneous entries. The notes and comments have been designed with both the independent student and the class instructor in mind. For the latter in particular we have occasionally added "Teaching Hints"; these are italicized and placed within parentheses.

Note 1

Dreifus, C. 1999. Primordial beasts, creationists, and the mighty Yankees. *New York Times,* December 31.

Note 2 (sample responses for Task Two)

a. One further strategy apparently common among our class participants is to keep a "word book"—a notebook for writing down useful or helpful phrases and expressions that the reader would like to incorporate into his or her own writing.

b. Many junior graduate students stress the importance of finding a mentor (Strategy 4). Many international students, especially when beginning their degree programs, look for mentors among their co-nationals, especially students or researchers more senior to them. Often these "informal" arrangements work very well, particularly with such important matters as choosing an advisor.

c. We don't offer complete answers here, but clearly collaboration (Strategy 9) may be harder for the historian than the physicist. On the other hand, stylistic development (Strategies 7 and 8) will be more important for the historian than for the other three.

Note 3

Names that refer only to the *means* of communication, such as a phone call or a letter, are not names of genres since they do not sufficiently indicate *communicative purpose.* However, a solicitation phone call or an application letter would be specific enough to be a genre. Genres are part of the history of a culture and are always evolving. That said, particular instances of a genre typically share similarities in organization (the same kinds of beginnings, middles, and ends) as well as similarities in style and content. Genres are increasingly common in modern professional life because they are "a means of getting jobs done when language is used to accomplish them." This powerful comment comes from Professor James Martin of the University of Sydney, who has been the leading proponent of a genre-based approach to language and literacy in Australian schools. The full reference is as follows.

Martin, J. R. 1985. Process and text: Two aspects of human semiosis. In *Systemic perspectives on discourse,* edited by J. D. Benson and W. S. Greaves. Norwood, NJ: Ablex, 248–74.

Note 4 (sample response for Task Three)

Master's students, in particular, are likely to be working within a simpler and more restricted genre network and one that will likely include such "school or pedagogical genres" as the term paper, the essay, or the lab report.

(Task Five Teaching Hint: Depending on the size of the class have one or two students present their genre plans each week either on an overhead or in a handout. Stress that you do not want every possible detail. Ask for comments at the end of the short oral presentations.)

Note 5

The source for the table is the following article.

Gibbs, W. Wayt. 1995. Lost science in the Third World. *Scientific American* (August): 92–99.

Figures 5 and 6 have also been taken from this source.

Note 6 (sample responses for Task Six)

1. Text A has no location statement and so could be questioned in this regard. Both B and C are fine.

2. Text A does this well, we think, and interestingly includes comments about countries missing from the table! Text B leaves it up to the reader to understand the table (except for the references to India and China). Perhaps a bit risky? Similar comments can be made about Text C.

3. All three texts seem to do this OK. Should it be "31%" in Text A?

4. Text A moves from general to specific, and its author has no problems with the data set. Text B *opens* with criticism; Text C gets to an alternative view rather quickly.

5. We think in each case the writer-researchers have adopted an interesting "position" for themselves; each seems to have some intelligent points to make.

6. Given their "unusual take" on the data, Texts B and C could have been a little longer.

7. Text A is basically an interpretation of the table, although in sentences 3 and 4, the author can (as we have seen) cleverly note which countries are not there! There is some nice highlighting as well as a speculative final sentence. Throughout the data is assumed to be accurate and not misleading in any way.

    Text B is very different, since it challenges all the assumptions built into the development of the data. It is perhaps rather more fluently written than Text A, but it needs to be because it offers persuasive argumentation rather than a summative interpretation. The problem remains, however, that the author of Text B does not quite know how to deal with the data. What *would* be a reasonable figure for the share of a wider pool of journal articles coming from the United States?

    Text C offers a re-analysis of the data and does so from the announced perspective of a researcher from a small country. Perhaps the writer should have provided the reader with the outcome of the simple calculation, showing that if Finland had been as populous as the United States its proportion would have risen to 40 percent (other things being equal).

8. Since this is an open-ended question, no answer can be given.

Note 7

Notice that in table 1.1 and in figure 5 country names are given in "legend format," while in the actual commentary those that refer to federations of some kind will need the definite article (the U.S., the U.K., the former Soviet Union, the European Community).

Note 8

The most complete scholarly survey to date of this growing area of special interest is Ulla Connor's volume *Contrastive Rhetoric* (New York: Cambridge University Press, 1996).

Note 9 (sample responses for Task Eight)

As many readers will recognize, the final question (regarding whether research writing should be "Americanized" for an American audience) raises some hotly debated issues. Here we just mention that some argue that it would be more "efficient" for everybody to write in the same way, and that way might as well be American—given the figures in table 1.1, and so on. Others argue that the United States should not be allowed to develop this kind of cultural domination. One set of arguments makes an analogy between biological diversity and academic cultural diversity, suggesting that if alternative rhetorics are suppressed this may in turn limit creativity and originality.

(Task Eight Teaching Hint: If time permits, the above activities could be restructured as a prepared panel discussion.)

Note 10

Einstein, Albert. 1934. *Essays in science.* New York: The Philosophical Library.

Note 11

Chang, Yu-Ying, and John M. Swales. 1999. Informal elements in English academic writing: Threats or opportunities for advanced non-native speakers? In *Writing: Texts, processes, and practices,* edited by C. N. Candlin and K. Hyland. London: Longman.

Note 12 (sample analysis for Task Nine)

We took a paper from a leading APA-style journal in our field published by Sage Publications. (P. Eubanks. Conceptual metaphor as rhetorical response: A reconsideration of metaphor, *Written Communication* 16 [1999]:171–99.) This was a long and substantial article. As instructed, we ignored texts in quotation and all notes. Working fairly fast, the task took us about an hour. Our findings were as follows.

Imperatives	9
I / my / me	46 (mostly *I*)
Initial *but*	5
Initial *and*	3
Direct questions	3 (One was a section heading.)
Contractions	0

Imperative verbs: *Consider* 3, *let* (me) 3, *suppose* 2, *see* 1 (this last being in parentheses and referring to a published work)

Overall, the results are quite comparable to those in table 1.2. Five of the six elements occurred, although only the first person usages were common and were especially frequent in explaining analytic procedures. Verb contractions do not appear to be an option for this journal, although initial *but* and *and* can be used for stylistic effect. In fact, one of the examples of *and* occurred in this striking sentence fragment: "And for good reason."

Note 13

While the change to "John M. Swales" reduces identity confusion, it has created problems for anybody who might want to cite his work before and after about 1987. As John knows to his cost, the minor name change can be very annoying for authors and editors. Moreover, the SSCI thinks there are two people, "J. Swales" and "J. M. Swales," with identical publications! The moral of this story is that it is best to make a decision about your academic name early in your career and stick to it. Hence the inclusion of this section in Unit One.

Note 14

We certainly do not have any firm opinions here. This is a sensitive matter of cultural identity and cultural affiliation. We think it is an individual choice.

Note 15 (sample responses for Task Fourteen)

1. Would everybody know what a GSRA is? No institutional affiliation? No degree program? A GSRA is a graduate student research assistant.

2. This might depend on whether the journal will allow an update in the bio-data at a later date.

3. Certainly, the history approach is less susceptible to the rewriting issue raised in item 2. On the other hand, it is standard journalistic practice to put the "freshest information at the top."

4. Two or three research areas would indicate your versatility; more than that might indicate that you are not yet "settled down" in your interests.

5. The first two are just fine, especially if the journals are well regarded and the fellowships are indeed somewhat "special." "Name-dropping" turns out with most of our participants to be highly controversial; the wisdom of doing this or not would seem to be highly field dependent.

Unit Two
Stepping onto a Wider Stage— the Conference Abstract

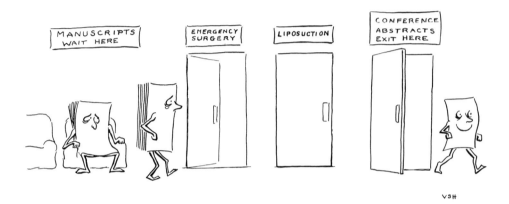

The first "genre" we deal with in detail is the conference abstract (CA), a text written in support of an oral presentation. A good reason for starting with CAs is that they are likely one of the first texts that a graduate student will submit to an outside audience—one outside your own institution. Your goal in writing a CA is to "sell" your research to the conference proposal reviewers, who in fact may have very little time to carefully read and assess your proposal.

Highlights of this unit include the following.

Unlike the abstract that precedes a research paper, CAs are independent texts and must stand on their own. Moreover, whether your abstract is accepted for a conference or not depends entirely on the impression that it makes on the CA reviewers. Since your purpose in writing and submitting a CA is to have an opportunity to present your work, your CA must be somewhat promotional—it must "sell" your work.

Task One

Consider the following questions and answer them for your area of study. If you are unable to answer a question based on your own experience, ask a more senior person in your field.

1. The CA typically has to be submitted months ahead of the actual conference. How far in advance of a conference are CAs usually submitted in your field?

2. Some small regional or local conferences may accept nearly all the CAs received; major national or international ones may reject up to 75 percent of the CAs received. What are typical acceptance rates for conferences in your field?

3. The CA is a freestanding (and often anonymous) document that has to impress a review committee. Are CAs in your field blind reviewed? That is, does the review committee select papers without seeing the names of the authors (and their institutional affiliations)?

4. Because of these characteristics, most CAs need to create a research space for themselves prior to reporting the actual findings. As a result, the first half of the CA may be devoted to "justifying the topic." Indeed, it has been persuasively argued that the conference abstract is much more like a research grant proposal than a journal article abstract. Would this be true for your field? (See Note 1.)

5. Conference abstracts often have rigorous word or space limits, and the number of words allowed never seems to be quite enough! What are the typical word limits in your field?

6. Because the CA is a challenging and complex promotional genre, it usually requires several drafts. If you can arrange it, input from colleagues and friends can be quite helpful. Who could you (or would you) turn to for help?

(See Note 2.)

2.1 A Close Look at the Structure of a Conference Abstract

One recent study of conference abstracts in our own field, applied linguistics, suggests the following five-part structure, although many abstracts will not have all five parts, or "moves" (Yakhontova, T. 1998. Cultural variation in the genre of the conference abstract: rhetorical and linguistic dimensions. Paper read at Conference on English as a conference language, 14–17 January, Halle-Wittenberg, Germany).

1. Outlining the research field
2. Justifying a particular piece of research/study
3. Introducing the paper to be presented at the conference
4. Summarizing the paper
5. Highlighting its outcome/results

Task Two

Here now is Tatyana Yakhontova's own conference abstract on conference abstracts! (Sentence numbers have been added here and elsewhere for ease of reference.) Read it carefully and mark up its "moves." Does it fit Tatyana's own model?

Cultural Variation in the Genre of the Conference Abstract: Rhetorical and Linguistic Dimensions

[1]The conference abstract is a common and important genre that plays a significant role in disseminating new knowledge within scientific communities, both national and international. [2]As a genre with the specific features of "interestingness" created to attract the attention of reviewing

committees, the conference abstract has been investigated by Berken-kotter & Huckin (1995) and Swales (1996). [3]However, the issue of cultural variation in the genre has not yet become a subject of research, although the conference abstract, like other genres of academic discourse, can be presumed to reflect national proclivities in writing.

[4]This paper attempts to describe the cultural-specific differences of English versus Ukrainian and Russian conference abstracts on the level of their cognitive structure and language, and to provide some tentative explanations of the cultural and ideological backgrounds underlying these rhetorical and textlinguistic preferences. [5]It will also be shown how the inherited cognitive patterns of Slavic writers interplay with the acquired stereotypes of English scientific discourse in the abstracts they construct in English. [6]These texts, hybrid from the viewpoint of their cultural shaping, can be regarded as evidence of the transition period typical of both sociopolitical and intellectual life of Ukraine and other states of the former Soviet Union. [7]As a result, this study raises a broader question: To what extent is it necessary to adopt the English conventions of this genre in order to be accepted and recognized by international fora?

[8]This issue will be discussed in connection with the pedagogical implications arising from the findings and observations of this study.

(minor editing)

(See Note 3.)

Task Three

Now, do the following with a partner, if you have one, for Tatyana's text.

1. Highlight or underline any words or phrases that you see as "promoting" or "selling" the abstract.

2. The abstract contains some interesting academic vocabulary. Be prepared to explain the meanings of the following words as they are used in this text (the sentence number is in parentheses).

   a. disseminating (S1)
   b. subject (S3)
   c. proclivities (S3)
   d. tentative (S4)
   e. interplay (S5)
   f. hybrid (S6)
   g. fora (S7)

3. As is typical, the second half of the CA contains a fair amount of *metadiscourse*. As its name suggests, metadiscourse is discourse about discourse, as when we write about our own text, such as "This paper has argued that . . . " Consider the following.

   a. (S4) This paper attempts to describe . . .
   b. (S5) It will also be shown how . . .
   c. (S7) As a result, this study raises a broader question: . . .
   d. (S8) This issue will be discussed in connection with . . .

   What is the purpose of the metadiscourse? Do you think all of it is necessary?

4. Notice how Tatyana alternates here between the active in sentences 4 and 7 and the passive in sentences 5 and 8. What is the effect? Why does she sometimes use the future rather than the simple present?

5. Would you have used *I* in this abstract (or *we* if a co-authored CA)?

6. Notice the subtle difference between, for example, "This paper" and "The paper." How do you react to the following commentary on *this* by Finnish linguist Anna Mauranen?

   > One rhetorical effect that *this* produces is an impression of closeness and solidarity between reader and writer. It has the effect of bringing the reader round to the writer's orientation, or point of view, by implying that the writer as well as the reader are both "here," on the same side, looking at things from the same perspective. (See Note 4.)

   Would it be safer to say that in using *this* a writer is *trying* to "bring the reader round to his or her orientation"?

7. The text is 254 words long, so it is fine for overall length. However, it consists of only eight sentences, thus giving an average sentence length of about 32 words. This is quite high for academic English, which overall averages around 25 words per sentence. Too high? If you think so, what suggestions do you have?

8. How do you react to Tatyana's argument that there may be a connection between academic texts and sociopolitical and ideological forces? Do you have any examples either for or against this claim?

9. The final sentence does not seem to be as well thought out as the rest of the CA. (A very common situation, in fact!) How do you feel about the following alternatives?

   a. Eliminate the sentence altogether
   b. Replace it with "Finally, the pedagogical implications of these trends and tensions are discussed."
   c. Replace it with "The paper closes with some suggestions for teaching the English conference abstract to Ukrainian and Russian academics."
   d. Do something else. If so, what?

(See Note 5.)

Language Focus: A Note on *Moves*

In the discussion of Tatyana's abstract, we introduced the term *move* without explaining more precisely what we mean by it. In linguistic description we see two types of terms: formal descriptors and functional descriptors. Formal descriptors include terms such as *paragraph, sentence,* and *verb,* while functional descriptors would include *description, suggestion,* and *purpose statement. Move* is a functional term that refers to a defined and bounded communicative act that is designed to achieve one main communicative objective. Because it is a functional category the length of a move can range from a single finite clause to several paragraphs.

To help you better understand what is meant by a *move,* let's take a look at a genre that you may be familiar with: the journal editorial, sometimes entitled "From the Editors" or "Editor's Note." The purpose of the editorial is to allow the editor(s) to make a more personal comment on some general aspect of the journal and/or to discuss its content.

Task Four

Read through this portion of a journal editor's comment. Identify the moves—the different communicative objectives—just as we did for Tatyana's CA. Put a box around the parts of the text that seem to go together. We anticipate that you will find that the text has (more or less) four moves.

> The journal is growing, especially following our decision to move to six issues a year. The introduction of blind reviewing and the inclusion of key words to facilitate database searching have also gone smoothly. The winner of the 1998 McArthur prize for the best article published in 1997 goes to . . . for their article entitled . . . The winner is determined exclusively by a vote of the members of the Editorial Board—the editors have no vote. This issue contains seven articles. In the first, Moreno and Sanchez develop a theoretical model to account for . . . In the second, . . . Once a year we also acknowledge the invaluable assistance of the additional readers for the journal, those who are not official members of the Editorial or Advisory Boards. For 1997 those readers were: Mary Abbott, Richard Alexander, Angela Antonioni . . .

Do you think the order of the moves you identified is "fixed," or do you think it could be changed? If it can be changed, in what way? (See Note 6.)

2.2 Conference Abstracts across Disciplines

So far we have focused on an abstract from the humanities. We now need to travel further afield.

Task Five

Now take a look at this abstract submitted to an automotive safety conference by two researchers, one from Australia and one from France. The abstract was submitted to the section dealing with crash tests in the laboratory. We have shortened the results section somewhat. What moves can you identify? Draw a box around each move. Are these the same as those suggested by Tatyana?

[1]Head biomechanics research is often interested in head or impacted structure modeling, but less often the study of impact itself. [2]In studies using an analytical approach, epidemiological studies, and in studies of structure aggressiveness, researchers often use a lumped parameter approach to model the structure and a single mass to model the head. [3]Often, in experimental studies, the real structure is impacted by a physical model of the head which is a single mass in structure and behavior (rigid head form or Hybrid 3 head).

[4]A collaboration between Institution 1 and Institution 2 has demonstrated that this approach may be criticized for two reasons. [5]First, the (analytical or physical) modeling of the head as a single mass rules out any interpretation of head injury mechanisms. [6]Second, the modeling of the head by a single mass produces a very different head-structure force interaction than that which would be produced if a more bio-faithful head model is used.

[7]The objective of this joint study is to propose an experimental and analytical method to analyze head impact which uses a more realistic model of the head. [8]In the past numerous studies have shown the importance of brain-skull decoupling on the mechanical behavior of the head under impact. [9]In the proposed approach, this phenomenon will be taken into consideration.

[10]In the experimental component of the study, the recently published dummy head "Bimass 150" is dropped onto beams with different characteristics. [11]The impacts are compared. . . . [12]The results show that the analytical model can simulate the experimental force interactions as well as intercranial dynamics. . . . [13]The results also show . . . [14]We conclude that the experimental or theoretical modeling of the head mechanical behavior has an important influence on the structure response and that this has to be taken into consideration in the analysis of structure aggressiveness. [15]It also appears that the proposed approach permits the prediction of a head injury mechanism for a given impact.

From C. Räisänen, *The conference forum as a system of genres* (Göteborg, Sweden: Acta Universitatis Gothoburgensis, 1999). Permission for use granted by Rémy Willinger.

(See Note 7.)

1. The title of the abstract is missing. Which of these do you think would work? Why?

   Experimental and Theoretical Modeling of Head Impact—Influence of Head Modeling

   Brain Decoupling and Its Influence on the Mechanical Behavior of the Head under Impact

   Theoretical Modeling of Head Impact for Predicting Head Injury Mechanisms using "Bimass 150"

2. The abstract contains some instances of metadiscourse (e.g., S7 and S9). What would be the effect if the metadiscoursal phrases were removed? What would be the effect of moving the third (metadiscoursal) paragraph to the first paragraph?

3. How would you rate the "positioning" of these research writers?

4. More detailed questions

   a. In S1 the beginning phrase *Head biomechanics research is often interested in . . .* sounds a little "funny." How might you reformulate it?

   b. In S3 the authors use the verb *impacted*. Until somewhat recently *impact* was used only as a noun as in *The development of new cloning techniques had a big impact on . . .* How does *impact* as a verb sound to you?

   c. S4 opens with the strange phrase *A collaboration between Institution 1 and Institution 2.* Why is this?

   d. As you may know, *-ed* passive participles can be used as modifiers. The first example in the CA is *impacted* in S1. How many other instances of such participles can you find?

(See Note 8.)

Task Six

Study a couple of conference abstracts from your field (your own and/or borrowed examples from colleagues or instructors). How are they similar to and different from Tatyana's model and text? What explanations might you have for any differences that you find? (See Note 9.)

2.3 The Rating of Conference Abstracts

Of course, finding an appropriate structure for your conference abstract and providing a suitable scene setting are only part of the story. There are additionally the matters of offering "interestingness" and of projecting a convincing and authoritative image. The Berkenkotter and Huckin study (see Note 10) referred to in Tatyana's abstract examined the properties of high-rated and low-rated abstracts submitted to the annual College Composition and Communication Convention in the United States. Table 2.1 shows basically what they found.

TABLE 2.1. Abstract Descriptors

High-Rated Abstracts	Low-Rated Abstracts
Topics were of current interest to experienced members of the community.	Topics were of lesser interest.
A problem was clearly defined.	No clear problem was defined.
Problem was addressed in a novel way.	Problem, if defined, received less interesting treatment.
Special terminology was current or "buzzy."	Terminology was standard.
Several explicit and implicit references to the scholarly literature.	Fewer citations and allusions were used.

Source: Data from C. Berkenkotter and T. N. Huckin, *Genre knowledge in disciplinary communication* (Hillsdale, NJ: Lawrence Erlbaum, 1995).

Of course, and as Berkenkotter and Huckin readily concede, each field will have its own perceptions as to what makes a conference abstract a "winning" one. Certainly, other fields, perhaps especially in science, may not associate "interestingness" so closely with novelty. Rather, they may value the cumulative addition of a new piece of evidence, such as a piece of research that confirms or updates previous findings.

Task Seven

Assume that you have been appointed as a member of the review committee for a conference in your field. You have been asked to make a list of the qualities that the committee should be looking for in the abstracts that they accept. Make that list. Here are two examples from our students that may be helpful as you think about this.

Mechanical Engineering

1. Novelty, originality
2. Applicability
3. Completeness
4. Hot topic

Environmental Sciences

1. Urgency of the problem
2. Good supporting data
3. Applicable to real world

(See Note 11.)

2.4 The Role of a Senior Author: An Example

As English language instructors and researchers, we are probably capable, at least most of the time, of assessing whether a draft abstract in our own field is well constructed and has that elusive quality of "interestingness." We are usually guessing in your fields and are probably better at asking questions rather than providing solutions. Here is a case in point.

Some years ago, John was helping an Iranian student in electrical engineering prepare a draft conference abstract for the major biennial conference on sensors. The abstract needed to be about 600 words long and be accompanied by a number of drawings. The third draft of the opening paragraph is shown on the left of the next page.

As you can see, the opening of the abstract draft on the left is rather flat. True, it identifies a need and goes on in S3 to offer a (partial) solution to this need, but it seems rather unimaginative and overreliant on technical detail. However, this was the third draft and seemed about the best a "lab rat" and a "grammar rat" could do after working together. The whole draft abstract was submitted to the lab director and senior professor for editing, a professor incidentally widely admired for his technical writing. He offered minor edits for the rest of the abstract but totally rewrote the opening paragraph. Professor Kenneth Wise's version is on the right.

A comparison of the third draft with the fourth draft (the submitted version) shows that the former text was situated—understandably enough—in the narrow and rather static world of technical problem solving within a laboratory setting. Draft 4, on the other hand, takes a confident and dynamic sweep across the field as a whole. In S1 certain questions are immediately identified as "major issues." Then in S2 certain things *are likely to evolve.* Finally, in the rapidly moving research front identified by the senior professor, the definition of standards *is currently*

3rd Draft	4th Draft with Dr. Wise's revision
[1]Present measurement and automated control systems need to have sensors with higher reliability and accuracy than is practical with discrete and isolated components. [2] In addition, issues such as cost optimization of testing, packaging and interfacing with higher level control systems have provided the motivations to change microsensors from "isolated components" to "integrated system elements." [3]This paper describes the design of an addressable VSLI smart sensor capable of handling up to eight sensors with 12 bit accuracy, introduces a custom designed bus, and describes a new method for data compensation.	[1]As integrated transducers are combined with increasing amounts of on-chip or in-module circuitry, where to partition the electronic system and how much electronics to include with the "sensor" become major issues. [2]Integrated sensors, particularly those associated with automated manufacturing, are likely to evolve into smart peripherals, and the definition of appropriate sensor interface standards is currently the subject of three national committees. [3]This paper describes a possible organization for such devices and appropriate interface protocols. [4]The device described is addressable, programmable, self-testing, compatible with a bidirectional digital sensor bus, and offers 12-bit accuracy using internally-stored compensation coefficients. [5]The design is sufficiently flexible to allow upward-compatible sensor designs to be inserted in existing equipment without reprogramming the host system and will accommodate differing sensor features.

From John M. Swales, *Genre Analysis: English in Academic and Research Settings,* 211. Cambridge: Cambridge University Press, 1990. Reprinted by permission.

the subject of three national committees. This last observation, in particular, indicates insider expertise and thus communicates an authoritative voice. Such authority, as this account has suggested, may well require the assistance of an experienced scholar in your area of interest.

The episode we have described had in fact a happy ending. The abstract was one of the 64 accepted for the conference. In fact, at this particular conference it is the reviewers' custom to rank the submissions numerically. The fourth draft was placed third! (If further evidence is needed of its high quality.) (See Note 12.)

2.5 The Problem of Promissory Abstracts

Academics and researchers make plans for the future, as in the genre plans in Unit One, Section 1.2. Alas, we often promise more than we can deliver. When looking to the future, we tend to assume a perfect world, one without illness, loss of data, technical problems, and so on. We may need to submit a CA to a conference with less of the work done than we anticipated as the deadline for submission approaches. We are now faced with writing a "promissory abstract," that is, one that *projects* what will be done by the time the conference comes around in several months' time.

Task Eight

Read through the following abstract and answer the questions that follow.

The Role of Natural Variation in Changing Amphibian[a] Populations

[1]In the last several years, numerous researchers (e.g., Doyle 1998; Lee 1997) have noted serious declines in the populations of many of the nearly 5,000 species of amphibians. [2]This reduction has caused concern because amphibians are generally regarded as sensitive indicators of the planet's overall health. [3]Although much recent research has pointed to habitat destruction, particularly the draining[b] of wetlands, as the cause of the declines, the declines and apparent extinctions are widely occurring in areas far removed from human populations, as in the case of the once abundant golden toad[c] in the cloud forests of Costa Rica.

[4]In order to provide a better understanding of the dwindling[d] amphibian population, my research will investigate whether the declines and extinctions are in fact indicative of a worldwide environmental crisis. [5]Analyzing data from as far back as the 1700s, I will show that amphibian populations are subject to year-to-year natural environmental variations, such as droughts and floods, that can affect egg laying and larvae survival and that much of the decline may in fact have less to do with human intrusion. [6]Along this same vein,[e] I will also investigate whether reports of increasing numbers of abnormalities in amphibians, such as missing eyes and limbs, can also be partly explained by natural environmental changes.

a. Frogs, toads, and salamanders
b. The removal of water
c. An animal similar to a frog, but with rougher, drier skin. Toads live mostly on land.
d. Declining, shrinking
e. Continuing this same line of thinking

1. Do you think that the research described in the abstract has actually been done? What in the abstract might suggest to a reviewer that it has not actually been completed?

2. What, if any, changes could be made so that it appears that some of the work has been completed?

3. What experience do you have with promissory abstracts? If you have written one, were you able to actually come through with what you promised?

Submitting a promissory abstract entails a certain number of risks. For one, you may not actually get the work done in time, which may cause you to withdraw your paper. For another, you may not get the results that you had hoped for. However, sometimes you have little choice but to write a promissory abstract, especially when abstract deadlines may be 8–10 months before the actual conference and you have just begun your research. In such cases you need to be especially careful to avoid language that may give you away. Keep in mind, though, that if an abstract includes only a research purpose and methodology without any substantive results, the reviewers will likely conclude that it is promissory. Moreover, many conferences require you to include some results as proof that the work has been completed. (See Note 13.)

Task Nine

A colleague has asked you to look over the following CA for a sociology conference on the impact of technology on society. What suggestions might you offer for improvement?

> In order to meet our growing population's demand for food, researchers have increasingly turned to genetic engineering. Put simply, genetic engineering involves inserting a gene from a plant or an animal into another organism. While the transfer of genetic information can occur naturally between similar kinds of plants or animals, genetic engineering allows researchers to insert any gene into another organism. For example, researchers developed a tomato that stays on the vine longer and holds up well during shipping because biotechnology allowed them to slow the ripening process.

The FDA has declared that the engineered tomato is as safe as tomatoes bred by conventional means. Moreover, since the tomato has all the characteristics of a conventional tomato, the FDA will not require the tomatoes to have special labels identifying them as genetically engineered. Although the FDA maintains that the tomatoes are completely safe, consumer reaction to them has been mixed. Thus, growers and marketers are very concerned given the potential for economic loss or profit from such products. This paper presents the result of recent research on consumer reaction to genetically engineered produce. Preliminary results reveal that consumer reaction is highly dependent on the type of genetically altered food and the type of alteration induced by the engineering.

(See Note 14.)

Task Ten

Now write your own draft conference abstract of 200–300 words based on one of your own research interests.

Language Focus: *this* + noun phrase (NP)

We have seen several examples so far of sentences in CAs opening with *this* as part of a noun phrase, such as

This paper attempts to describe . . .
The objective of this joint study is to propose . . .

There is, however, another use of this kind of sentence subject. Consider the following sentences.

This issue will be discussed in connection with the pedagogical implications. In the proposed approach, *this phenomenon* will be taken into consideration.

This device links the current sentence with the previous one by putting "old" or "given" information before "new" information at the beginning of the sentence.

Consider the following statement.

1. The government expects a budget surplus for the next year. This surprised economists.

First notice that the writer has a strategic choice as to how much "old" information to place at the beginning of the second sentence. Which of the following do you prefer?

This surprised economists.
This announcement surprised economists.
This unexpected announcement surprised economists.
This unexpected announcement by the government surprised economists.

In *AWG* we described this structure as *this* + summary word. In this more advanced work, we would like to suggest that the noun phrase can sometimes be seen as being *interpretive,* or designed to persuade the reader how to "read" the previous sentence.

Which of the following opening nouns do you consider to be functioning as *summary* (S) and which as *interpretation* (I)?

2. The graduate students said they wanted a final examination.

	S	I
a. This *statement* surprised the instructor.	—	—
b. This *request* surprised the instructor.	—	—
c. This *hope* surprised the instructor.	—	—
d. This *desire* surprised the instructor.	—	—
e. This *demand* surprised the instructor.	—	—
f. This *ultimatum* surprised the instructor.	—	—

(See Note 15.)

Of course, the *this* + NP structure is not necessarily confined to the subject position.

So far in this section we have focused entirely on the important role of *this* in maintaining links across sentences. However, confusion can sometimes arise between the roles of *this* and *it* (and between *these* and *they*) as a means of "picking up where the previous sentence left off."

Consider this sentence and the beginnings of the following sentences. Which do you accept/prefer and why?

3. The weather in January was much warmer than usual.

   a. It was the second warmest on record.
   b. This was the second warmest on record.

   c. This was even warmer than December.
   d. It was even warmer than December.

   e. It has led to large savings in snow removal costs.
   f. This has led to large savings in snow removal costs.

   g. This may be connected to global warming trends.
   h. It may be connected to global warming trends.

As you have probably realized, *it* is the correct choice for the first two sentences and *this* for the last two. *It* is used to refer to the main subject of the previous sentence (the weather), while *this* refers to the proposition asserted (the above-average temperature in January).

So far so good. But now let's look at a more complex case. Make your choices below.

4. The vowel sounds in English can be adequately described in terms of their tongue position (unlike in French where the amount of lip rounding is also important).

   a. They have several advantages.
   b. These have several advantages.
   c. This has several advantages.
   d. It has several advantages.

   e. This can be plotted on a two-dimensional grid.
   f. It can be plotted on a two-dimensional grid.
   g. They can be plotted on a two-dimensional grid.
   h. These can be plotted on a two-dimensional grid.

As far as a–d are concerned, the answer is fairly obviously *this* since the follow-up sentence refers to the classification scheme in general. Indeed, there would be a good case for following *this* with a summary noun, such as

4c. This system/classification has several advantages.

For e–h the situation is much more complicated. We can see this if we introduce the appropriate noun phrases.

4e. This tongue position can be plotted on a two-dimensional grid.
4f. The tongue position can be plotted on a two-dimensional grid.
4g. The vowel sounds can be plotted on a two-dimensional grid.
4h. These vowel sounds can be plotted on a two-dimensional grid.

In both pairs, the noun phrases from sentence 4 are simply repeated, so we might expect 4f and 4g to be the preferred choices. While 4e and 4h are certainly possible, notice that the subjects move the discourse forward and do not actually provide further information about the noun phrases themselves. Compare the following sentences.

4i. This moves in both vertical and horizontal planes.
4j. It moves in both vertical and horizontal planes.
4k. They number about 20 in most dialects.
4l. These number about 20 in most dialects.

Here there would indeed be a preference for *it* and *they*, while the situation in e–h has a more open-ended meaning. In such circumstances, there is therefore a case for repeating the noun phrase, as in the alternatives, at least in part (*This position; These sounds*).

So far we have focused on the use of *this* + NOUN. In some cases, however, expanding *this* + NOUN may be necessary to establish an unambiguous reference within the text. Read the following short text that discusses two ocean birds—the albatross and the white-chinned petrel. Which of the choices following 5 do you prefer? Why?

5. It has been estimated that about 9,000 white-chinned petrels are inadvertently caught annually in longline fishing for hake in the Southern Hemisphere. In addition, more than 40,000 albatross are hooked and drowned every year after trying to eat the squid bait used on fishing lines set for bluefin tuna.

   a. It is threatening the continued existence of these ocean birds.
   b. This is threatening the continued existence of these ocean birds.
   c. This level is threatening the continued existence of these ocean birds.
   d. This level of mortality is threatening the continued existence of these ocean birds.

In terms of grammar any of the four choices can follow. However, the use of *it* in choice a results in an unclear reference. Is *it* the fishing lines or the hooking and drowning? Is *it* the fact that these birds are inadvertently caught? Choice b, on the other hand, might be better since *this* often refers to something larger; in this case perhaps being caught, eating, hooking, and drowning. Choice c might actually be somewhat confusing, causing the reader to pause and ask what *level* the writer is referring to. It could, for example, refer to the level of fishing activity. Finally, d conveys the clearest meaning for the reader, who may not have immediately considered that it is specifically the number of white-chinned petrels and albatross lost each year that poses the threat to their existence.

Now take a look at 6 and the options that follow. Which option (or options) do you prefer? Why?

6. Web-based learning approaches often use a paradigm that completely separates learning material and assessment. The typical learner experience is to "cover" a specific learning module and then immediately complete a short assessment process (usually multiple choice) that tests for immediate recall of the information. The learner is then free to return to the module or move on to the next based on performance within the assessment.

   a. It has some serious instructional shortcomings, however (Elstein 1994; Ramsden 1993; Page 1995; White and Gunstone 1992).
   b. This has some serious instructional shortcomings, however (Elstein 1994; Ramsden 1993; Page 1995; White and Gunstone 1992).
   c. This approach has some serious instructional shortcomings, however (Elstein 1994; Ramsden 1993; Page 1995; White and Gunstone 1992).
   d. This assessment has some serious instructional shortcomings, however (Elstein 1994; Ramsden 1993; Page 1995; White and Gunstone 1992).
   e. This approach to assessment has some serious instructional shortcomings, however (Elstein 1994; Ramsden 1993; Page 1995; White and Gunstone 1992).

(See Note 16.)

Task Eleven

Provide an expanded *this* + summary word phrase (*this* + NOUN + PREPOSITION + NOUN) to complete the following. If you feel an adjective might also help to establish the best connection, do not hesitate to use one.

1. Over the last hundred years, the North American diet has become increasingly imbalanced. The percentage of calories derived from complex carbohydrates has dropped, while the proportion of fat calories has risen dramatically. This _____ is an important factor in the growing rate of cardiovascular disease.

2. Researchers once believed that poor nutrition led to brain damage and cognitive disability in children. However, recent studies have shown that young malnourished animals did poorly on tests of mental ability, such as maze running, not because they had suffered brain damage but because they had no energy. Lacking energy, they withdrew from everything in their environment, including other animals. Also, mothers did more for the less active infants, further hindering their development.

    These studies have led researchers to conclude that cognitive disability in malnourished children can partly be attributed to reduced interaction with the environment and people. This _____ has led to greater optimism that programs to improve the social and academic skills of disadvantaged children can counteract past deficits.

3. The invention of the wheellock was a major achievement. Previous gun locks required an external heat source, such as a glowing ember or lit match, to ignite the gunpowder. After the invention of the wheel-lock, guns could be concealed yet kept ready for instant action without having to pause to light a match. This _____ forever changed the role these weapons played in society.

(See Note 17.)

Task Twelve

Complete the blanks in the following CA with suitable nouns. Above the nouns you provide indicate whether you think they are "summarizing" or "interpretive." A single summary noun may not be sufficient; you may need a noun phrase (NOUN + prepositional phrase such as *this shift in attitude*).

Up until the 1980s, the typical immigrant to the United States was poor, not well educated, and had few marketable skills. Over the last decade, however, increased global economic interdependence has given rise to growth in transnational migration among the generally well educated middle class. In fact, in some urban areas of the United States middle class migrants have a stronger presence than poorer, struggling immigrants. Despite this _____ , however, social work and psychological theories of migration and acculturation have continued to focus on poorer immigrants and U.S.-born minority populations (Sherraden & Martin, 1994; Drachman, 1992; Mayadas & Elliot, 1992; Jabob, 1994).

As a migrant population, the middle class has a unique set of problems that is often exacerbated since this group is unable to gain access to social services and other support mechanisms for the less well off. This _____ has led to a unique set of vulnerabilities. Among this population, the group least understood is that of graduate and postdoctoral students and their families (academic migrant families), who have come to the U.S. for education opportunities. The number of academic migrants in the U.S. is not insignificant, with more than half a million students and scholars studying in the U.S. annually— triple the number 20 years ago.

This paper reports on a recent investigation of the problems faced by graduate students, scholars, and their families at a large midwestern university. Preliminary analysis of a survey questionnaire reveals that after migration, men perceive their lives as having changed very little, while women believe their lives have drastically changed, especially since they typically maintain the home, care for young children, and must learn to navigate the "ins" and "outs" of a new culture. This _____ may explain why women uprooted from their countries for the sake of their husbands' education often report greater feelings of frustration and homesickness. . . . This presentation concludes by describing interventions for migrant students and scholars that reflect the complicated nature of their vulnerability.

Note the number of summary phrases. Does it seem about right? Also note the location of the metadiscoursal *this* phrases. (See Note 18.)

2.6 Reformulations

In a reformulation, another person rewrites without consultation what she or he understands the original writer to be saying. In this process the reformulator attempts to impose greater clarity and explicitness on the original. If it works, this procedure should achieve three purposes.

1. It should improve the language of the original;
2. it should offer clarification of the original message;
3. it may well reveal places where the reformulator has—for whatever reason—misunderstood or misinterpreted the original writer's meaning.

Although some experts in teaching L2 writing argue that the reformulator should not be the instructor, we prefer to use ourselves for this task. Our reasoning provides a fourth purpose.

4. We can reveal something of the thinking that underlies the changes we have made.

Samiri Hernandez-Hiraldo's Conference Abstract

Below is Samiri's draft conference abstract as originally written. At the time she wrote the draft, Samiri was a third year Ph.D. student in anthropology. Her first language is Spanish, and as we will immediately see, she writes academic English quite fluently and with an extensive academic vocabulary. Read through Samiri's first draft and compare it to the second one that follows. Highlight the changes that you notice in the reformulated text. Are all of these changes for the better? If so, why? If not, why not? Try to anticipate Samiri's reactions.

Religious Coexistence in Puerto Rico

[1]The recent dramatic changes in the religions and the new religious movements all over the world counter modernization theory and historical materialism. [2]Religious studies demonstrate that the continuing role of religion is due to its capacity for restructuring and assuming various forms (Wuthnow 1988 & Kepel 1994). [3]Anthropologists and Latin Americanists interested in conversion emphasize the role of world/traditional religion in the articulation of local and global specificities, so necessary

for coexistence (Stoll 1990, the Comaroffs 1993 & Hefner 1993). [4]Prevailing paradigms, however, limit their analysis by concentrating exclusively in the ideological and scriptural analysis, by considering the official point of view, and by elevating the more palpable or heroic manifestations of coexistence that are, religious conferences, assemblies, ecumenical agencies, academic seminars, special purpose groups, etc. [5]This paper elaborates the processes of religious coexistence in a small municipality of Puerto Rico. [6]From archival research, life histories, interviews and participant observation, results show that types of conversion relate to patterns of coexistence. [7]They also demonstrate that coexistence is determined by the interplay of processes from above and from below, by the immediate social contact of the daily life and by discursive and non discursive aspects of doing ritual or the whole religious experience.

Now here is Samiri's revised, post-reformulation version. It is not identical to the full reformulation given in Note 19 because Samiri (quite rightly) did not accept all of the suggestions for change.

Anthropological Insight:
The Case of Religious Coexistence in Puerto Rico

[1]Recent dramatic changes in religions, especially the resurgence of old and the rise of new religious movements in many areas of the world, run counter to the assumptions of both modernization theory and historical materialism. [2]In fact, research suggests that the continuing role of religion is due to its capacity for restructuring and assuming various alternative forms (Wuthnow, 1988; Kepel, 1994). [3]More specifically, Latin Americanists, anthropologists and other specialists interested in religious conversion have stressed the way in which both traditional and world religions have contributed to the articulation of local and global specifics, thus preserving religious belief within changeable and/or pluralist societies (Stoll, 1990; Comaroff & Comaroff, 1993; Hefner, 1993). [4]Prevailing paradigms, however, limit their analyses by concentrating on ideological or scriptural interpretations, by privileging the official point of view, and by elevating the more visible or "heroic" demonstrations of coexistence as manifested through religious conferences or assemblies, or through ecumenical agencies or academic seminars. [5]In contrast to this orientation, this paper investigates the processes of religious coexistence in a small municipality in Puerto Rico at a more basic level. [6]Using a combination of archival research, life histories, interviews and participant observation,

this study will allow an evaluation of the relationship between conversion and coexistence processes. [7]More specifically, the study will demonstrate the extent to which religious coexistence is determined by the interplay of processes at various levels—from the official and popular point of view, and from the discursive/non-discursive aspects of ritual engagement and the immediate social contact of daily life.

We give below the thinking behind the revisions of the title and the first sentence. The details of the thinking and classroom discussion that underlie the remaining parts of the reformulation can be found in Note 19. Not being anthropologists, we do not know whether we have done enough to help Samiri; maybe the abstract is still not specific enough. Regardless, soon after she wrote it, she was thinking of submitting a version of it for a conference in Puerto Rico.

Rationale for the Suggested Changes

(Key: O = the original; R = our reformulation; J = our justifications for the changes; C = class opinions)

Title

O: Religious Coexistence in Puerto Rico

R: Anthropological Insight: The Case of Religious Coexistence in Puerto Rico

J: We didn't like the original title much; it seemed to be rather dull; it also seemed very narrow and specific for an anthropological conference, especially as Samiri appeared to be arguing for a different approach to the phenomenon. So, we chose a title split by a colon, the first part being general and the second specific.

C: General agreement, including from Samiri.

First Sentence

O: The recent dramatic changes in the religions and the new religious movements all over the world counter modernization theory and historical materialism.

R: Recent dramatic changes in religions, especially the resurgence of old and the rise of new religious movements in many areas of the world, run counter to the assumptions of modernization theory and historical materialism.

J: OK, this looks like a great start, but *all over the world* looks risky. There is always somebody who will object, "But in my country this doesn't apply." And does she mean changes in terms of religions declining as well as religions gaining? Probably not, so let's put that "especially" phrase in. Does the rise of religion actually *counter* modernization theory (whatever that is)? Finally, a very interesting question of whether to start with the definite article (*The recent . . .*) or with the indefinite (*Recent*). In fact, the deletion of *the* now looks like a switch from old information to new information. We could go either way; so let's make the change because it will make a good discussion point in class.

C: Class decided by a clear majority that the "breaking story" strategy was more effective than the "as you know" strategy. The first word would not be *The*.

(See Note 19.)

2.7 Conference Abstract Titles

Given the word and space constraints for abstracts, abstract titles carry a lot of weight. Although abstracts may need to be considerably shortened as they are revised, often the titles can remain long and convey a lot of information. Indeed in recent years, biology in particular has become notorious for the length of its titles.

Task Thirteen

Here are 17 titles and opening sentences of unedited draft CAs from international students or visiting scholars we have worked with. Look at the titles and opening sentences from an area of study that seems closest to your own. Finally, considering that the title and first sentence make the first impression on the reviewer, decide in each case whether

a. they are basically OK as they are;
b. they need some minor editing;
c. they require some substantial work.

For at least one of the cases you marked as requiring substantial work, offer a trial reformulation. Include some account of the thinking behind the suggested changes.

Business

___ 1. Marketing and Economic Development: One More Time

> One of the problematic issues in macromarketing is the question of whether marketing is a consequence of economic development or if economic development is a consequence of marketing.

___ 2. Psychology and Rapid Social Change in China

> The outcome of the rapid transformation of China to a democratic and market-oriented society involves not only political and economic changes but crucial psychological factors as well.

Anatomy/Medicine

___ 3. The Medical Geneticist's Perspective on NDI Research

> Nephrogenic diabetes insipidus (NDI) is an inborn error of water homeostasis that presents in early infancy.

___ 4. A Novel Target of Cancer Treatment

> Currently, metastatic cancers remain incurable diseases.

Chemistry

___ 5. Chemical Speciation of Thallium in Natural Waters Using Catio Exchange Resin

> Thallium is a potential pollutant, which is more toxic than lead and mercury.

___ 6. Quantitative and Regulatory Aspects of Polymorphism

> It is increasingly important to fully characterize solid state pharmaceutical systems at the bulk, particulate, and molecular levels.

Engineering

___ 7. Low Temperature Polycrystalline Silicon Thin Film Transistors with In-situ Doped Source and Drain

> We have fabricated novel polycrystalline silicon thin film transistors (poly-Si TFTs) employing in-situ doping process in order to implement poly-Si CMOS TFT technology.

___ 8. The Worst Case Scenario Generator

> In recent years, the auto industry has been focused on active safety systems, which can help the drivers to avoid traffic accidents.

English Language Teaching/Education

___ 9. Syllabus Design in ESP: Teachers' Problems in Estonia

> One of the problematic issues in ESP teaching is the choice of the suitable syllabus.

___ 10. The Effectiveness of Teacher Questions in Eliciting Responses from ESL Students Education

> ESL teachers ask questions of their students to encourage students to practice speaking English.

___ 11. How Asynchronous Learning Technologies May Expand the Need for Computer Skills Training of Education Majors

> The Web has become one of the most informative and diversified educational tools available to university instructors.

Theater

___ 12. Arthur Miller's Holocaust Plays

> An American dramatist, Arthur Miller achieved his major success with his early works, such as *Death of a Salesman* and *The Crucible.*

___ 13. Do the New Technologies Create New Opportunities for Performing Arts?

> Brenda Laurel said in her book *Computers as Theatre* (1991) that new media are dramatic because of the way they present information.

Anthropology

___ 14. "Hoabinhian" Lithic Assemblages from Lang Kamnan Cave, Western Thailand

> The status of "hoabinhian" has long been questioned by archaeologists for several decades.

___ 15. A Case Study of Agroecosystem Health in Honduras: Focusing on the Roles of Livestock in Agricultural Communities

> Small scale livestock production in the Tascalapa watershed of Honduras is an important method in which semi-subsistence farmers secure their livelihoods.

Sociology

___ 16. Analysis of Socio-cultural Influences on Japanese Families and the Social Welfare Policies in the Future

> This paper examines the following questions: what has influenced and will influence the cultural norms in Japanese families; how they have developed and will develop; and how will current social welfare policies in the U.S. and Japan need to be adjusted in order to accommodate with the transitions in social circumstances of Japanese and other families?

___ 17. The Ethnic Relations between Caucasian and Chinese Workers in California from 1849 to 1882

> This paper talks about the work of Bonancich and Hechter and suggests several factors affecting the process of institutionalizing discrimination: the number of migrant workers, the growth rate of the migrant workers, the economic situation of the area, the number of migrant workers in the threatening jobs, and the organizational strength of the local workers.

(See Note 20.)

2.8 Reviewing Conference Abstracts

By now, if you are taking a class, you will have submitted your revised CAs. Depending on the size and composition of the class, the instructor will divide you into two or more review panels. The (imaginary) regional conference is multidisciplinary, covering all fields. You might, for example, be divided into different fields of study. Whatever the outcome, you will not be reviewing your own CA!

Task Fourteen

Appoint a review panel chair. The chair will then ask you to rate each of the abstracts as one of the following.

1 = strong/excellent—must be included in the program

2 = fairly good—should get on the program if at all possible

3 = problematic/unconvincing/weak—only include if space needs to be filled up

Use this score sheet.

Name of abstract group _____

Abstract Number Score

1. __   5. __

2. __   6. __

3. __   7. __

4. __   8. __

The panel chair will then call a short meeting to tally the rankings and make final decisions. Not more than 50 percent of the abstracts should receive any one of the ratings (1–3).

When the panels reconvene, a representative of each panel should then announce which abstract received the highest rating and why. Congratulations will be in order. Before the class breaks up, each participant should choose an abstract and agree to send an e-mail message to the author giving the panel's rating and explaining why the rating was given. A copy of this should also be sent to the instructor. But first, look at the following Language Focus.

Language Focus: Good and Bad News E-mail Messages

Good News

The good news messages are relatively easy. Take a look at these two sent out by two of our former students.

1. Hi, congratulations! Your abstract was evaluated by our panel as among the best of those received. We very much hope that you will be able to present at the conference. If this is not possible, please let us know within a few days since we have a waiting list. Once again, congratulations.

2. Hi (name). We thought your abstract was excellent; indeed, it received an overall rating of 1.2. In consequence, we have reserved a place on the conference program for your paper. Please confirm as soon as possible that you will be attending.

What do you think of this e-mail message sent to Chris regarding a conference proposal?

```
To: Christine Feak
Subject: Case reading skills for students of law

Your proposal has been accepted for presentation at the ESP
Reading and Writing Conference in Seattle. You will receive
official notification by mail shortly. This mailing will
also include the time of your presentation as well as regis-
tration information.

There is no need to reply to this e-mail message unless you
need to provide a change of address. Your official notifica-
tion letter will be sent to the address below:

Thank you.
```

Did you note the absence of any congratulations? What effect does this have? (See Note 21.)

"Bad news" usually requires some preparation. Also the communicator of bad news may wish to "hide behind" the panel! Consider the following messages.

1. Unfortunately, due to the unusually large number of applicants and the limited amount of space on the program, the review committee was unable to accept your abstract this year. If you would like further details, please feel free to e-mail me. In the meantime, good luck with your future research.

2. A large number of strong abstracts were submitted to this year's conference, and we have only space to select the very best. After carefully reviewing your abstract, we cannot recommend that your paper be accepted at this time. However, we were sufficiently impressed by your work to place you on a waiting list. If this is acceptable to you, please let us know ASAP. On behalf of the review committee, (name).

3. Although the committee was interested in your project, we did not feel that your study would be "ready" for this year's conference. We remain confident, however, that you will be successful next time.

Recommendations and Suggestions

When sending a "bad news" message many of our students felt compelled to offer some kind of explanation for the rejection or some advice, as in the following. Please notice the difference in verb form between

1. Your abstract would have been more acceptable if you had included a sentence describing the methodology. (too late now!)
2. Your abstract would be more acceptable if you were to/could include a sentence describing the methodology. (maybe not too late!)

Notice also the role of a "prefacing" conditional designed to give the recipient *space* and to make the advice seem less imposing.

3. If you are planning to resubmit a version of this abstract to another conference, you might like to consider the following points which were made by members of the review committee: . . .

4. If you are in a position to submit a revised version by the end of this week, we would suggest that you focus attention on . . .

5. If you were to revise your abstract for another occasion, the sub-committee's advice would be to give more emphasis to the purpose of the research and less to the previous literature.

Task Fifteen

Now send your e-mail message to one of the abstract authors informing him or her of your committee's decision.

Task Sixteen

Prepare your third and final draft of your own CA taking into consideration the comments made by the committee.

2.9 The Ordering of Author Names and Short Versions of Conference Abstracts

No doubt you have worked hard on your conference abstract; we hope you are pleased with the final result and will actually submit it to an upcoming conference. In the real world, of course, your name may not be the only one associated with a CA. If there are other names you will need to decide how to order them, a decision which may require considerable thought.

Partly because of the way citation indexes (like the SCI and the SSCI) work, the *ordering* of names can be important—and can give rise to stress.

Task Seventeen

What are your preferences and/or expectations?

1. Ceteris paribus (other things being equal), names should be ordered alphabetically.

2. The first name should be that of the person who did most of the writing.

3. The first name should be that of the most senior person.

4. The first name should be that of the person who did most of the work.

5. The first name should be that of the person who needs the first-name credit the most.

6. Irrespective of any other factors, the first name should rotate when you work with the same people on different CAs and publications.

(See Note 22.)

The final bit of business concerning your successful CA may well be to produce a shorter version to appear in the conference program. These short versions are typically no more than 50 words—not necessarily an easy task. The 50-word summary should convey the key points of the paper and function as an advertisement to attract an audience.

Task Eighteen

Once again here is Tatyana's abstract, followed by three versions of a 50-word summary of her paper. Can you identify the first, second, and third (final) drafts of the summary?

Cultural Variation in the Genre of the Conference Abstract: Rhetorical and Linguistic Dimensions

[1]The conference abstract is a common and important genre that plays a significant role in disseminating new knowledge within scientific communities, both national and international. [2]As a genre with the specific features of "interestingness" created to attract the attention of reviewing committees, the conference abstract has been investigated by Berkenkotter & Huckin (1995) and Swales (1996). [3]However, the issue of cultural variation in the genre has not yet become a subject of research, although the conference abstract, like other genres of academic discourse, can be presumed to reflect national proclivities in writing.

[4]This paper attempts to describe the cultural-specific differences of English versus Ukrainian and Russian conference abstracts on the level of their cognitive structure and language, and to provide some tentative

explanations of the cultural and ideological backgrounds underlying these rhetorical and textlinguistic preferences. [5]It will also be shown how the inherited cognitive patterns of Slavic writers interplay with the acquired stereotypes of English scientific discourse in the abstracts they construct in English. [6]These texts, hybrid from the viewpoint of their cultural shaping, can be regarded as evidence of the transition period typical of both sociopolitical and intellectual life of Ukraine and other states of the former Soviet Union. [7]As a result, this study raises a broader question: To what extent is it necessary to adopt the English conventions of this genre in order to be accepted and recognized by international fora?

[8]This issue will be discussed in connection with the pedagogical implications arising from the findings and observations of this study.

a. As a genre with specific features of "interestingness" created to appeal to reviewing committees, the conference abstract has been attracting some scholarly attention. However, the issue of cultural variation in this genre has not been addressed. This paper describes and interprets the differences among English, Ukrainian, and Russian conference abstracts. (50 words)

b. Conference abstracts (CAs) are an important "gatekeeping" genre with interesting promotional features. Although these features are known in general terms, cross-cultural preferences and modifications have been little studied. Here, I compare English CAs with those written by Ukrainian and Russian specialists and explain those differences in cultural and ideological terms. (50 words)

c. The conference abstract is a common and important genre that plays a significant role in disseminating new knowledge within scientific communities. This paper describes the culture-specific differences of English versus Ukrainian and Russian conference abstracts. It then provides an explanation of the cultural and ideological backgrounds underlying these differences. (50 words)

Do you think Tatyana needs a fourth version? If so, why? (See Note 23.)

2.10 Notes and Comments for Unit Two

Note 1

Faber, B. Rhetoric in competition: The formation of organizational discourse in Conference on College Composition and Communication abstracts. *Written Communication* 13 (1996): 314–54.

Note 2 (sample responses for Task One)

1. Answers have ranged from two months to up to a year.

2. Most participants observe that it is much easier to get a poster accepted than a presentation; indeed, often an attempt to give a presentation gets "down-graded" to an opportunity to exhibit a poster.

3. Blind reviewing seems to be an increasing practice in most fields.

4. Some science fields, such as chemistry and biology, seem to be much more results oriented; their CAs are less like grant proposals.

5. The range seems to be from about 150 words to about 600.

6. Advisors and supervisors are often willing to be helpful here.

Note 3 (sample response for Task Two)

Broadly speaking, Tatyana's abstract fits her own model quite well, although there is a partial exception.

S1 and S2.	Outlining the field
S3	Justification
S4	Introduction of paper
S5 and S6	Summary of details
S7	?
S8	Discussion of consequences

Note that in S7, Tatyana does not so much "highlight the outcome" as she uses her research "to raise a broader question." This strikes us as an interesting variant.

Note 4

Mauranen, A. 1993. *Cultural differences in academic rhetoric: A textlinguistic study.* Frankfurt: Peter Lang.

Note 5 (sample responses for Task Three)

1. S1 common / important / significant role / both national and international
   S3 not yet become a subject of research / national proclivities
   S4 cultural and ideological backgrounds underlying these rhetorical and
      textlinguistic preferences
   S5 inherited cognitive patterns . . . acquired stereotypes

2. disseminating (S1)—spreading
   subject (S3)—topic
   proclivities (S3)—tendencies
   tentative (S4)—provisional, preliminary
   interplay (S5)—interact with
   hybrid (S6)—in this case made up of elements from two different kinds of texts
   fora (S7)—plural of *forum*, in this case a conference or professional meeting

3. The metadiscourse is intended to help guide the reader through the text so
   that it is read the way the author intended it to be. Metadiscourse is quite
   common in North American academic writing; however, it is less common in
   the academic writing of other cultures. For a fuller discussion see pages 169–74
   in Unit Five. The question of whether it is necessary typically generates debate in our classes. Some students feel that it is gratuitous and perhaps even
   condescending. Others find it quite helpful.

4. In S5 the use of the passive is useful as a stylistic variation. In this way she
   can avoid using *show* with an inanimate subject and also avoid using *I*. Compare the alternative wording: *In addition, I intend to show* . . . In S8 the choice
   of passive voice keeps the focus on the question raised in S7.

   It's hard to say with certainty why she sometimes uses the future. Tatyana
   had already completed the work in the abstract, and so it is not "promissory"
   (see Section 2.5). It could simply be a stylistic variation, or perhaps she just
   wants to emphasize her intent by using *will*, as something the audience can
   look forward to.

5. Whether or not *I* is appropriate in any academic text raises considerable discussion. Most of our students argue against using *I* since it sounds too self-
   promotional, as we found in Unit One. Using *we* seems more acceptable, but
   then the question arises as to whether *we* can always be used, even when there
   is a single author. Students in the sciences have generally said *we* is fine in all
   cases and is much preferred over *I*.

6. Perhaps using *this* can help "bring some readers round to an author's orientation," but whether it necessarily does seems open to question.

7. One possibility is to break S4 into two sentences to ease the cognitive load on the reader. Another is to remove some of the appositives and put the information contained there into its own sentence. For example, in S6:

> [6]These texts can be considered hybrids from the viewpoint of their cultural shaping. As hybrids, they can be regarded as evidence of the transition period typical of both sociopolitical and intellectual life of Ukraine and other states of the former Soviet Union.

8. It seems reasonable to us that there may be a connection between academic texts and sociopolitical and ideological forces.

9. In our experience, almost everybody answers this question (correctly) by saying, "It depends on the context." If the conference has a theoretical orientation, the last sentence could be left out. If it is a conference with many language teachers attending, keep the original or replace it with the b alternative. If it is a conference with a particular focus on Slavic academics, then c would work well.

Note 6 (sample responses for Task Four)

1	The journal is growing, especially following our decision to move to six issues a year. The introduction of blind reviewing and the inclusion of key words to facilitate database searching have also gone smoothly. The
2	winner of the 1998 McArthur prize for the best article published in 1997 goes to . . . for their article entitled . . . The winner is determined exclusively by a vote of the members of the Editorial Board—the editors have no vote. This
3	issue contains seven articles. In the first, Moreno and Sanchez develop a theoretical model to account for . . . In the second, . . .
4	Once a year we also acknowledge the invaluable assistance of the additional readers for the journal, those who are not official members of the Editorial or Advisory Boards. For 1997 those readers were: Mary Abbott, Richard Alexander, Angela Antonioni . . .

The first move deals with general business of the journal, while the second contains a specific announcement. The third summarizes the contents of the articles in the issue. The final one is devoted to professional courtesy, namely, thanking those who had helped the journal by providing reviews.

The third move is likely fixed and obligatory; however, what comes before and after probably depends on whether there is "business" to be taken care of as well as the nature of the business. Move 2 and Move 4, for example, likely occur only once a year. If there is little or no pressing business, the beginning may also include a general introduction to the issue, discussing current concerns or directions of the field.

Note 7 (sample analysis for Task Five)

1. Outlining the field	[1]Head biomechanics research is often interested in head or impacted structure modeling, but less often the study of impact itself. [2]In studies using an analytical approach, epidemiological studies, and in studies of structure aggressiveness, researchers often use a lumped parameter approach to model the structure and a single mass to model the head. [3]Often, in experimental studies, the real structure is impacted by a physical model of the head which is a single mass in structure and behavior (rigid head form or Hybrid 3 head).
2. Justifying by indicating a gap	[4]A collaboration between Institution 1 and Institution 2 has demonstrated that this approach may be criticized for two reasons. [5]First, the (analytical or physical) modeling of the head as a single mass rules out any interpretation of head injury mechanisms. [6]Second, the modeling of the head by a single mass produces a very different head-structure force interaction than that which would be produced if a more bio-faithful head model is used.
3. Introducing the paper	[7]The objective of this joint study is to propose an experimental and analytical method to analyze head impact which uses a more realistic model of the head. [8]In the past numerous studies have shown the importance of brain-skull decoupling on the mechanical behavior of the head under impact. [9]In the proposed approach, this phenomenon will be taken into consideration.
4. Summarizing the work	[10]In the experimental component of the study, the recently published dummy head "Bimass 150" is dropped onto beams with different characteristics. [11]The impacts are compared. . . . [12]The results show that the analytical model can simulate the experimental force interactions

5. Highlighting
   conclusions

{ as well as intercranial dynamics . . . . [13]The results also show . . . [14]We conclude that the experimental or theoretical modeling of the head mechanical behavior has an important influence on the structure response and that this has to be taken into consideration in the analysis of structure aggressiveness. [15]It also appears that the proposed approach permits the prediction of a head injury mechanism for a given impact.

From C. Räisänen, *The conference forum as a series of genres* (Göteborg, Sweden: Acta Universitatis Gotholourgensis, 1999). Permission for use granted by Rémy Willinger.

Note 8 (sample responses for Task Five)

1. Theoretical Modeling of Head Impact for Predicting Head Injury Mechanisms using "Bimass 150"

   This title seems to be the best since it reflects the objective stated in S7.

   > Experimental and Theoretical Modeling of Head Impact—Influence of Head Modeling

   This title doesn't capture the focus of the work. Head modeling is not new, as indicated in S1, so it has little news value.

   > Brain Decoupling and Its Influence on the Mechanical Behavior of the Head under Impact

   This title seems too narrow. The decoupling phenomenon is only part of the study as stated in S9.

2. In S7 the metadiscourse announces the purpose of the study. Without such an explicit statement, the reader may have to infer what the objective is. In S9 the metadiscourse ("proposed") helps the writer establish what sets this research apart from other research. Removing the metadiscourse would pose a greater challenge for the writer in terms of convincing the reader of the importance of the work. If the metadiscourse in S7 were moved to the first paragraph, the abstract would have a rather narrow and abrupt beginning. There would be no background or justification for the work before the purpose of the study is revealed.

3. We think, despite some uncertainties in language, the two researchers have established their authority and expertise quite well; certainly, they have worked hard to try to establish the superiority of their approach. As in Tatyana's case, however, we feel the final sentence does not quite get them where they might want to be.

4a. Stating that "the research is interested in . . . " seems a bit odd to us. Here are two alternatives.

> Recent head biomechanics research has tended to focus on head or impacted structure modeling but less often on the study of impact itself.

> While head or impacted structure modeling has been the focus of much head biomechanics research, the study of impact itself has received much less attention.

4b. *Impact* as a verb still sounds "funny" to Chris, and she does not use it; however, *impact* as a verb has spread like wildfire throughout the United States and can be widely heard and read. Check journals in your field to see whether *impact* has achieved verb status in your research area. In the MICASE spoken data about one-sixth of the occurrences of *impact* are verbs.

4c. This has occurred almost certainly because the requirements of blind reviewing do not permit the authors to mention their own institutions.

4d. S1: impacted structure modeling
S2: a lumped parameter approach
S10: recently published dummy head "Bimass 150"
S9 and S15: the proposed approach

Note 9

Naturally we cannot provide any answers here, but we would anticipate that in science and engineering conference abstracts would be more technical and contain less justification in the openings.

(Teaching Hint: If your class is ready for it, they can do Task Ten about now, rather than waiting until later.)

Note 10

Berkenkotter, C. and T. N. Huckin. 1995. *Genre knowledge in disciplinary communication.* Hillsdale, NJ: Lawrence Erlbaum.

Note 11

Other suggestions have included the scale of the research reported, good statistical support, a sophisticated model, the "neatness" of the experiment, and a connection to recent theory.

Note 12

This little story has been included to emphasize that the experienced researcher in your area is the best person to anticipate how other experts will react to your draft. A nonexpert cannot offer this valuable perspective.

Note 13 (sample responses for Task Eight)

1. Perhaps some thinking has been done on the topic, but there is little in the abstract to suggest anything substantive has been done. In S4 *my research will* and in S6 *I will also investigate* suggests that the work must still be done. Also no preliminary results have been given, nor has a method been outlined.

2. At the very least, some detail on where the research will be carried out and on what species should be added. Our best advice would be for some work to be done before submitting the abstract.

3. We have both written promissory abstracts, which, we suspect, is easier to do in our field than it might be in others. While neither of us has failed to come through with what was promised (or at least something close), we know of others who have been less fortunate.

(Teaching Hint: Here's an activity that our students have enjoyed. After the students have turned in their abstracts, retype the first sentence of each (without the author's name) on a handout. Distribute the handout in class and have the students guess who wrote which sentence.)

Note 14 (sample response for Task Nine)

Here is one response. Note all the hedges.

> This seems interesting, and there has been a lot of public interest in the issue. The topic is timely and therefore of possible interest to the conference goers. Since this proposal is for a sociology conference, the simple description of genetic engineering is probably helpful. The preliminary results indicate that the work has likely already been done—this is not a promissory abstract. Also, it is good that the need to be investigating the issue is given: there is a potential for great economic loss or gain.
>
> Still the abstract could be improved with the addition of references to previous work. The second paragraph seems a bit repetitious. Given the space constraints of typical proposals, is it really necessary to say twice that the FDA considers the tomatoes to be safe? If there is sufficient space, it might also help to say something about how the data was obtained (Was it a questionnaire or an interview?

What kind of interview or questionnaire?) and to describe some general characteristics of the individuals involved in the study. Should you say anything about
the method of data analysis? Also I think it would be a good idea to give the full
name of the FDA—the Food and Drug Administration—since usually the full
form is used first and then subsequently the acronym.

Note 15 (answer key for item 2, Task Ten)

2. The graduate students said they wanted a final examination.

	S	I
a. This *statement* surprised the instructor.	✓	__
b. This *request* surprised the instructor.	✓	__
c. This *hope* surprised the instructor.	__	✓
d. This *desire* surprised the instructor.	__	✓
e. This *demand* surprised the instructor.	__	✓
f. This *ultimatum* surprised the instructor.	__	✓

In c–f the writer is indicating his or her subjective interpretation of the event.
However, choices c and d convey less of an interpretation than choice e and
much less than f.

Note 16 (sample responses for item 6, Task Ten)

All of the choices are grammatically correct, but not all convey the writer's
intended meaning. Choice a, *it,* is unsuccessful because the referent is unclear.
What is *it?* Is *it* the fact that the learner is free to choose what to do next? Is *it*
Web-based learning? Typically, *it* will refer to a single noun phrase rather than
a whole point. Thus, using *it* to refer to a larger point can be confusing to the
reader. Choice b, *this,* is perhaps only slightly more successful than a, again because the referent is not clear. While *this* can refer to a larger chunk of text, in this
case, *this* could perhaps be thought to refer to any of the points. *This approach* in
choice c seems better but may still lead to confusion in the reader. The first sentence refers *to Web-based learning approaches,* so given the plural the reader would
rule this out as a referent. The reader would look for a singular referent. Is *this
approach* referring to simply using the Web to learn? To taking multiple choice
tests? Choice d does not seem successful since it suddenly shifts the focus to one
small part of the text, namely, the use of multiple choice to test recall of information. This focus seems too narrow; something broader is necessary. Finally, choice
e seems to have the appropriate focus. *This approach to assessment* here refers to
students learning via the Web but being assessed in traditional ways that separate learning and the assessment of that learning.

Note 17 (sample responses for Task Eleven)

1. This change in preferences; This reverse in habits; This change in proportion; This shift in diet

2. This fundamental shift in understanding; This change in our understanding; This improved understanding of the link between malnutrition and cognitive ability

3. This advance toward more convenient guns; This advance in gun technology; This improvement in weapons technology

Note 18 (sample responses for Task Twelve)

Up until the 1980s, the typical immigrant to the United States was poor, not well educated, and had few marketable skills. Over the last decade, however, increased global economic interdependence has given rise to growth in transnational migration among the generally well educated middle class. In fact, in some urban areas of the United States middle class migrants have a stronger presence than poorer, struggling immigrants. Despite this <u>growth / change in demographics / shift</u>, however, social work and psychological theories of migration and acculturation have continued to focus on poorer immigrants and U.S.-born minority populations (Sherraden & Martin, 1994; Drachman, 1992; Mayadas & Elliot, 1992; Jabob, 1994).   *all summarizing*

As a migrant population, the middle class has a unique set of problems that is often exacerbated since this group is unable to gain access to social services and other support mechanisms for the less well off. This <u>lack of access / difficulty / problem</u> has led to a unique set of vulnerabilities. Among this population, the group least understood is that of graduate and postdoctoral students and their families (academic migrant families), who have come to the U.S. for education opportunities. The number of academic migrants in the U.S. is not insignificant, with more than half a million students and scholars studying in the U.S. annually—triple the number 20 years ago.   *Difficulty* and *problem* are interpretive; *lack of access* summarizes

This paper reports on a recent investigation of the problems faced by graduate students, scholars, and their families at a large midwestern university. Preliminary analysis of a survey questionnaire reveals that after migration, men perceive their lives as having changed very little, while women believe their lives have drastically changed, especially since they typically maintain the home, care for young children, and must learn to navigate the "ins" and "outs" of a new culture. This <u>difference (in attitude) / disparity / contrast</u> may explain why women uprooted from their countries for the sake of their husbands' education often report greater feelings of frustration and homesickness. . . . This presentation concludes by describing interventions for migrant students and scholars that reflect the complicated nature of their vulnerability.   *Disparity* seems more interpretive; *difference* and *contrast* summarize

The density of summary words seems right. Some texts may, in fact, have few summary words, while others may have more. There are two instances of metadiscoursal phrases: *This paper* and *This presentation.*

Note 19 (discussion of Samiri Hernandez-Hiraldo's conference abstract)

Samiri's text was selected for reformulation for reasons that are not hard to imagine. The subject matter is likely to be interesting and broadly accessible to classmates coming from many different fields (although many will be reaching for their dictionaries). The syntactic errors are sufficiently insignificant to not distract attention from the more "macro" questions. The abstract also looks like a pretty successful draft; certainly, Samiri seems to have found an appropriate balance and organization for her text.

So here is the rest of our reformulation, with the further thinking behind our changes to the text. Again, note that Samiri did not adopt all of the suggestions. (Key: O = the original; R = our reformulation; J = our justifications for the changes; C = class opinions)

Sentence 2

O: Religious studies demonstrate that the continuing role of religion is due to its capacity for restructuring and assuming various forms (Wuthnow 1988 & Kepel 1994).

R: In fact, research suggests that the continuing role of religion is due to its capacity for restructuring and assuming various alternative forms (Wuthnow, 1988; Kepel, 1994).

J: Up-to-date references, good; Berkenkotter and Huckin would surely approve (see table 2.1). Interesting, we don't often see an ampersand (&) used to join *different* publications; this will make a small but technically useful point in class. *As it did.* Samiri's *religious studies* seems ambiguous—academic studies or study of sacred texts by true believers? As probably the former, let's change to *research;* also add a sentence connector. That *demonstrate* looks far too bold: shooting her research in the foot before she has started? We need a softer verb here.

C: Points all taken by the class

Sentence 3

O: Anthropologists and Latin Americanists interested in conversion emphasize the role of world/traditional religion in the articulation of local and global specificities, so necessary for coexistence (Stoll 1990, the Commaroffs 1993 & Hefner 1993).

R: More specifically, Latin American anthropologists and other specialists interested in religious conversion have stressed the way in which traditional world religions can intersect with local or global specifics, thus preserving religious belief with a secular culture (Stoll, 1990; Comaroff & Comaroff, 1993; Hefner, 1993).

J: This is a tough sentence, highly dense and abstract—evidence of Hispanic academic argumentation? We need to try to break it out a bit. How do *anthropologists and Latin Americanists* line up? Let's experiment. Why the slash between *world* and *traditional?* "Coexistence" with what? Other religious groups? Or with the nonreligious as well? We like "the Comaroffs" as a warm and friendly way of making a reference, but, unfortunately, it will not go with the formal tone of the text.

C: There was major debate on this. First, we had misread Samiri's intentions with the opening subject; second, Samiri made it very clear that "world" and "traditional," that is, local, were completely different; and third, where did we get this idea of religious-secular coexistence from? Especially given the title. On the last point at least, we clearly needed to have our heads examined. (See Samiri's final revised version (p. 53) for a third sentence rather different from both her original and the reformulation.

Sentence 4

O: Prevailing paradigms, however, limit their analysis by concentrating exclusively in the ideological and scriptural analysis, by considering the official point of view, and by elevating the more palpable or heroic manifestations of coexistence that are, religious conferences, assemblies, ecumenical agencies, academic seminars, special purpose groups, etc.

R: The prevailing paradigms, however, limit their analyses by concentrating on ideological or scriptural analyses, by privileging the official point of view, and by elevating the more visible or "heroic" manifestations of coexistence as manifested through religious conferences or assemblies, or through ecumenical agencies, religious pressure groups or academic seminars.

J: This is an impressive sentence, in length, language, and content. Don't want to do much here. An extra article before *ideological* can go. We don't understand *palpable;* change? Put *heroic* in scare quotes to maintain judicious academic distance? What are these *special purpose groups?* Pro-life or something like that?

C: Several members of the class jumped on the unnecessary repetitions of *analyses* and *manifest.* The instructors acknowledged that they would try to do better in the future. Lengthy class discussion with Samiri about what she meant by *special purpose groups.* This turned out to be groups of hospital visitors, and the like. Clearly not "pro-life" types of groups. She finally agreed that it was hard to explain and not necessary anyhow.

Sentence 5

O: This paper elaborates the processes of religious coexistence in a small municipality of Puerto Rico.

R: In contrast to this orientation, this paper investigates the processes of religious-secular coexistence in a small municipality in Puerto Rico.

J: OK, here is the switch to the present study, so let's build up the contrast. *Elaborates* looks like a Spanishism.

C: Changes were approved, especially after the instructors themselves deleted the word *secular.* Learning from their mistakes!

Sentence 6

O: From archival research, life histories, interviews and participant observation, results show that types of conversion relate to patterns of coexistence.

R: Using a combination of archival research, life histories, interviews and participant observation, the study shows that patterns of conversion can be related to patterns of coexistence.

J: *From* is a bit awkward here as is *results show.* A better connection is needed.

C: Samiri observed that, although the repetition of *patterns* showed an attractive parallelism, it wasn't in fact accurate; it was *processes* that she was concerned with. Very interesting discussion, especially from the scientists, about the merits and demerits of saying, "The results show" (there they are, for all to see), as opposed to "the study shows" (results are hard to get at, but after my analysis . . . !).

Sentence 7

O: They also demonstrate that coexistence is determined by the interplay of processes from above and from below, by the immediate social contact of the daily life and by discursive and non discursive aspects of doing ritual or the whole religious experience.

R: More specifically, the study demonstrates that coexistence is determined by the interplay of processes at various levels—from the whole religious experience, from the discursive and non-discursive aspects of ritual engagement, and from the immediate social contact of daily life.

J: Add a connecting phrase; keep with "the study" orientation; how many levels? In any case, put them in order from macro to micro.

C: Typing error. It should read *contract*, not *contact*; otherwise the class (and Samiri) thought the changes were basically successful. (But see the changes made in Samiri's revised version on p. 53.)

Note 20 (sample responses for Task Thirteen)

Business

1. The opening sentence seems OK, but the title is not very informative. A good title should suggest what the paper is about.

2. Both the title and first sentence are fine.

Anatomy/Medicine

3. The title is fine. The first sentence, a definition, is rather uninteresting but may be fine.

4. The title is a bit vague. What kind of cancer? What kind of target? The first sentence could use a little work, too.

Chemistry

5. The title is sufficiently specific. It reveals the focus of the paper. The first sentence is much like that of number three—it seems to be saying something that would be generally known in the field.

6. The title appears to be OK. The opener is good. By stating the importance of fully characterizing solid state pharmaceutical systems at the bulk, particulate, and molecular levels, the author presents him- or herself as an authority and familiar with issues in the field.

Engineering

7. Title is fine. Interesting opening sentence beginning with *we* and announcing what has been accomplished.

8. The title here is very broad. What kind of generator will this paper discuss? The connection of the first sentence to the title is unclear.

English Language Teaching/Education

9. The title could do a better job at revealing the actual focus of the paper. ESP (English for specific purposes) is actually a broad field that includes business

English, English for medicine, English for law, hotel English, and a whole host of other professional areas. The title here leaves the reader wondering what area will be dealt with. Consequently, the first sentence also needs to be tightened up.

10. The title seems fine, but the first sentence is simply stating the obvious. An opener such as this would likely suggest to the reviewer that this was written by someone fairly new to the field.

11. Good title and pretty good first sentence, which expands on the title.

Theater

12. The title is too broad as it fails to indicate what aspect of Miller's Holocaust plays will be discussed. It's unlikely that all aspects can be discussed in a conference paper.

13. Interesting title. The first sentence suggests the writer has some familiarity with the field, a definite plus.

Anthropology

14. The title is highly specific, suggesting expertise on the part of the writer. The first sentence works well to counter the possible "dullness" of the title by raising a general issue.

15. Very specific, informative title. It could be improved by using *A Focus on* rather than *Focusing on*. The opening statement of fact seems fine.

Sociology

16. The title is fine, but opening with a series of questions does not seem to be the best strategy.

17. The title is fine. However, the opening sentence seems to suggest that the paper will be a review of Bonancich and Hechter. It's not clear whether a contribution to the field will be made.

(Task Fourteen Teaching Hint: The arrangements for this activity are a little complicated, so here are some suggestions. Give each panel four to five abstracts for review, making sure that nobody on a panel reviews his or her own abstract. That said, try to make sure that the members of the panel work on areas not too distant from the areas they are reviewing. For example, five engineers could review five science abstracts, and five scientists could review five engineering abstracts. Finally, make sure that a panel chair is appointed at the outset, who will have the responsibility of announcing the "winner" and delegating the follow-up e-mail messages.)

Note 21

The message seems rather cold and uninviting. Adding a simple "congratulations" would be an improvement.

Note 22 (sample responses for Task Seventeen)

This is a minefield. Arrangement of names can easily lead to bad feelings and bitterness, even if great care is taken in deciding the order. People with names beginning with A, B, or C may favor the first approach. Many scientists of our acquaintance follow approach 2. In some fields, especially where there are several co-authors, the convention is that the most senior person is placed last. We believe that approach 2 is more common than approach 4. In some cases, such as when someone is looking for a job or being considered for a promotion, approach 5 may be appropriate. The sixth option is fine if there is a regular and well-established research group.

   Arranging names alphabetically may be the easiest thing to do, but it may be problematic. It's best to have some reason for the names appearing in the order that they do. Although names are often ordered according to the amount of work done, you may decide to do otherwise, particularly if you work with the same group on various projects. Seniority should not outweigh the level of contribution individuals have made.

Note 23 (sample response for Task Eighteen)

The short program abstract may be your only opportunity to advertise your presentation to conference participants. Thus, you want to take a reasonable amount of time preparing it. The short abstract should say enough about your presentation so that the reader has a fairly good idea of what your talk is all about. Abstract a was written first, followed by c, and then b. There is not a great deal of difference among the three proposed abstracts; however, it's not clear that it is necessary to say anything about the characteristics of the CA. Anyone potentially interested in the teaching or research of CAs will already be familiar with their characteristics. Perhaps a fourth version should be considered.

d. Although the conference abstract has been attracting some scholarly attention, the issue of cultural variation in this genre has not been addressed. This paper describes the culture-specific differences of English versus Ukrainian and Russian conference abstracts. It then provides an explanation of the cultural and ideological backgrounds underlying these differences. (51 words)

Unit Three
Research on Display—
the Conference Poster

"Haven't I seen this poster somewhere before?"

The main topic of this unit is both similar to and different from that of Unit Two. It is similar because it also focuses on writing in connection with an academic oral event. It is different because the writing is now visible, public, and open for all to see. That is why we have entitled the unit "Research on Display—the Conference Poster."

The unit has the following sections.

   3.1. Introductory Activities

   3.2. Poster Layouts

   3.3. Types of Compressed Language

3.1 Introductory Activities

Today most conferences and meetings have special sessions designed for the presentation of posters. For many years posters have been the poor country cousin of papers, but recently they have gained in status. In the United States in some fields, for instance, it used to be difficult to receive any funding to present a poster at a conference. Today, however, the story is changing and funding is more available. At some conferences, monetary prizes may even be awarded to the student who presents the best poster. It's no wonder then that many resources such as Internet sites and commercial software are widely available to help in the preparation of posters.

The experience of a poster "presenter" is quite different from that of a paper presenter. Papers are given under strict time constraints (rarely more than 30 minutes) and usually permit only limited interaction at their close between presenters and the fixed audience. Posters are on official display for a much longer period of time (typically two hours or more). Members of the audience are free to move around and are free to either read the poster or to engage in a one-on-one discussion, and they will typically do both. As a result, although the term *poster presentation* is conventional, it is not quite accurate; the "poster presenter" is more like an exhibitor.

Task One

Posters have several potential advantages over papers. Here are three.

1. They allow research to be presented at an earlier stage than do papers.

2. They provide the presenter an opportunity to have a direct exchange of professional ideas, thus providing some feedback that may in fact influence the remaining or future research.

3. They enable a new researcher to begin making personal contact with others in the field.

Can you think of other advantages of doing a poster? If so, list them here.

_____

_____

_____

What are the possible disadvantages? List them here.

_____

_____

_____

(See Note 1.)

On the next page you will find a short critical article, written in the style of a letter to the editor. The article appeared in the *British Medical Journal* and argues for greater evaluation of posters in medical science. In our view, however, the article raises some general issues that need to be considered in all fields. As background to the article, we offer the following observations.

Medical research, like pharmacy and computer science, is one of those areas where the relationships between the academy and industry are particularly complex. However, even in the humanities there are times when industry and the academy converge, such as at conferences that have large publishers' exhibits. Some conferences may also provide publishers with a place on the conference program for authors of new books, particularly textbooks, to "advertise" their new products.

Further, in many fields, national associations for particular disciplines may see their annual conferences as key opportunities for raising money. Getting as much as possible of the membership to attend is therefore important. At the same time, however, obtaining funding from one's home institution for travel, registration, and hotel accommodation has traditionally been tied to paper presentation, which, of course, is generally limited to some percentage of the conference paper abstracts submitted (as discussed in Unit Two).

Ways of increasing the number of active and official participants have included making more official the duties of chairs and associate chairs of presentation sessions and of organizers of panels, symposia, and so on. The most significant development in many fields, however, has been the rise of the poster session.

Here now is Dr. Leach's contribution to the Personal View column in the *British Medical Journal.* The title is somewhat of a pun—on a literal level, posters are indeed *writing on the wall.* However, the phrase *the writing is on the wall* has its roots in the Old Testament of the Bible (Daniel 5) and also means that the end is near. Some language glosses have been provided for your assistance.

The Poster Session: Is the Writing on the Wall?

Despite the global improvement in telecommunications, the size and number of international medical conferences continue to grow. Demand for such meetings is fuelled[1] by the often exotic locations, which have been made more accessible by the increasing ease of intercontinental travel. As conferences grow, delegates' fees and subsidies from the pharmaceutical industry ensure that they are now rather profitable and more about business than about education or research.

1. Driven, powered

Large medical meetings traditionally allow "experts" to lecture large audiences from high podiums.[2] For some reason, probably a hangover from the over-reaching 1980s,[3] it is rather unfashionable to attend a conference merely to learn something. So in an attempt to involve as many people as possible—that is, increase revenue—organising committees have come to rely increasingly on the poster presentation, where new research work (and new researchers) can be presented to smaller groups of interested delegates.

2. Impressive and authoritative places of delivery
3. Something left over from the over-ambitious 1980s

There are positive aspects of poster sessions. They allow research to be presented at an earlier stage, and provide a source of feedback which can shape the final work. For non-English speaking or inexperienced researchers, posters will always be less threatening, allowing any grammatical or scientific difficulties to be ironed out[4] in advance. Some people would argue that the threshold for accepting poster abstracts should be low, on the grounds that it encourages talent from underdeveloped medical cultures. It is a rather cynical encouragement, however, which necessitates the handover of substantial amounts of money in conference registration fees.

4. Taken care of, smoothed away as with a laundry iron

The main incentive for many people—despite the attractions of travel—in presenting a poster is that the abstracts for any self respecting congress will be published, usually in one of the relevant specialty's more highly regarded journals. My recent conference experience would suggest, though, that this trend is having less than beneficial effects on research and researchers.

At one session at the recent World Congress of Neurology, 24 out of 78 poster sites remained vacant, the remaining sites being occupied by small audit projects, or poorly constructed, ill conceived and (by implication) unethical trials, or even (despite the conditions stated in the original call for abstracts) single case studies. Anyone looking for respite[5] from the demands of randomisation or control groups would have been delighted.

5. Relief, escape

You might wonder why you should pay any attention to this, my own small uncontrolled study? Admittedly, if the only negative aspect of poster sessions is that delegates have to bear the sight of[6] some rather poor science, while avoiding eye contact with the nervous authors, then I would accept that abolishing the sessions would be unnecessarily harsh. The matter, however, is somewhat more sinister.[7]

6. Tolerate

Automatic acceptance of abstracts for poster presentations means that unscrupulous doctors can gain citable publication (and therefore academic credence) with work that might never have been seen in public, never mind subject to adequate peer review. The potential for such abuse is realised when abstracts appear with eponymous[8] titles, reading more like advertisements than considered science.

7. Here serious, dangerous, worrying

In four years' time the next World Congress of Neurology will be held in London. I hope that there will be some vigorous vetting[9] of the submitted abstracts, imitating those meetings where acceptance of an abstract is an honour, not a basic right. Ideally, the need for income will come second to the desire to see good clinical science rewarded before bad. Evidence from other conferences, though, would suggest that the profit motive will win once again.

8. The name of the author of a work is part of the title, e.g., *Roget's Thesaurus.* One could envision a poster entitled "Goddard's Miracle Cure" presented by Dr. Goddard!
9. *British* checking, assessing

—John Paul Leach, specialist registrar in neurology and neurophysiology, Liverpool

This article was first published in the BMJ. (J. P. Leach. The poster session: Is the writing on the wall? *BMJ* 1998; 316:157) and is reproduced by permission of the BMJ.

Task Two

Number the paragraphs of Dr. Leach's commentary. In your view, which paragraph contains Dr. Leach's strongest point? (See Note 2.)

From the perspective of your own field, do you agree with Dr. Leach's rather critical assessment of posters in his own field of neurology, which could be summarized as presenting "junk work"? If not, why not?

Posters are, of course, situated in a particular time and place, and efforts are continually being made to make them more prominent. According to one of our students, Jin Nam Choi, at the meetings of the American Psychological Association, posters now have to be printed in a much larger font and to contain more graphics. As a result, the number of words available has decreased.

Task Three

A colleague has prepared her poster for a conference. She has used a large font and given space constraints cannot include everything she would like to present on the poster. She is not quite sure what else to take with her. Here are four options. Which would you advise? Or do you have a fifth?

1. There should at least be a list of references available.
2. Interested viewers should be directed to a Web site that contains a more complete write-up of the work that they can download.
3. Hard copies of the complete paper should be available.
4. Interested viewers should be encouraged to provide their names and addresses on a sign-up sheet so that they can be sent a more complete write-up later. (Keep in mind a recent study that revealed presenters follow through at best about 50 percent of the time!)

(See Note 3.)

One problem with poster sessions is that they tend to have a very loose and freely organized structure (although this can also be an advantage, of course). For example, one poster might attract a big crowd, while another might be completely ignored. One way of adding structure to poster sessions is to have a *poster review session* during which a senior member of the field is invited to give his or her reactions to a subset of posters at a particular time. (The International Applied Linguistics Congress introduced this at the 1996 congress in Finland. John was asked to do one of the first of these, and he had to struggle to make a few comments about each of the 24 posters in his set and to try to find connections among them. The authors of the posters sat on the floor in the poster area for the hour's commentary and discussion. John is unsure if he'll ever agree to do something like this again!)

Do you have any experience with this kind of forum? What do you think of it?

3.2 Poster Layouts

Regardless of Dr. Leach's criticism of posters in his field, posters are often a good first step into the conference arena. They are also sometimes the preferred mode of presentation by some researchers because of the advantages discussed in Task One. Thus, in the next part of this unit we will highlight some considerations in poster preparation. But first, take a moment and test your poster knowledge.

Task Four

Answer Y (yes) or N (no) to those statements that you think apply to posters in your field. Compare your results with those of a partner.

___ 1. The success of a poster presentation depends on visual and inter-personal skills as well as content.

___ 2. Posters should be modeled on the sections of a journal article and include an abstract, an introduction, methods, results, discussion, a conclusion, references, and acknowledgments.

___ 3. Photographs, figures, diagrams, and other types of visuals should take up more space than does the written explanation.

___ 4. Posters should contain only those results that are necessary to validate your conclusions.

___ 5. Information in posters should be presented in newspaper style (in columns so that the viewer reads from top to bottom first and then moves to the right).

___ 6. Posters should have a lot of "white space" to limit the amount of reading required of the viewer.

___ 7. Figures should be simplified so that the viewers can easily understand them.

___ 8. A poster should be self-explanatory, requiring no input from the presenter.

___ 9. Information, except for captions, should be presented in full sentences.

___ 10. Some information should be WRITTEN IN ALL CAPITAL LETTERS.

___ 11. Posters should not contain the pronouns *I, we, my, mine,* or *our.*

___ 12. Acronyms should be spelled out in their entirety the first time used.

(See Note 4.)

Of course, one of the major concerns in poster preparation is determining the most effective layout. Presenters want their posters to attract the attention of those walking through the session. Thus, your title needs to be readable from around 10 feet away, and the layout needs to be appealing. Although we want to devote most of our attention in this unit to language issues related to posters, we will first offer some general formatting suggestions.

1. Follow the guidelines given by the conference.

2. Arrange your information into vertical columns across the poster, using subheadings, if necessary.

3. Make sure there is sufficient white space between blocks of information and that there is not too much text (use bullets).

4. Clearly label all figures and graphs.

5. Use a large typeface so that everything can be read from a comfortable distance.

6. Use no more than two fonts throughout.

7. Try not to overdo the formatting. Bold, italicize, and underline only as necessary. Too much fancy formatting will distract your audience.

8. DO NOT WRITE IN ALL CAPITAL LETTERS.

Task Five

Figures 6 and 7 provide two pilot versions of the same poster material. Does each of the posters tell its story well? Which of these versions do you prefer, and why? What special circumstances might affect your decision?

From Information Transfer to Data Commentary
J. M. Swales and C. B. Feak
English Language Institute
The University of Michigan
Ann Arbor, MI 48109

Abstract

This paper demonstrates the need for a wider concept of data commentary, in which a proactive and critical approach to "reading" the data is encouraged, and in which the written output provides an opportunity to demonstrate intelligence, analysis, and that elusive characteristic of "interestingness"...

Introduction

Right from the early days of English for Specific Purposes (ESP), the use and value of incorporating technical non-verbal material in teaching texts and tasks was widely recognized (e.g., Herbert 1965). By the mid-70s the use of formulas, diagrams, graphs, and tables had become a major feature of ESP materials...

Method

Under present policy, the University of Michigan, like many anglophone universities around the world, re-evaluates the English ability of most new international graduate students. For the writing part of the re-evaluation two tasks are required: one a 30-minute composition based on source material and the other a data commentary. Four student commentaries were analyzed for language and rhetorical effect ...

Results

Scores on the commentary task ranged from a low of 63 to a high of 97 on a ten-point scale. The texts ranged in length from 51 to 105 words total. The text contained an average of five propositions...

Discussion

The weaker, less successful texts clearly relied on a simple information transfer (IT) approach.

These texts merely repeated information that was obvious from the visual, resulting in rather flat, unimaginative writing. The stronger texts tried to offer interpretations...

Conclusion

EAP writing instructors must go beyond teaching syntax, morphology, and typical genre conventions and attempt to reach out to students' critical intelligence. Writing accompanying nonverbal material typically takes the form of a selective interpretive *commentary*...

References

Herbert, A. 1965. *The Structure of Technical English*. London: Longman.

Fig. 6

(See Note 5.)

There is considerable variation within and across disciplines with regard to poster presentation. For example, in a Department of Molecular Biology poster session that we attended, most but not all posters had an abstract, an introduction, methods, results, discussion, and a conclusion. Other posters had an introduction, a problem statement, a description of a solution, and a conclusion. Still others began with an introduction, which was

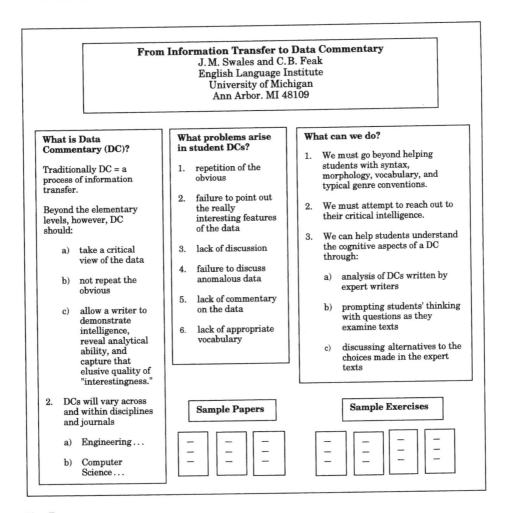

Fig. 7

then followed by objectives and a description of the study. Some posters were very dense in terms of written text, consisting of full sentences (like figure 6), while others had a lot of white space, bulleted lists, and sentence fragments (like figure 7).

Because of this stylistic variation within and across fields, it is difficult to address all of the language issues that might arise in the preparation of a poster. Instead, we have chosen to focus mainly on various kinds of *reduction*—or ways of saving words. These reductions may also be of use in other genres, such as in instructional manuals and other kinds of documentation.

Task Six

With a partner look over the process presented in a poster given at a bio-statistics conference (fig. 8). What do you notice about the text on the extreme left and right? And how is this different from the language toward the bottom of the main box?

(See Note 6.)

3.3 Types of Compressed Language

Words are at a premium in posters—perhaps even more so than in abstracts. Conciseness, compression, and clarity are compelling virtues. One of the principal devices used to achieve conciseness in academic and technical English is noun compounding. Noun compounds in English are always "unpacked" from the right. So, a *shoe factory site announcement* is a type of announcement and a *computerized weather observation station* is a kind of station.

Look at the following two titles, the first from the preceding poster. Underline the compound nouns.

1. The Use of Edit-Query Tables as a Database Management Tool in Clinical Trials

2. Predicting Nitrate-Nitrogen and Atrazine Contamination in the High Plains Aquifer in Nebraska

Some languages, of course, do not unpack from the right. Speakers of these languages have to be especially careful in processing English compound noun structures.

The amount of noun compounding that is appropriate is a complex issue that involves a trade-off between compression and comprehension. Consider that the above two titles could have also taken the following forms.

3. Edit-Query Table Utilization as a Clinical Trial Database Management Tool

4. Predicting Nebraska High Plains Aquifer Nitrate-Nitrogen and Atrazine Contamination

The Use of Edit-Query Tables as a Database Management Tool in Clinical Trials

Glen A.B. Feak, Brenda W. Gillespie, Kenneth E. Guire, David C. Musch

Department of Biostatistics, The University of Michigan, Ann Arbor, Michigan 48109

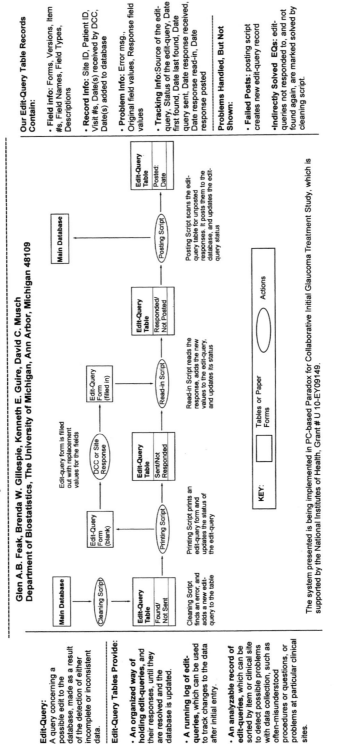

Edit-Query:

A query concerning a possible edit to the database, made as a result of the detection of either incomplete or inconsistent data.

Edit-Query Tables Provide:

• **An organized way of** holding edit-queries, and their responses, until they are resolved and the database is updated.

• **A running log of edit-queries,** which can be used to track changes to the data after initial entry.

• **An analyzable record of** edit-queries, which can be sorted by item or clinical site to detect possible problems with data collection, such as often-misunderstood procedures or questions, or problems at particular clinical sites.

Our Edit-Query Table Records Contain:

• **Field info:** Forms, Versions, Item #s, Field Names, Field Types, Descriptions

• **Record Info:** Site ID, Patient ID, Visit #s, Date(s) received by DCC, Date(s) added to database

• **Problem Info:** Error msg., Original field values, Response field values

• **Tracking Info:** Source of the edit-query, Status of the edit-query, Date first found, Date last found, Date query sent, Date response received, Date response read-in, Date response posted

Problems Handled, But Not Shown:

• **Failed Posts:** posting script creates new edit-query record

• **Indirectly Solved EQs:** edit-queries not responded to, and not found again, are marked solved by cleaning script.

The system presented is being implemented in PC-based Paradox for Collaborative Initial Glaucoma Treatment Study, which is supported by the National Institutes of Health, Grant # U 10-EY09149.

Fig. 8

Alternatively, the titles could have been

5. The Use of Edit-Query Tables as a Tool for Managing Databases in Clinical Trials
6. Predicting Contamination by Nitrate-Nitrogen and by Atrazine in the High Plains Aquifer in Nebraska

Which of the three title variations would you prefer to have written? And why? (See Note 7.)

Compression into noun compounding removes certain prepositional and verbal information from the linguistic surface. The presenter thus assumes that the reader can work out the relationships among the various elements. These relationships can in fact be surprisingly variable, even in just a two-word compound, as shown in the next task.

Task Seven

Explain the meaning of the following.

1. an oil tanker
2. the oil industry
3. an oil heater
4. an oil can
5. oil pollution

One constraint on compounding is that sometimes we need to preserve the NOUN + *of* + NOUN structure because it has a difference in meaning from the compound alternative.

Are the following pairs of phrases the same or different in meaning?

1. a pipeline   a line of pipes
2. a ink bottle   a bottle of ink
3. a book collection   a collection of books
4. a cornfield   a field of corn
5. a pencil case   a case of pencils

(See Note 8.)

Now take a look at another poster (fig. 9 on page 94) that was prepared by one of our former students, Chia-ho Hua, for presentation at a biomedical engineering conference. You will probably notice that the subheadings consist of noun phrases rather than full sentences or questions (except for the first and final two subheadings). Why is this desirable? Do you notice any grammatical elements missing from the noun phrases? What are they?

(See Note 9.)

Notice the amount of white space and text to be read. Does it seem about right? Too much? Too little?

Language Focus: Gapping

Gapping is the deletion of certain elements in your text to achieve smoothness or conciseness. Instances of gapping can be seen in titles (legends) or captions, as in *Results from First Experiment* or *Imperfections Found*. Gapping is also a common feature of written instructions, as in *Remove cap with care* or *Flip support foot out until in locked position*. Gapping is also found in everyday prose. Gapping is common in English and can be achieved in different ways. For instance, an element can be omitted, as in the first option below, rather than repeated, as in the second.

a. The tides rise and fall because of the influence of the moon.

   The tides rise and the tides fall because of the influence of the moon.

Within the noun phrase

b. All of the boys and girls were observed while completing the task.

   All of the boys and all of the girls were observed while completing the task.

It can also occur with complements.

c. Collect questionnaires and file in project office.

   Collect the questionnaires and file them in the project office.

Decoding Penalty Calculation for a Ring Compton Camera Using Uniform Cramér-Rao Bound

C.H. Hua[1], N.H. Clinthorne[2], S.J. Wilderman[3], J.W. LeBlanc[3], W.L.Rogers[1,2]

[1]Department of Biomedical Engineering, [2]Division of Nuclear Medicine, [3]Department of Nuclear Engineering and Radiological Sciences, The University of Michigan, Ann Arbor, MI 48109, USA

What is a Compton camera?

1. A Compton camera is a single-photon imaging system that utilizes electronic collimation rather than mechanical collimation.

2. The idea of applying electronic collimation to single photon imaging in nuclear medicine was first proposed by Todd et al. in 1974.

3. The Compton camera principle is based on detecting a sequential interaction of the emitted gamma rays with two position and energy sensitive detectors.

4. Two advantages in using ring geometry for a Compton camera: (1) the count rate in the second detector is limited to events scattered in the first detector, (2) ring geometry limits detected coincidence events to those having scattering angles with minimum angular uncertainty.

Three reasons to study Compton cameras

1. Potential for a substantial joint improvement in sensitivity and spatial resolution.

2. Greatly improved performance for medium and high energy imaging.

3. It may require development of new tracers labeled with medium and high energy gamma emitters.

Problems with Compton cameras

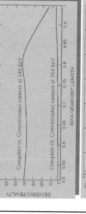

1. Because of the use of spatial multiplexing, information conveyed by each detected photon in Compton cameras is typically less than that in a mechanically collimated camera.

2. Large angular uncertainty of scattered photons due to Doppler broadening and finite detector resolution make such information loss even worse.

3. Doppler broadening of energy spectra is due to the fact that electrons in the scattering detectors are bound electrons rather than free electrons. They can have substantial kinetic energy. The momentum distribution of these electrons add uncertainty in the angle of the scattered gamma-rays.

4. The effects of Doppler broadening and finite detector energy resolution on angular uncertainty of scattering photons are shown as upper right figure. Simulations are based on the assumption of a crystalline silicon detector with 0 eV, 500 eV, 750 eV, and 1 keV FWHM resolution.

5. Simulated projection images for 140 keV incident photons (upper) and 364 keV photons (lower) are calculated based on single point sources, 60 degree scattering angle, and crystalline silicon detector with 750 eV FWHM resolution.

6. Angular uncertainty is larger for lower energy photons.

Our quantitative description — decoding penalty

1. We describe the information loss for Compton cameras as decoding penalty, defined as the ratio of variance of reconstructed pixel intensity for a pixel of interest for a Compton camera to a mechanically collimated camera normalized to a per-detected-photon basis.

2. This ratio can be described as a function of bias or bias gradient length.

3. The rationale comes from information theory, where the mean square error performance of an estimator can be described in a bias-variance tradeoff curve. Different estimators can be compared to each other on the same tradeoff plane.

4. For the ideal estimator, the tradeoff curve is seen the limiting performance of the system.

5. Due to information loss, Compton cameras usually have a higher tradeoff curve per photon compared to conventional mechanically collimated cameras. In this case, the decoding penalty will be greater than 1.

Our mathematical tool — uniform Cramér-Rao bound

(1) Unknown object intensity: $\underline{\theta} = [\theta_1, \theta_2, ..., \theta_p]^T$

(2) Projection data: $\underline{Y}$

(3) $\hat{\theta}_i$ is an estimator for a pixel of interest θ_i from $\underline{Y}$

If the estimator $\hat{\theta}_i(\underline{Y})$ satisfies the constraint on bias gradient length:

$$\|\nabla_\theta b_\theta(\underline{\theta})\| \le \delta < 1$$

where δ is a prespecified maximal tolerable bias gradient length, then the estimator variance satisfies the following lower bound:

$$\mathrm{var}_\theta(\hat{\theta}_i) \ge B(\delta)$$
$$= \lambda^2[\nabla b_\theta]^T[F_\theta + \lambda F_\theta]^{-1}F_\theta[F_\theta + \lambda F_\theta]^{-1}[\nabla b_\theta]^T$$

where F_θ is the $p \times p$ Fisher information matrix for the unknown $\underline{\theta}$ and λ is a positive scalar determined by the equation :

$$\delta^2 = [\nabla b_\theta]^T[F_\theta + \lambda F_\theta]^{-1}[\nabla b_\theta]^T.$$

Results

- The scattering detectors of ring Compton cameras — crystalline silicon with 750 eV FWHM resolution
- Conventional cameras— parallel-hole collimated gamma cameras
- Bound curve are calculated for the central pixel of the 7.5 cm diameter uniform disk.
- 9x9 cm² silicon detector and 1 cm thick second detector are assumed for relative efficiency calculation.

What do we learn from this study?

Each detected photon in ring Compton cameras usually conveys less information than that in mechanically collimated cameras, especially at low energy.

The amount of information loss not only depends on incident photon energy but also strongly relates to detector energy resolution and Doppler broadening which is an inherent property of detector material.

At 364 keV and higher, there is a potential for large estimation performance increase for ring Compton cameras. At 140 keV (Tc-99m), Compton cameras need high efficiency to break even in terms of estimation performance with the illustrated geometry.

We are deeply grateful for …

the support from the US DHHS under NIH grant R01 CA32846.

the computing services provided by the University of Michigan Center for Parallel Computing, which is partially funded by NSF grant CDA-92-14296.

Visit us at http://www.personal.engin.umich.edu/~chua/

Fig. 9

Within the verb phrase

d. The score reports were checked and mailed to the candidates.

   The score reports were checked, and they were later mailed to the candidates.

Note, however, that compressed language of all kinds can also lead to ambiguity and confusion, even to unintended humor.

Task Eight

Can you explain the ambiguities in the following?

1. Shake before drinking. (a fairly common instruction for bottled juices and liquid medicines)
2. All entrées come with bread and soup or salad.
3. Visiting relatives can be boring.
4. He decided on the boat.
5. All the old men and women were examined first.
6. The accused was observed with binoculars.
7. Two cars were reported stolen by the local police.
8. Heat the Orlon solution. Cool by bathing in (40°F) water.

(See Note 10.)

Task Nine

Here are four stylistic variations for the opening of a poster. Rank the four alternatives from most preferred to least preferred. Why did you rank them as you did? What title for this poster might you want to suggest?

1. This study provides an analysis of camel herders in Kazakhstan whose flocks graze the launch site of the International Space Station and proposes a plan for relocating them to other nearby areas.

2. This study provides:
   a. an analysis of camel herders in Kazakhstan whose flocks graze the launch site of the International Space Station;
   b. and proposes a plan for relocating the camel herds to other nearby areas.

3. This study:
   a. provides an analysis of camel herders in Kazakhstan whose flocks graze the launch site of the International Space Station; and proposes a plan for relocating the camel herds to other nearby areas.

4. What does this study offer?
   a. An analysis of camel herders in Kazakhstan whose flocks graze the launch site of the International Space Station.
   b. A proposal for relocating the camel herds to other nearby areas.

(See Note 11.)

3.4 Captions

Gapping and other kinds of compression are close to inevitable when you are writing captions or titles for your figures, charts, graphs, tables, and other nonverbal material. Elements that would be required in academic prose, such as articles, prepositions, and modal verbs, may well be omitted.

Task Ten

What has been gapped in the following captions? In other words, what might these look like if they were part of a regular sentence?

1. Fig. 1. Predicted nitrogen level
2. Fig. 2. Relationship between assembly hours and output
3. Fig. 3. Theoretical model
4. Fig. 4. Mean number of attributes accurately recalled
5. Fig. 5. Raw experimental data obtained

6. Fig. 6. Predicted atrazine concentration

7. Fig. 7. Overview of previous research

8. Fig. 8. Seismic activity Mt. Pinatubo 1950–1998

9. Fig. 9. Postdiscussion scores as function of interactive goal and subject gender

10. Fig. 10. Perceptions of kinds of help by institution

(See Note 12.)

Task Eleven

The captions that follow are written in full sentences. With a partner try to "gap" them in order to save space.

1. Figure 2 provides the results from the simulation.

2. Below are some sketches of the formation of the flower instability that we have found thus far.

3. Figure 1 shows the percentage of electricity obtained from nuclear power plants.

4. Table 1 provides the amount of radiation absorbed after treatments.

5. Figure 4 shows the change in film thickness over time.

6. Figure 5 shows the ion spectra that were obtained from a boron trichloride discharge.

7. The figure provides an estimate of natural vegetation variation if there had been no fire.

8. Figure 6 shows a hydrophone mooring that is being deployed in the NE Pacific in 1995.

9. Figure 10 shows the kinds of bacteria that eat oil and are used to clean up soil that has been contaminated by fuel.

10. In Figure 8 you can see the emerging technologies compared for the United States and Japan.

(See Note 13.)

3.5 Further Notes on the Technical Noun Phrase

In this section, we will briefly review some of the complexities in the grammar of the technical noun phrase. These include problematic cases of noun status (uncountable or countable; exceptions to the rule that noun modifiers lose their plurals; and finally, some discussion of academic names in research texts).

Tricky Cases of Countable and Uncountable Nouns

The basic grammatical rules are clear and are typically learned by non-native speakers of English fairly early in their acquisition of the language. Countable nouns can take the indefinite article in the singular and can pluralize; uncountables do neither. Students more or less know the rules for which is which (e.g., *dollars* vs. *money*). Tricky standard cases are a bunch of words that are noncountable in English but can be countable in other (European) languages. Prime suspects here are *information, machinery, training, equipment, furniture.*

But beyond that, there can be changes from uncountable to countable status in the types of highly technical professional communication that occur in research writing.

Here are some examples. Can you think of one more, especially from your own field? Write it in the space provided.

Among agriculturalists: grasses, wheats, soils . . .
Among chemists: sugars, starches, oils . . .
Among metallurgists: steels . . .
Among psychologists: behaviors, treatments . . .
Among linguists: grammars

_____ : _____

Clearly, we can at least partly see the above phenomenon as a move toward language compression. It is more economical and more technical to write "grasses" rather than "several types of grasses" or "several species of grasses."

Now for some of the most important special cases.

Work

Work is usually uncountable ("He does good work"; "Previous work on this topic is unsatisfactory"). However, it becomes countable when it refers to individual creations, particularly of a creative nature.

The Collected Works of Shakespeare
She is interested in classical works of art.

There is also the old phrase *good works,* which is still used to refer to "charitable activities," although sometimes today in an ironic manner.

Finally, there are signs that the traditionally uncountable *homework* is becoming countable on United States campuses.

There will be eight homeworks in this class.

Research/Researches

At present, *research* remains an uncountable noun, although it is quite commonly used by nonnative speakers as a countable noun (*a research / researches*). One reason of course is that its equivalent easily pluralizes in many (European) languages. Whether nonnative speaker pressure and pressure for conciseness ("researches" as opposed to "pieces of research") will cause a gradual change in its status is an open but interesting question. (See Note 14.)

Data

This is currently the most uncertain case. Historically, of course, *data* is plural, being the Latin plural of the Latin word *datum.* However, *datum* is very rare now, even in its last stronghold, philosophy. So, should we write and say

"This data" or "These data"?
"The data is" or "The data are"?

A recent British study shows the following.

1. In research articles, *data* tends to be plural.
2. In scientific journalism, *data* can be either singular or plural.
3. In quality (British) newspapers, *data* tends to be singular.

4. *Data* in its traditional sense of information tends to plural, but in its newer sense of computer bytes it tends to the singular.

(See Note 15.)

Exceptions to the Rule that Noun Modifiers Lose Their Plurals

A very powerful rule in English (a "robust" one, as the engineers might say) is that modifiers, like all adjectives, are invariable. "A generator of pulses" thus becomes a "pulse generator." But, as usual, there are exceptions. One we have already seen in Section 3.3 is "High Plains Aquifer." Here are some more.

Civil *rights* legislation
A *means* test (cf. *a mean—unkind—test!*)
Communication *skills* courses (cf. a single skill course)
Industrial and *operations* engineering
A *manuals* survey (cf. a manual survey)
A public *works* department
A family *values* program
Materials science (cf. material assistance)
The Student *Activities* Building (cf. a police activity report)

We can find fairly reasonable explanations for most of these (except perhaps the last). The loss of the plural could lead to ambiguity between noun and adjective (*right, mean, manual, material*) or to ambiguity about the noun (i.e., "a fellowship committee" might be one established to create good fellowship or friendliness among a group). We could also see that these exceptions seem to be mainly used with "official" or "titular" entities.

Task Twelve

Here are three more exceptions to the rule that noun modifiers lose their plurals. Explanations? Examples from your field?

1. A systems approach is widely used in modern management.
2. A new administrative programs director has recently been appointed.
3. The Graduate Library has an extensive serials collection.

(See Note 16.)

More on Names in Academic Texts

Names of previous scholars and researchers occur frequently in academic texts. They can occur in association with quotations, as subjects or agents in sentences, in parentheses, in footnotes or in endnotes, and consolidated in lists of references and bibliographies.

Certain names become established as identification devices. These we can call *named modifiers*. Recall the title of Chia-ho's poster: "Decoding Penalty Calculation for a Ring *Compton* Camera Using Uniform *Cramér-Rao* Bound." As you can see from the two italicized sections, he uses two named modifiers in this title.

Named Modifiers

In technical fields, the use of a person's name (or the names of two people) as a modifier is a common identification device. (Doubtless it also bestows honor, priority, and reputation on the so-named people.) A question arises, however, as to the use of a possessive genitive (Boyle's law) as opposed to a modifier (the Compton effect). Are there rules here? Or at least tendencies that it might be useful to know about?

Task Thirteen

Consider this data set.

1. a Geiger counter
2. the Stefan-Boltzmann law
3. Avogadro's hypothesis
4. the Kelvin scale
5. Lincoln's sparrow
6. Kiliani's reaction
7. Fermatt's last theorem
8. Spearman's rank order correlation
9. Scheffe's S method
10. the Fischer-Tropsch process
11. the Liebig method
12. Ohm's law
13. a Rorschach test
14. Hinsberg's method
15. Hodgkins' disease
16. the Schumacker-Levy comet
17. Fourier transforms
18. a Tukey-Duckworth two-sample test
19. Clarke's gazelle
20. a Dewar flask

Can you now add up to five more from your own field?

21. _____

22. _____

23. _____

24. _____

25. _____

It is clear from the data that "double (hyphenated) names" (examples 2, 10, 16, and 18) always (or nearly always) take the modifier form. But what about the single names? What kinds of explanations occur to you? Can you form a rule that will account for (most of) the data? (See Note 17.)

Adjectival Names

Perhaps one of the final stages of recognition is for a scholar's or researcher's name to become an adjective. Doubtless the final stage is when that individual's work becomes assimilated into general knowledge!

Task Fourteen

Here is a scrambled list of adjectival names and fields. Can you match them up?

1. Euclidean   A. ethics
2. Newtonian   B. sociology
3. Bayesian   C. biology
4. Chomskyan   D. cultural theory
5. Skinnerian   E. geometry
6. Aristotelian   F. statistics
7. Foucaultian   G. physics
8. Keynesian   H. linguistics
9. Darwinian   I. psychology
10. Durkheimian   J. economics

(See Note 18.)

Often such people are, in Foucault's term, *founders of discursivity;* in other words they changed the way we think and write about their own specialized worlds. In consequence, these "naming" adjectives can also take the prefixes *pre-* and *post-*, as in

Pre-Linnaean botanical descriptions
Post-Bloomfieldian linguistics
Post-Keynesian economic theories
Pre-Durkheimian social theory

What named adjectives are common in your field? Does using such "labels" come easily to you in your writing?

Task Fifteen

You have two options here. Produce your own poster or with a partner or partners, present the following research in a poster format, completing the following subtasks.

Using the information below, along with figures 10–13, make a miniature version of the poster (as on p. 89) to submit as a group. Work in two stages.

Thinking and Planning

1. Create a title.
2. Decide how and where to list "author" names and institutions.
3. Determine your sections and decide on section headings.
4. Photocopy the charts given.
5. Create suitable captions.
6. Consider the content. What information should be included?
7. Consider what elements can be gapped.

Putting It All Together

8. Decide on fonts and font sizes.
9. Print and then cut apart the various sections of your poster so that you can experiment with your layout.

10. Put the final layout together and then try photocopying it at a reduced size so that all of your poster is on one sheet.

Information to Work With

- Computer models used by traffic planners studying the impact of road closures assume that closing one main road will cause traffic to shift to another, thus causing traffic congestion.

- Automobile use is increasing day by day. People prefer using their own vehicles to using public transportation.

- The research presented here is a small part of a larger project investigating the impact of road closures. Our research focuses on changes in road use habits as revealed through questionnaires of drivers affected by or about to be affected by road closures. This poster presents the results of this questionnaire.

- From 1997 to 2000 we analyzed five cases each in London (a European city of over 7 million), Amsterdam (a European city of over 700,000), Boston (a city in the United States of over 500,000), and Mexico City (a North American city of over 8 million) where roads were closed or underwent a reduction in their ability to carry traffic due to road repairs. Twenty project members administered questionnaires to 250 users of roads in each of the 20 cases (pre- and postclosure) to determine how the road closure affected their driving.

- The roads that were closed carried an average of 30,000 vehicles (e.g., passenger cars, buses, trucks) a day (A Roads). The roads to which traffic was anticipated to shift carried an average of 17,000 per day (B Roads).

- Postclosure or reduction, A Roads carried no or fewer than 200 vehicles per day (for roads that permitted some traffic such as buses or emergency vehicles [ambulances and fire trucks]). B Roads experienced an increase in traffic but little or no congestion postclosure. B Roads carried an average of 39,000 vehicles per day.

- After they were reopened A Roads carried approximately 23,000 vehicles per day. B Roads carried approximately 21,500 vehicles per day.

Fig. 10. How people traveled the A roads before closure

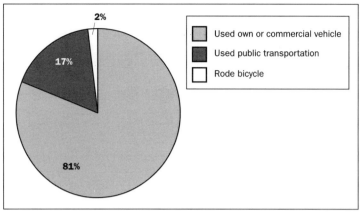

2%

17%

81%

Used own or commercial vehicle

Used public transportation

Rode bicycle

This figure is reproducible.

Fig.11. How people traveled the B roads before closure

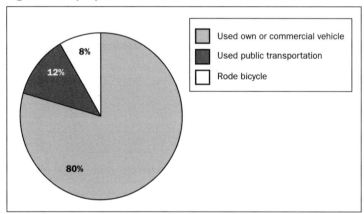

8%

12%

80%

Used own or commercial vehicle

Used public transportation

Rode bicycle

This figure is reproducible.

Fig. 12. How people traveled the A roads after they were reopened

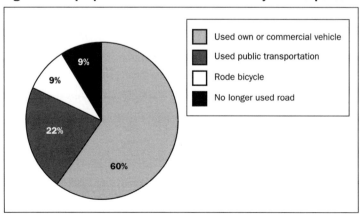

9%

9%

22%

60%

Used own or commercial vehicle

Used public transportation

Rode bicycle

No longer used road

This figure is reproducible.

Fig. 13. How people traveled the B roads after they were reopened

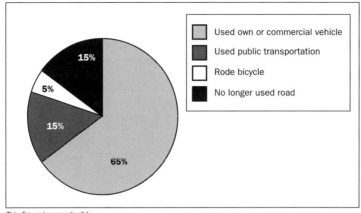

This figure is reproducible.

3.6 Etiquette on "the Day"

Congratulations! Your poster was accepted. You have decided, as considered in Task Three, what extra materials you might take. You also have packed a few spare stationery items such as tape and pins. Now there are some other things to think about. Everybody seems to want to give you advice.

Task Sixteen

Here are some of those suggestions. Do you think each is a good (Y) or a bad (N) piece of advice?

___ 1. It's very easy to put posters up and take them down, so arrive in the poster session area a few minutes before your session is due to start. You can spend the time better by going to presentations. That way you won't be so nervous as well.

___ 2. Have a good supply of business cards visible, so people can pick them up if they want to. Don't *force* your cards on passersby, however.

___ 3. Have a list where those interested in your work can give you their names and e-mail addresses.

___ 4. Wear your most formal clothes. This makes you look more professional.

___ 5. Focus on your own situation and don't be distracted by what is happening at nearby posters.

___ 6. Strike up conversations with the other poster presenters near you. This will help you relax and can help pass the time if things are slow.

___ 7. Bring something to do during the poster session in case few viewers come by.

___ 8. Approach viewers of your poster to see if they have any questions.

___ 9. Consider viewers of your poster to be valuable resources and seek their input on your work.

___ 10. Don't wander away from your poster (except in an emergency). Murphy's law will guarantee that you will miss the key encounter.

(See Note 19.)

Task Seventeen

Further congratulations! Your poster is attracting quite a lot of attention. What might you say in response to the following?

1. "This really is an outstanding poster; I'm really impressed."
2. "Haven't I seen this poster before somewhere?"
3. "I know that you don't get much space for your poster, but my impression is that the data looks pretty thin."
4. "Have you read _____'s latest paper in _____ journal?"
5. "I don't see any references to the work of our research group."
6. "How do I quote your work?"

(See Note 20.)

3.7 Notes and Comments for Unit Three

Note 1 (sample responses for Task One)

Other advantages: They allow the "presenter" to adjust his or her explanations to the level of expertise of the inquirer; they do not require such a high level of skill in spoken English; and they do not exert such a toll on the nerves.

Disadvantages: Lack of space to do your research full justice; no captive audience; potential embarrassments as people pass your poster by with a brief look.

Note 2 (sample response for Task Two)

There are a number of candidate paragraphs, but to us the strongest criticism is that expressed in paragraph 7.

Note 3 (sample response for Task Three)

In discussions with our class participants, all four strategies have their supporters. Indeed, it appears that experienced poster presenters have experimented at one time or another with most of these arrangements. Option c is the most expensive and the most risky. Maybe you will have lots of extra copies to carry home! On the other hand, . . .

Note 4 (sample responses for Task Four)

Many of our reactions are given in the suggestions that follow. If the conventions of your field permit it, we see nothing wrong with using *we* for a multi-authored poster, especially as it might save some words (point 11). The need to spell out acronyms probably depends on how specialized you anticipate your audience to be. For a narrow-focus gathering of experts, probably not.

Note 5 (sample responses for Task Five)

The first version is boxed and captioned like a minipaper. It is written in full sentences, which are hard to follow given the narrowness of the columns. The numerical data looks rather lost. The second version is much "snappier" with its white space, its lists, its clear sequence of bolded questions along the top, and its illustrative material at the bottom. We have little doubt that the second version is a "better" poster in layout terms.

Note 6 (sample responses for Task Six)

The leftmost column opens with a definition but with a colon rather than the word *is*. It then gives three advantages in bullet format, using a fair number of passives. In the rightmost column we find a summary of the records with many acronyms and abbreviations ("info," "msg," etc.). Note the interesting element at the bottom right-hand corner ("Problems Handled, But Not Shown"). The four sentences along the bottom have a very nice parallelism. Notice how the active verbs in the present tense give a lively impression of the processes at work.

Note 7 (sample responses to poster title questions)

Compound nouns: Edit-Query Tables; Database Management Tool ("clinical" is an adjective); Nitrate-Nitrogen and Atrazine Contamination; High Plains Aquifer. As for the stylistic choices, we have a slight preference for the originals (1 and 2). Alternatives 3 and 4 strike us being a bit overcompressed, while 5 and 6 may be a little "loose."

Note 8 (sample responses for Task Seven)

1. a tanker designed to carry oil
2. the industry that extracts, refines, and sells oil products
3. a heater that burns oil
4. a can used to contain oil
5. pollution caused by oil. See what we mean!

1. "A pipeline" is a line of connected pipes; "a line of pipes" will usually be interpreted as separate pipes that are not yet connected.

2. "An ink bottle" may be empty, "a bottle of ink" not.

3. These two are close, but "a book collection" looks like a planned and organized accumulation, while the latter might be more like a haphazard heap.

4. "A cornfield" is a field used for growing corn (but which may now be harvested), while "a field of corn" must have corn in it.

5. Similarly, "a case of pencils" needs some pencils in it.

Note 9

The noun phrases convey the message in a quick and efficient manner. Articles *a, an,* and *the* are the most obvious missing elements, which is typical in headings and subheadings.

Note 10 (sample responses for Task Eight)

1. Do you shake the bottle or do you shake yourself?!

2. Is it "with either bread and soup or with salad" or is it "with bread and either soup or salad"?

3. Is it "relatives who visit you," or is it "relatives whom you go to visit"? In the former case, it would be "visiting relatives are boring" and in the latter "visiting relatives is boring."

4. "He decided on which boat to buy" or "He made a decision while on the boat"?

5. Is it all the women (of any age) or only the old women?

6. Was the accused observed wearing/carrying binoculars, or did somebody observe the accused through binoculars?

7. Did the local police do the reporting or do the stealing?

8. Is the solution or the experimenter cooled in the water?!

Note 11 (sample responses for Task Nine)

The full sentence in 1 will look long and awkward if shown in column format. Variation 2 is sensible and quite discreet, but there is a minor problem with parallelism (see 4 below). Variation 3 has too short a stem ("This study:"). Variation 4 is attention getting (too much so?), and the opening noun phrase in b ("A proposal") corrects the lack of parallelism in 2.

Note 12 (sample responses for Task Ten)

1. the predicted nitrogen level
2. the relationship between assembly hours and output
3. a *or* the theoretical model
4. the mean number of attributes which was accurately recalled
5. the raw experimental data that were obtained
6. the predicted atrazine concentration
7. an overview of previous research
8. the seismic activity on Mt. Pinatubo 1950–1998
9. postdiscussion scores as a function of interactive goal and subject gender
10. the perceptions of different kinds of help as arranged by the type of institution

Note 13 (sample responses for Task Eleven)

1. Fig. 2. Simulation results
2. (below) Sketches of flower instability formation found to date
3. Fig. 1. Percent of electricity from nuclear power plants

4. Table 1. Post-treatment amounts of absorbed radiation
5. Fig. 4. Film thickness changes over time
6. Fig. 5. Ion spectra from a boron trichloride discharge
7. Estimate of natural vegetation variation (no-fire condition)
8. Fig. 6. Deployment of hydrophone mooring (NE Pacific, 1995)
9. Fig 10. Oil-eating and soil-cleaning bacteria
10. Fig 8. Comparison of emerging technologies in U.S. and Japan

Note 14

There is one example of countable *research* in the MICASE data, out of about a hundred examples of *research* as a head noun.

in terms of actually being *a research* that goes beyond the educational classroom

Note 15

The MICASE data is/are (?!) interesting in this regard. There is about a 2:1 preference for the uncountable. Compare the following statements.

1a. The data's gonna be introspective.
1b. That data is still sitting there waiting to go into the code.
1c. They take the data, and they analyze it in a particular way.

2a. If you're going to approach any kind of analysis of these data in a rigorous way, you have to follow the rules.
2b. The data are a lot better than some others.
2c. Do your data really allow you to say that?

What do you think are the preferences in the written English of your field?
How does your professor/advisor use *data?*
Do you hear countable or uncountable uses in academic talk?

Note 16 (sample responses for Task Twelve)

1. *Systems* as in *systems management* has developed a special meaning that requires the preservation of the *s.* Compare *system failure,* where *system* is used in a more general sense.

2. Since there is presumably a range of *administrative programs,* using the singular would probably cause some ambiguity.

3. Similarly, there might be an ambiguity with *serial collection;* also *serials* has become a well-established word in library science.

Note 17 (sample response for Task Thirteen)

A useful rule of thumb here is to ask whether the named phenomenon was invented or discovered. So discovered items, such as animals, diseases, and laws of nature, tend to take the possessive form. Invented items, instruments, and so on, are more likely to take the nominal form. Admittedly, there are some residual problems, particularly with regard to methods (9, 11, 14).

Note 18 (answer key for Task Fourteen)

1. E (geometry) 2. G (physics) 3. F (statistics) 4. H (linguistics) 5. I (psychology) 6. A (ethics) 7. D (cultural theory) 8. J (economics) 9. C (biology) 10. B (sociology)

Note 19 (sample responses for Task Sixteen)

1. Not a good piece of advice. Check out the location well ahead of time and assemble your poster well ahead of time. That way you will avoid any last-minute crises.
2. Yes, this is sensible advice.
3. It's a good idea to think ahead and plan how you might collect such information from viewers. Getting a business card would be the easiest.
4. This might be right in some circumstances but by no means in all. Get some further advice from a colleague.

5 and 6. It may depend somewhat on your personality, but we prefer 6 to 5.

7. Not a good idea
8. If someone looks like they would like to talk to you but seems a bit shy, then you might want to approach him or her. We think it's best to not approach viewers, unless one of them is someone you really would like to meet. Usually, if viewers want to talk with you, they will.
9. You never know who might come to look at your poster. If someone whose work you respect is viewing your poster, you may want to seek his or her input.
10. Yes. Because of this one of John's Ph.D. students missed meeting the one professor she most wanted to meet in the world.

Note 20 (sample responses for Task Seventeen)

1. Compliments are nice to receive but for most of us hard to deal with. A graceful "Thank you very much; I'm glad you like it" will probably work OK.

2. Uh-oh. If you have shown this poster before, you might as well admit it. "You're right; I had a trial run with it at the regional conference in . . . " If not, politely question the speaker since he or she may have seen some work that you might very well need to know about.

3. "Well, as you know, there are considerable space restrictions for these posters. Can I show you more detail from my handout?"

4. Even if this is an implied criticism (which it may or may not be), assume that the speaker is trying to be helpful. "No, that sounds interesting. Can you give me a reference or tell me a little about it?"

5. Another "uh-oh." Of course express interest, even if the work strikes you as outside your direct interest.

6. This is up to you or perhaps up to your advisor. It may also depend on how fully the poster is abstracted in the conference handbook.

Unit Four
The Literature Review

Review of the Literature

Reference to prior literature is a defining feature of scholarly and research writing. Such references enable you to demonstrate how your current work—and that of your colleagues, if any—builds upon or deviates from earlier publications. In effect, successful academic writing depends in part on situating current work within a larger disciplinary context. This situating is once again an aspect of graduate/junior researcher positioning.

In this unit we will cover the following areas.

4.1 Types and Characteristics of Literature Reviews

A review of the literature can serve numerous functions, but literature reviews (LRs) fall into two basic types:

1. a survey article (sometimes called a "review article" or a "state-of-the art" paper) and
2. a literature review as part of a research paper, proposal, thesis, or dissertation.

Survey articles are typically written by senior and well-known scholars and researchers, often by invitation. These LRs can be highly prestigious. We will not be dealing with this type of LR in this chapter, although of course much can be learned from seeing how the "experts" sort, survey, describe, and evaluate aspects of the literature in your field.

A literature review that forms part of a research paper, proposal, thesis, or dissertation may occur in one of three forms.

1. It may be a separate, independent section, a part of a chapter, or an entire chapter, which is likely called "A Review of the Literature" or something like that.
2. It may be incorporated more organically into the wider text.
3. It may be integrated throughout the whole work as the need for comparison and evaluation arises.

Task One

There is considerable debate about the advantages and disadvantages of these three approaches. How would you answer the following questions?

1. Would one of the forms be preferred over the others for a thesis or dissertation in your field?
2. What is your own preference?
3. Would different considerations as to form have to be made for a journal article? If so, what might these be?

(See Note 1.)

The LR as part of a research paper, proposal, thesis, or dissertation is often thought of as being a boring but necessary chore. Such LRs are often criticized (see Unit Five) but are rarely praised. After all, one rarely hears comments such as "The most brilliant part of your thesis was the literature review"! This kind of literature review also tends to be conservative in style and substance. In fact, we know of only one really experimental and original literature review written by a graduate student. This occurs as Chapter Two of Malcolm Ashmore's 1985 doctoral dissertation from the University of York (United Kingdom), subsequently published virtually unchanged by the University of Chicago Press. (Note 2 contains more information on Ashmore, if you are interested.)

As you may already have experienced, advisors, supervisors, and senior scholars are often not as sympathetic as they might be to the efforts of newcomers to the field, such as graduate students, to construct literature reviews. "Old hands" conveniently forget that they have grown up with certain bodies of literature over many years, indeed perhaps decades. They have a firm sense of how the research has evolved over time and have very possibly contributed themselves to that evolution. They may have forgotten what it takes to start from the beginning or somewhat close to it.

Task Two

Check your literature review knowledge. Make a check mark (✓) next to the items that would seem to apply to your writing situation, that is, whether you are writing something for publication or preparing the literature review for your thesis or dissertation.

___ 1. The preparation of a literature review is a three-step process: finding the relevant literature, reading, and then writing up the review.

___ 2. Your literature review should be as long as possible to persuade your reader that you have read very widely.

___ 3. You need to include all of the previous research that relates to your topic.

___ 4. You can safely ignore literature that is not directly related to your topic.

___ 5. Your literature review is important because it demonstrates that the findings, theory, or analysis that you will present are a contribution to a cumulative process.

___ 6. Your literature review needs to explain clearly which potential areas for inclusion have not been covered in the review and why they have been omitted.

___ 7. Your literature review should discuss problems and/or controversies within your field.

___ 8. Your literature review should be presented in chronological order.

___ 9. Your literature review can help you discover conceptual traditions and frameworks used to examine problems.

___ 10. Your literature review should focus on very recent publications because they are likely the most relevant.

___ 11. Your literature review should help you reveal gaps in the existing body of research.

___ 12. In your literature review you should critically evaluate each piece of work included.

(See Note 3.)

Writing an LR is a hybrid act of literacy in that the LR requires you to be both a reader and a writer. You are reading texts by others in order to create your own new text, a research story that sets up your discussion of your own research. Perhaps the following analogy will explain this point. In a group conversation, somebody may tell a story of something that happened to him or her (or someone else), say, a story about having a difficult time at Customs. At the end of this story, it is likely that another person may begin to tell another story. This phenomenon is known as *second-storying* to discourse analysts. The first point to note is that this second story must somehow be connected to the first. In the case of our example, the second story could be yet another story about a difficult Customs experience. The second point is that for the second story to "succeed" it must go beyond the first one in some way; for example, the second story should describe an even more difficult time than the first one did. We can now see that you, the researcher, have, in essence, a second story to tell after your first story—the LR. This first story must carefully be constructed so that the second story both is thematically related to and goes beyond the first one.

In this and the following unit, we address issues in the production of an LR partly through three case studies, the first one created by us using our experiences with graduate students and the last two based on actual cases.

4.2 Organizing the Literature: Creating an Architecture

Fulan A. Fulani is writing his prospectus. The proposed topic for his dissertation is

> A Formative Evaluation of Current Problems in Engineering Education

He is now at work on the literature review. He has divided this into six sections. He has reached Section Five, which deals with the teaching of communication skills to engineers.

He has managed to find nine items for this section. This was hard work, as the papers were scattered across a wide range of journals. He has made notes on the articles and has assembled photocopies of the abstracts on separate pieces of paper.

He is now looking at the abstracts and trying to puzzle out which studies go with which and for what kind of reason. As an ex-student of

ELI writing classes, he knows that he cannot just describe or summarize each one separately.

He knows that he has to (a) impose some order on the material in order to demonstrate that there is an organizing mind at work; and (b) exhibit some appropriate level of evaluation.

He recollects his advisor's comment, but he is not quite sure if he fully understands it: "One final thing, Fulani. Either you control the previous literature, or it will control you."

But what order and organization? That is his first problem. What can you suggest?

Task Three

For this task you will use the following nine abstracts. (Don't look for the actual articles in the library. All of them have been made up!) Draw a tree-diagram or other kind of visual of the abstracts (using number or first author's name) to reveal your proposed scheme for organizing them. Keep in mind that there is no one right way to order or group the abstracts. Be prepared to explain the thinking processes behind your choices.

1. Van Hoek, J. 1996. Information in manufacturing systems and the needs of the graduating engineer. *European Journal of Professional Education* 17:67–77.

    > Few opportunities for developing communication skills exist in the crowded curricula of most bachelor of science engineering courses in Western Europe. It is thus important that those few available are spent on fundamental aspects of the most relevant areas. The course developed at the University of Amsterdam is built around case studies of actual manufacturing problems. Students are required to form engineer-manager groups as task forces to solve problems as they arise. In this way they become socialized into the engineering community. Evidence is presented from student evaluations as to the success of this approach.

2. Scott, J. 1995. The logical structure of technical reports: software support. *Journal of Technical Documentation* 11:273–82.

    > The "expression" problem in writing engineering technical reports is secondary to the "comprehension" problem—that is, the ability to perceive relevance, organize material into sections, and then organize sections into

a logical order. This paper begins by considering the question of efficiency and the contributions that "logical sections in logical order" can make to the effectiveness of reports. It then presents an algorithmic IBM-compatible software program which encourages the kind of analysis and organization underlying effective report writing.

3. McWrath, A. 1990. Communication skills for engineering undergraduates: an engineer's response. *Professional Engineer* 47:21–23.

The growing employment of "specialists" in communication skills has recently become problematic in many engineering schools. As a professor of engineering, I am committed to helping my undergraduates improve their writing and speaking abilities. I argue that this is best achieved in the context of real engineering courses taught by real engineers, not by "outsiders" to the profession who often fail to understand the nature and purpose of engineering communications.

4. Leon, A., and W. Deng. 1998. Developing communication skills in civil engineering students. *Civil Engineer* 73:507–19.

Civil engineers are responsible for devising economic practical solutions to satisfy the needs of the community for roads, bridges, water supplies, and other major works. Throughout their education and training it is unlikely that they will receive much formal training in effective communication. To remedy this, a new course of communication studies was introduced two years ago at Manchester University. The essential feature is to have all the communication topics set in the context of civil engineering practice. Thus, a large civil engineering contract is simulated, and all aspects of communication skills are related to the simulation. Preliminary results suggest that the students have appreciated the linking of communication studies with civil engineering work.

5. Ahmed, S., and B. Williams. 1997. Content in engineering courses for engineering students. *Studies in Higher Education* 33:74–92.

Communication courses for engineering undergraduates vary widely in content, from mass media on the one hand to the social responsibility of the engineer on the other. As a rule, students find little interest in such courses because of their distance from their immediate concerns (Olsen, 1992). In contrast, our research shows good responses—as measured by interview and questionnaire—for courses that focus on the day-to-day communication problems of engineers, both with their colleagues and the general public.

6. Lo, C., and C. S. Li. 1998. Empowering female students in engineering education. *Cross Currents* 24:96–109.

> Many reports speak of a "chilly climate" toward women engineering students (EEGR Survey (1996) for an overview). Our experimental program provides opportunities for women students to develop their communication skills in sheltered, women-only environments and then apply their newly found confidence in mainstream situations. Follow-up studies report improved grades, more effective participation in class, and increased job offers ($p = 0.5$; $QZ = 4.78$; $ff = X4+$ on the Fittori scoring rule).

7. Pradip, S., and R. Rahim. 1997. Moving from national to international prominence: Computer engineering in Bombay. *UNESCO Journal of Technical Education* 23:2–14.

> There has been much talk of the "Bombay Miracle" (e.g., *Time*, August 3, 1996) but rather less of the communication failures of the computer engineers and scientists in the city. We have developed training courses for engineering graduates stressing cross-cultural differences in negotiation, writing styles, patent laws, and contractual obligations among Indian, Japanese, and North American leaders in technological change. Although no empirical evidence is yet available, there are signs that the case approach to success and failure in Indian computer engineering initiatives for export is having beneficial results.

8. Sullivan, P. 1996. Problems in communication skills courses. *Journal of Technical Education* 24:23–40.

> A survey of undergraduate technical communication programs in the United States ($n = 77$) suggests that the acceptability of the program to both students and faculty does not depend on the quality of the program (as measured by staff profiles, curriculum analysis, and level of integration with engineering courses). Rather, the prime determinant is engineering faculty support (or otherwise) for the program. The study suggests that the way forward lies more in canvassing for faculty support than in internal improvements.

9. Fredrickson, K. 1998. Provision for the non-native speaker in graduate engineering programs. *English for Specific Purposes* 12:222–33.

> The increasing numbers of NNS in U.S. graduate engineering programs have caused various kinds of strain, including faculty burnout (Perillo, 1991), tension between NS and NNS populations for financial support

(Luebs, 1995), and dissatisfaction with NNS after graduation when their English skills are shown to be less than promised (Swales, 1995). An experimental program of "English internships" with U.S. research associates and scientists has proved highly effective in helping NNS students develop their technical writing skills in English. The conclusions suggest that such programs should be expanded to other campuses.

Perhaps the most important *rhetorical* characteristic of LRs is that they are different from most other academic genres or part genres in one crucial respect. They do not easily fall into those stages or "moves" (Unit Two) that have proved helpful for structuring abstracts, conference posters, introductions, discussions, and so forth. In effect, and as we will see, the range of options for structuring the LR is much greater. This then constitutes a further difficulty.

We begin our search for a possible solution by providing two architectures suggested by former students. The first plan, as you will see, is rather straightforward.

Task Four

Look over these two proposed organizational schemes, or "architectures" in figure 14. Can you explain the reasoning behind each of them? In the boxes provided, write what you think holds the citations together. The first box has been done for you. After you finish labeling, decide which, if either, of the plans is close to the way you organized the information. For the purposes of discussion we have simplified the architectures for this exercise so that each item is used only once.

(See Note 4.)

As you might have guessed Architecture 2 came under criticism for stressing the wrong things. Below is the author's eloquent e-mail defense of her primary choice of territory and local educational context.

```
My architecture reflected the categories that I, as a stu-
dent of literature, would have chosen, not what an engineer-
ing student would. I think I did not see the relevance of
```

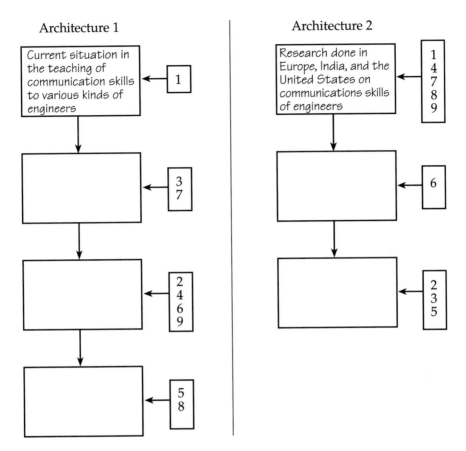

Fig. 14

other choices and the biased side of mine. Maybe the tendency to classify by the literary production of a country comes, among other things, from the awareness of territory that I see in post-colonial countries such as mine. So, this explains, in a way, my inclination to do what I did in my classification. Maybe that also explains the devotion of one category for considering engineering women. I see that this classification was not really a "scientific" one as the other approaches showed in class, where the categories were a result of a very different way of thinking. Personally, doing this exercise was very important to me mainly because it showed me the way I am used to thinking, the ideas I have about other fields, and my criteria for forming categories.

—Angeles (minor editing)

As we have seen, different organizational approaches are feasible and, as far as we can see, likely to reflect disciplinary training. However, not all architectures are easy to write up. Some need more rhetorical work than others. For example, one proposed architecture submitted by one of our students began with the Fredrickson abstract (9) and then Pradip and Rahim (7), thus focusing on why communication courses are most badly needed. These two abstracts seem less central to the main research trend and therefore pose a challenge as opening choices.

Task Five

Which of the following LRs opening with Fredrickson 1998 do you think are successful? Why?

1. There have been several studies that have investigated the communication skills of engineering students. Some of these also offer proposals for remediation and improvement. For example, Fredrickson (1998) describes a program in which non-native speakers of English are placed in "English internships" with U.S. mentors.

2. Of the nine relevant papers only one focuses directly on the communication problems of non-native speakers in engineering education. Fredrickson (1998) suggests that a program of "English internships" will likely reduce such problems.

3. In recent years, there has been some attempt to deal with weaknesses in the communication skills of engineering students and graduates. Among those most obviously at risk are non-native speakers of English in English-medium degree programs. A possible partial solution is Fredrickson's curricular experiment in which non-native speakers are placed in "English internships" with U.S. researchers (Fredrickson 1998).

4. The available literature on the teaching of engineering communication skills can be viewed as a series of graded responses from a more critical to a less critical situation. At the former extreme is the plight of students with limited English proficiency in English-medium degree programs, particularly in the U.S. Fredrickson (1998) has tackled this problem with her program of "English internships" for such students in which they are paired up with other U.S. researchers.

(See Note 5.)

Language Focus: Articles and Complex Prepositional Noun Phrases

Consider these opening noun phrases from the nine abstracts.

1. Few opportunities for developing communication skills . . .

3. The growing employment of "specialists" in communication skills . . .

5. Communication courses for engineering undergraduates . . .

8. A survey of undergraduate technical communication programs in the U.S. . . . .

9. The increasing numbers of NNS in U.S. graduate engineering programs . . .

Such NOUN + PREPOSITION + NOUN structures are a common feature of academic writing. The issue of article usage before the first noun is complex and can often cause problems for non-native speakers. In what follows we offer some guidelines about article usage with the first of the nouns in a sequence. These guidelines are not perfect and will work only part of the time. In so doing, we have relied in part on Marco's (2000) useful study of *the . . . of . . .* and *a . . . of . . .* in a hundred medical research articles. (See Note 6.)

Certain prepositions, especially *of, in, to,* and *for,* are some of the most common words in English and as we have seen often form part of NOUN + PREPOSITION + NOUN structures. The issue is whether the first noun should be preceded by a definite or indefinite article.

Task Six

Consider the following data. What would you conclude about articles and the first noun?

1a. The increase of temperature caused the equipment to malfunction.
1b. An increase in temperature can cause equipment to malfunction.

2a. Skills in oral presentation are now expected of engineers.
2b. The communicative skills of this candidate are very impressive.

3a. Interest in this area is growing.
3b. The interest of this area lies mostly in its potential for interdisciplinary work.

4a. The contributions of this research group are substantial.
4b. Contributions to this project are truly multinational.

5a. Participants in the meeting agreed on a common goal.
5b. The members of the committee agreed on a common goal.

6a. The link between malnutrition and mental performance is not straightforward.
6b. Researchers have discovered a link between laughter and immune system enhancement.

(See Note 7.)

We see then that there is a probabilistic rule that favors *the* before a following *of* phrase but favors indefinite articles before following phrases governed by other prepositions. This rule doesn't always work, however. Look back at the opening to Abstract Two. Can you come up with some other counterexamples?

Now let's look at the *of* phrase situation in more detail, if only because it is the most common structure. Marco's corpus of one hundred medical articles produced 9,900 examples of *the . . . of . . .* phrases but only 780 examples of *a . . . of. . .* So far, so good, then.

Marco provides a useful list of nouns that have a greater than 50 percent chance of occurring in the *the . . . of . . .* framework. There were twelve of these in the medical corpus, the first of which—*start*—actually occurred 100 percent of the time in this position!

80–100%	*start / basis / presence*
60–79%	*absence /percentage /administration /number / importance*
50–59%	*extent / development / effect*

Overall we can see that a number of these are connected with numerical quantities (*number, percentage*), with existence (*presence, absence*), and with treatment (*start, administration, development*).

The *a . . . of . . .* structure, as we have seen, is much less productive. Marco's data for proportion of occurrences in this structural context is interesting.

variety	100%	*total*	24%
minority	87%	*percentage*	16%
history	87%	*number*	11%
series	43%	*range*	10%
proportion	28%		

Task Seven

Complete the blanks with either *a* or *the*.

1. Malnourished children tend to have _____ history of health problems.

2. _____ history of the battle against smallpox is an inspiring one.

3. Side effects were noted in _____ minority of the patients.

4. Side effects were noted in _____ minority of patients who had had pre-existing conditions.

5. _____ percentage of subjects reporting stress rose sharply.

6. _____ percentage of subjects reported increased levels of stress.

7. The research group is planning _____ series of experiments to test this hypothesis.

8. After an initial setback, _____ series of experiments produced useful results.

9. _____ number of students who failed has increased over the last decade.

10. _____ number of students have failed, presumably because of poor preparation.

(See Note 8.)

Task Eight

Now write your first draft literature review of the nine items for Section Five of Fulani's literature review chapter.

4.3 Citations

How to best report prior work is an important and complex problem for all academic writers. Issues of accuracy, fairness, plagiarism, selection, style, and evaluation in your text will emerge and re-emerge. However, matters are somewhat simplified by the fact that different disciplines—as represented by their associations' style sheets and guidelines for their major journals—have distinct preferences that tend to limit the potential options. As a result, we deal with these formal elements first.

Hyland's study of citation pattern in eight disciplines revealed some interesting differences (see Note 9). A first difference that emerges is the way in which the cited work is handled. Below are the basic options.

1. Within-sentence quotations

   According to Kim (1999), "The World Trade Organization still has many obstacles to overcome, particularly with regard to decision-making processes (10)."

2. Block and indented quotations (quotations of more than 40 words)

   As Kim (1999) has indicated:

   > Although the WTO is a major improvement over the old GATT system, it is still a young organization and leaves much to be desired. Mostly, the organization lacks both the competence and the resources to deal with new trade areas such as investment and information; its formal and binding structure as well as rigid decision-making process hinders and even sometimes blocks any harmonization effort in new trade-related areas.

3. Paraphrase/summary

   According to Kim (1999), the World Trade Organization needs to improve the processes by which decisions are made.

4. Generalization (combining several sources)

> The ways in which decisions are made within the World Trade Organization are typically inefficient (Mitchell 1997; Kim 1998; Kim 1999; Kirgis 1999). (See Note 10.)

Task Nine

Working with a partner, if possible, examine table 4.1 and answer the questions that follow.

TABLE 4.1. Percentages for Each Citation Option according to Discipline

Discipline	Quotation	Block Quotation	Summary/ Paraphrase	Generalization
Biology	0	0	72	38
Physics	0	0	68	32
Electrical engineering	0	0	66	34
Mechanical engineering	0	0	67	33
Marketing	3	2	68	27
Applied linguistics	8	2	67	23
Sociology	8	5	69	18
Philosophy	2	1	89	8

Source: Data from K. Hyland, "Academic attribution: Citation and the construction of disciplinary knowledge," *Applied Linguistics* 20 (1999): 341–67.

1. What percentage of citations in your field would likely involve a quotation? What about the field of your partner?

2. How do you account for the fact that sociology and applied linguistics have the highest percentage of citations in the form of quotations from previous authors' work?

3. Note the percentages for generalizations. If you had to guess, would you say the differences might reflect (a) the size of the field, (b) the integration of the field, or (c) some other cause?

4. Note that no quotations at all were found in the science and engineering research papers. Under what circumstances might one occur?

5. Can you come up with one more question?

(See Note 11.)

Another important variable is whether the cited author is part of the syntax of the citing sentence or stands outside it, either in parentheses or as represented by a number. (See style sheets in your field to see how this is done.) The former are often called *integral* citations and the latter *nonintegral* ones. Integral citations tend to focus the attention more on the researcher and rather less on the research. Here are some examples.

Integral

Hyland (1999) showed disciplinary variation in citation patterns.

Disciplinary variation in citation patterns has been shown by Hyland (1999).

According to Hyland (1999), there is considerable disciplinary variation in citation patterns.

Nonintegral

There would appear to be considerable disciplinary variation in citation patterns (Hyland 1999).

Research shows considerable disciplinary variation in citation patterns.[5]

Task Ten

Reflect again on the eight fields in Task Nine (and your own if not mentioned) and rank them in terms of the percentage of *nonintegral* citations that you might expect to find. Put the field with the most at the top. According to Hyland's study, integral citations made up the majority of citations in only one of the fields. Which field do you suppose it was? (See Note 12.)

In Hyland's corpus of 80,000 words from the 80 research articles, over 400 different reporting verbs were used to introduce the citations. Nearly half of the verbs used occurred only once, however, with some of the more unusual ones coming from philosophy. Here are sample sentences (adapted by us) using some of these uncommon verbs.

1. Lee (1998) *got mileage out of* the model by applying it to a wide range of environments.

2. Initially Ohara (1987) *was seduced by* the encouraging results of the pilot study.

3. Jarvannen (1997) *laments* that such discussions have all but disappeared.

4. Sandoval (1989) *espoused* the benefits of biofeedback in the treatment of migraine headaches.

5. Berg (1999) *holds out hope that* this new class of antibiotics will be effective in dealing with drug-resistant strains of *enterococcus*.

In contrast, here in table 4.2 are the most frequent reporting verbs by discipline.

TABLE 4.2.   High Frequency Reporting Verbs

Discipline	Verbs						
Biology	describe	find	report	show	suggest	observe	
Physics	develop	report	study	find	expand		
Electrical engineering	propose	use	describe	show	publish	develop	
Mechanical engineering	describe	show	report	discuss	give	develop	
Marketing	suggest	argue	find	demonstrate	propose	show	
Applied linguistics	suggest	argue	show	explain	find	point out	
Sociology	argue	suggest	describe	note	analyze	discuss	
Philosophy	say	suggest	argue	claim	point out	hold	think
Overall	suggest	argue	find	show	describe	propose	report

Source: Data from K. Hyland, "Academic attribution: Citation and the construction of disciplinary knowledge," *Applied Linguistics* 20 (1999): 341–67.

Task Eleven

Take one or two short published articles from your field that appear to contain some reporting verbs. Highlight all the verbs used to report previous research. Count the occurrences. Ignore citations based on comments by important public persons or literary figures that are not part of the research literature. For example:

> As Benjamin Franklin once said, "Either write something worth reading or do something worth writing."

Be prepared to add your findings to those in the table and to discuss how they compare. (See Note 13.)

V S Hixson

"Look, they cited your article! You're on your way
to becoming an important footnote!"

Language Focus: Ambiguity in Citations

Citations can sometimes be ambiguous or partly ambiguous as to whether the writer means to imply that somebody else said/claimed/ concluded something or actually did/found/carried out something. Such citations have been called "hanging" citations by at least one editor in our field, who recently announced that he would no longer accept them. Even experienced research writers can run into problems here, whether they are using author-date references or number references. Ambiguity may be particularly difficult to avoid in number systems, especially if reference numbers are placed at the ends of sentences. Regardless, care should be taken so that the references are as clear as possible. Consider the following citations.

1. The causes of illiteracy have been widely investigated (Ferrara 1990; Hyon 1994; Jones 1987).

2. Much has recently been published on the relationship between culture and the successful treatment of hypertension (Brown 1996; Edward 1998; Koch 1997; Lee 1998).

In these two sentences, we can probably safely presume that the authors cited for each are those engaged in the research and are thus provided to exemplify the point. But suppose the sentences were written like this.

3. The causes of illiteracy have been widely investigated (Clement 1993).

4. Much has recently been published on the relationship between culture and the successful treatment of hypertension (Lee 1998).

Now, it is no longer clear how the citations should be read. Are Clement and Lee major researchers in their fields, with the references thus referring to books they have published—perhaps their crowning works? Or are they perhaps commentators, with the citations referring to review or summary articles? Since we cannot easily answer these questions, these "hanging" citations should probably be rewritten so that the intended meaning is conveyed.

Task Twelve

Consider this set of in-text citations. Are they citations of research or of commentary, or are they ambiguous? Put an A next to those that you feel are ambiguous.

___ 1. Many researchers believe that per capita food production will continue to increase (Smith 1993; Chavez 1998; Chen 1999).

___ 2. Very few studies of this sort have been done on chronically malnourished individuals (Braun 1999).

___ 3. No studies of this sort have been done on chronically malnourished individuals (Braun 1999).

___ 4. Some studies of this sort have been done on chronically malnourished individuals (but see Braun 1999).

___ 5. One of the classic studies of family behavior was conducted in Polynesia (Malinowski 1932).

(See Note 14.)

Look at this extract from the *Journal of Personality and Social Psychology* (full information on the source is given in Note 15). The citations you should focus on have been italicized. Answer the questions that follow.

> Until recently, these two lines of investigation have had different emphases, posing a threat to their integration. The most robust risk factors in epidemiological research have an interpersonal theme *(Adler & Matthews, 1994).* These include explicitly interpersonal processes (e.g., social networks and social support) and characteristics of people that are likely to color their relationships (e.g., hostility). By contrast, traditional studies of psychophysiological mechanisms have focused on the responses of single individuals to nonsocial stressors, such as mental arithmetic or reaction time tests (for reviews, see Blascovich & Katkin, Katkin, 1993; Manuck, 1994). Cardiovascular responses to these tasks are not closely related with CVR in response to social stressors (Lassner, Matthews & Stoney, 1994; Matthews, Manuch, & Saab, 1986; Smith & O'Keefe, 1988). Thus, it is not clearly established that the psychophysiological mechanisms described in psychosomatic models of CVD occur in the interpersonal circumstances identified as risk factors *(Smith & Christensen, 1992).*

1. What did Adler and Matthews actually do? Did they write a review article? Did they do a statistical analysis of some data? Or did they undertake some major research?

2. Did Smith and Christensen identify risk factors, or did they show what was not clearly established?

3. Look at the following citations from the article. Would you now change your answers?

Adler N. & Matthews K. (1994) Health psychology: Why do some people get sick and some people stay well? *Annual Review of Psychology*, 45, 229–259.

Smith T.W. & Christensen A.J. (1992). Cardiovascular reactivity and interpersonal relations: Psychosomatic processes in social context. *Journal of Social and Clinical Psychology*, 11, 279–301.

(See Note 15.)

Task Thirteen

Rewrite the two "hanging" citations of Clement and of Lee on the top of page 133, first to indicate that they are books and then that they are review articles.

Book

_____

_____

Review Article

_____

_____

(See Note 16.)

4.4 Paraphrase and Evaluation

In Section 4.3 we mentioned issues of "accuracy, fairness, plagiarism, selection, style, and evaluation" in reporting the work of others. In this section, we will investigate these issues, using restatements of the Pradip and Rahim abstract (from Section 4.2), which were written by some of our students.

We provide the abstract again for you for convenience.

Pradip, S., and R. Rahim. (1997)

> There has been much talk of the "Bombay Miracle" (e.g., *Time*, August 3, 1996) but rather less of the communication failures of the computer engineers and scientists in the city. We have developed training courses for engineering graduates stressing cross-cultural differences in negotiation, writing styles, patent laws, and contractual obligations among Indian, Japanese, and North American leaders in technological change. Although no empirical evidence is yet available, there are signs that the case approach to success and failure in Indian computer engineering initiatives for export is having beneficial results.

Task Fourteen

Carefully read these four "treatments" of Pradip and Rahim. Evaluate them in terms of information and language, using the codes below.

Information (or the amount of detail in Pradip and Rahim that is retained)

I O (The amount is about right.)

I + (More information is retained than really necessary.)

I – (The information is insufficient.)

Paraphrase (or the amount of rewriting of the original)

P O (nicely done; captures the essence of the original in rather different words)

P + (perhaps too much changed; doesn't accurately represent the original)

P – (too much lifted from the original; raises issues of plagiarism)

___ 1. Another communication program is developed by Pradip and Rahim (1997) for engineering graduates. All of these programs show appreciable results.

___ 2. Pradip and Rahim (1997) have developed training courses for engineering graduates stressing cross-cultural differences via a case study approach of success and failure in Indian computer engineering initiatives for export, and again find signs of beneficial results.

___ 3. In their article Pradip and Rahim (1997) talk about the successes in Indian computer engineering and also point out its weakness as a result of communication failures. They relate this with cross-cultural differences and have developed a program for training graduate students stressing cross-culture differences in negotiations, writing, laws, and contractual obligations among Indian, Japanese, and North American leaders in technology.

___ 4. Pradip and Rahim have designed training courses stressing cross-cultural differences in engineering communications.

Which one of the "treatments" would you prefer to have written? Why?

(See Note 17.)

We have now worked our way through most of the thorny issues confronting the writer of an LR. But three important issues remain: tense choice in reporting previous work (which we will deal with in the next unit); evaluation of the work reported; and dealing with literature that does not "fit" the second story you want to construct.

At the beginning of this unit (Task Two) we saw that not every piece of research should be evaluated, but providing some kind of evaluative commentary gives the impression of an intelligent and organizing mind at work. Being able to provide such an impression substantially contributes to research positioning.

Several strategies can successfully be used to reveal your stance toward the literature. One is to provide a closing assessment that focuses on shortcomings in the body of literature to date or suggests future directions. Here is one good concluding paragraph written by one of our students.

> Overall, researchers seem to agree with the importance of real-life context in engineering communication courses. Despite the apparent consensus about *what* to teach, there still remains the problem of *how* to teach. Researchers have tried various methods to teach engineers how to communicate and each method appears to be successful for a specific purpose and a special population. Considering that the effectiveness of a specific method depends on some moderating variables, future studies should focus on the effects of these moderating parameters, such as the purposes of the course, educational and cultural settings, and target population. (original emphasis)
>
> —Jin Nam Choi (unedited)

You may have noticed that Jin Nam hedged or qualified some of his statements. How necessary was this? Why?

Another strategy is to open the LR with a general assessment such as those presented in the following task.

Task Fifteen

Which of the following general assessments seem appropriate for the abstracts on engineering communication (Section 4.2)? Make a check mark (✓) next to those that seem to fit.

__ 1. There have been surprisingly few studies on the teaching of communication skills to engineers.

__ 2. The 1990s saw an upsurge of interest in the teaching of communication skills to engineers.

__ 3. To date, studies on the teaching of communication skills to engineers are scattered, poorly controlled, and have had very small sample sizes.

__ 4. One impressive feature of the literature on the teaching of communication skills to engineers is its international scope.

__ 5. There have been a surprisingly large number of studies devoted to the specialized topic of teaching communication skills to engineers.

(See Note 18.)

A third strategy would be to make occasional comments within the LR on selected papers. Along this same line, a well-chosen adjective or adverb may help you intersperse your evaluation.

Task Sixteen

Which of the following could apply to work described in one or several of the abstracts? Indicate the abstract(s) by author name(s) in the space provided.

1. short _____

2. large-scale _____

3. preliminary _____

4. early _____

5. quantitative _____

6. limited _____

(See Note 19.)

"Misfits"

The final issue is how to deal with literature that just does not seem to fit well with your story. Looking at the engineering communication abstracts again, we see that the egregious paper is Sullivan (number 8) since it argues that any attempt to develop a communication skills program for engineers is doomed to failure unless the engineering faculty support it. One convenient strategy for dealing with Sullivan is to simply drop it. What, if any, are the implications of ignoring it?

Another possible solution (albeit perhaps temporary) is demonstrated by the following.

> The only large-scale study is that of Sullivan (1996), which suggests that the key factor to the acceptability of the program (and by inference to its success) is not the quality of the program itself, but faculty support for it. This issue deserves further consideration, not only because of its intrinsic importance, but also because of its implications for the formative evaluation proposed in this dissertation. This discussion, however, is better suited for the next chapter.
> —Hamilton de Godoy Wielewicki (minor editing)

Task Seventeen

Revise your draft LR of teaching communication skills to engineers or prepare a revised draft of a section of an LR you are currently preparing.

4.5 A Postscript and a Warning

The Fulan A. Fulani case that we have extensively discussed here is situated at the proposal stage. Most doctoral students (and proposal writers) tend to believe that when their research is finished, they can simply cut the LR from the proposal and paste it into the dissertation or research article. In the vast majority of cases this strategy will be unsuccessful. First, during the research process additional items from the literature will be discovered. Second, in the interim, new research will likely be published. Third, the scope and direction of your research will likely have changed; for example, it will be agreed that certain lines of inquiry discussed in the prospectus need not be pursued. Fourth, and most important, you now have a second story, a body of research findings, and this will effect your construction of a first story. None of this is to say, of course, that the hard LR work put into a proposal cannot form some kind of basis for a dissertation-level treatment of previous research.

Task Eighteen

Look at this tenth abstract that deals with teaching communication skills to engineers. How might this new piece cause you to revise your LR?

10. Fulani, A. F. (in press). Meeting the communication needs of engineers in contemporary Egypt. *Technical Education Quarterly.*

> Privatization trends in Egypt today have created a need for a new cadre of engineers. The traditional engineering curriculum in state universities, with its heavy reliance on mathematics, is slowly transforming itself to meet these new demands, despite much faculty opposition. This paper analyzes the revised "English for Engineers" course at Helwan University. Results suggest that the new emphasis on oral skills and the writing of memoranda and other engineering correspondence, while welcomed by the business community, has negatively affected student performance in other courses—particularly those that require the reading of research articles. This, in turn, seems to have contributed to a rising failure rate in the Engineering College.

(See Note 20.)

So far in this unit we have primarily dealt with issues concerning the write-up of an LR without considering how you might choose the actual literature you include. In doing so, we have been able to highlight several points. First, as a hybrid act of literacy involving reading and writing, creating an LR is a challenging and complex activity. As you read the texts of others you weigh them against what you know about your field and build meaning, which in turn forms the basis of your LR. Second, there is no magic formula or a preferred way to write up an LR. And finally, how you weave the work of others into your work through citation varies from discipline to discipline. In the next unit, we will turn our attention to the rather challenging task of choosing what to include in the LR by presenting the cases of two writers. As you may see, simply having read a lot in your own discipline, and possibly in other disciplines, is just the beginning.

4.6 Notes and Comments for Unit Four

Note 1 (sample responses for Task One)

It seems clear that 1 will generally be easiest and that this is a clear advantage. It offers compartmentalization: "OK, that's one job done—now I can move on to something else." On the other hand, this compartmentalization will work to prevent your work from seeming to be fully integrated into the wider picture. Approach 2 is usually only a cosmetic improvement on 1, but it certainly *looks* more integrated. Approach 3 is the harder and more ambitious road. However, it can lead to awkward problems of repetition when certain studies need to be referred to again and again.

In linguistics dissertations there would seem to be some small preference for approach 3; in articles approach 2 is common.

Note 2

Malcolm Ashmore defended his Ph.D. thesis in 1985 at the University of York (United Kingdom). The work was entitled "The Reflexive Thesis: Wrighting Sociology of Scientific Knowledge," and, as its title suggests, his research area is sociology. The dissertation was published four years later. Ashmore deliberately switches the genres around: The opening chapter takes the form of an introductory lecture by the candidate with the advisor/supervisor sitting at the back; the LR second chapter is cast as a 60-page encyclopedia on the topic with entries for people, terms, and schools; and the final chapter takes the form of a transcript of a mock dissertation defense. A flavor of Ashmore can be sensed from this opening to his endnotes.

> Chapter One
>
> Welcome to the notes. I hope you will visit this section of the text regularly. Quite a lot will be going on here and it would be a shame to miss it all. But to get to the business of this particular note: May I ask by which route you arrived at Chapter One, note 1? (227)

Note 3 (sample responses for Task Two)

1. This comment suggests that preparing your literature review is a linear process when in fact you will at times be doing all three of these activities simultaneously. If only it were so simple.

2. Length does not necessarily equal quality. Of course, your LR needs to be thorough. But you need to concentrate on work that helps you establish your research story.

3. You might initially give an unqualified *yes* to this one, but the question is what will your criteria for relevance be? *All* is a rather strong modifier here. For some research areas there may be a small, manageable amount of relevant literature. For other areas there may be quite a lot of relevant work, and you may need to exclude some pieces.

4. Your first instinct may be to brush aside work that does not seem to be directly related. However, similar work in another area that is particularly interesting or novel but not necessarily exactly on your topic, can often offer insights into your own work. Those of you working on interdisciplinary topics have probably already realized this.

5. Yes, your research adds another "chapter" to the research story that has been developing on your topic. Some stories, such as those in medicine, have their roots in antiquity. Others, however, such as cloning, are relatively new.

6. Your reader will approach your text with certain expectations, including what areas would likely be covered. Consider your audience. If you are excluding certain areas that one might expect to be included, explain the scope of your work and the reasoning behind your choices.

7. Yes. These are precisely the sorts of things that make your work interesting.

8. No, not quite. While the overall organization of an LR should be more or less chronological, an LR should not follow a strict chronological order in which research is presented precisely in the order in which it was done. Such LRs suggest a rather narrow understanding of the field you are working in. Unless you are writing a reflective piece looking back at where your field has been, you should resist any urge you might have to present research in sequence without synthesizing or presenting the big picture.

9. Yes

10. In certain fields, particularly those that are changing quickly, such as the hard sciences, this is generally the norm. However, in others, such as law, history, or philosophy, older works may still be highly relevant.

11. Yes

12. Providing a critique of each piece would not only be tedious for you as a writer but also possibly tiresome for your reader. Critiquing each piece would serve to isolate previous work, making it difficult for you to show trends, patterns, and directions. Reserve your critiques of individual research for key work that deserves individual attention; otherwise it is best to focus on general trends, traditions, or approaches.

(Task Three Teaching Hint: Do not attempt to do all the architectures in one class. Choose several students to go first. Then encourage a second group of students to build upon what the earlier group has constructed.)

Note 4 (sample responses for Task Four)

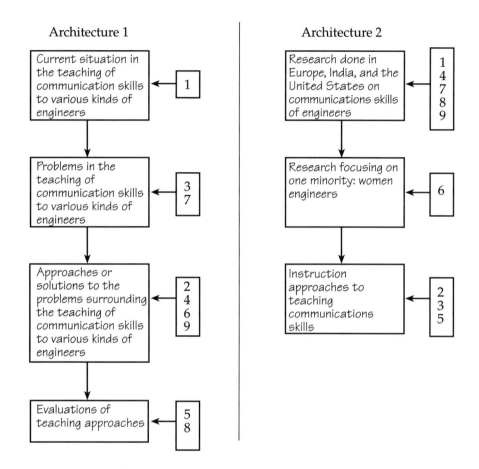

Note 5 (sample responses for Task Five)

1. This is bland and jumps abruptly with *For example, Fredrickson.* Fair.

2. So why start with this? Especially since it is not an English as a second language dissertation.

3. This strikes us as pretty good. Over its three sentences, it justifies starting with Fredrickson.

4. This is definitely smart! It makes a real and successful effort to justify the choice of Fredrickson as the opening paper for inclusion. Excellent. (*Plight* means *desperate situation.*)

Note 6

Marco, M. J. L. 2000. Collocation frameworks in medical research papers: A genre-based study. *English for Specific Purposes* 19:63–86.

Note 7 (sample response for Task Six)

In all these cases, a following *of* phrase requires the first noun to take *the,* while a different preposition selects an indefinite article before the first noun. As we will see, this is partly a statistical preference but still offers useful general guidance in cases of severe doubt! *Between* does not follow the rule, however. Hyland's corpus (see Note 9) shows a 3:1 preference for *the* with nouns preceding a prepositional phrase with *between.* You may also have noticed that in some cases, such as 1 and 2, the *the* + *of* phrase is more specific. There are also occasions where the presence or absence of *the* seems to have little effect, as in

Evidence of malnutrition in this region is widespread.
The evidence of malnutrition in this region is widespread.

Note 8 (answer key and analysis for Task Seven)

1. a   2. the   3. a   4. the   5. the   6. a   7. a   8. the   9. the   10. a

In speech, there are a number of *a . . . of . . .* patterns that are also common, particularly the very common phrase *a lot of.* Also note that *the number of students* follows the regular rule, takes a singular verb, and is specific (*The number of subjects in the study was limited to 25*). On the other hand, *a number of students* is exceptional in taking a plural verb; that is, in this case the verb is determined by the *second* noun (*A number of subjects in the study were unable to complete the task*). Also note that *a number of* refers to some unspecified number within a group. Other exceptions concern percentages, proportions, and fractions, as in *70 percent of the candidates have passed.* One final group of expressions that deserves mention here is partitive phrases with unit nouns such as *a piece of paper* or *a cup of coffee.* Here are some examples of other partitive phrases that are indefinite.

Area	*Depth*	*Length*	*Weight*	*Volume*
a hectare of land	a millimeter of water	a meter of copper wire	an ounce of gold	a pint of blood
five acres of farmland	two meters of snow	three inches of foil	two kilograms of rice	five quarts of motor oil
	an inch of rain	a millimeter of bone growth	a ton of steel	a watt of electricity

Note 9

Hyland, K. 1999. Academic attribution: Citation and the construction of disciplinary knowledge. *Applied Linguistics* 20:341–67.

Note 10

The standard APA practice is to place multiple citations in chronological order. If two citations have the same year, then they are arranged alphabetically.

Note 11 (sample responses for Task Nine)

1. No answer possible

2. Sociology is a field (like English) dominated by big names, often of historical proportions, such as Marx, Durkheim, and Weber. Hence the direct quotations from the "founders." In applied linguistics, unlike sociology, it is common practice to quote short memorable phrases from previous authors.

3. Well, we are also pretty much in the dark here. The low figures for philosophy clearly reflect the focus on *individual* philosophers. The predominance of "big names" mentioned in 2 might partly explain the situation in sociology. Marketing will probably use some quotations from famous people in the field.

4. Famous oldies? Nobel Prize winners? Famous people who are not scientists or engineers?

Note 12 (answer key for Task Ten)

1. biology (90%) 2. electrical engineering (84%) 3. physics (83%) 4. mechanical engineering (71%) 5. marketing (70%) 6. applied linguistics (66%) 7. sociology (65%) 8. philosophy (35%).

As you probably guessed, philosophy alone had a preponderance of integral citations.

Note 13 (sample analysis for Task Eleven)

For our part, we took three articles from the *Journal of Business and Technical Communication*. Here are all the reporting verbs that occurred three times or more and the number of occurrences.

note 11; argue 9; claim 5; point out 5; suggest 5; call 3; describe 3; report 3

We noticed that there seemed to be individual preferences; two authors preferred *argue,* while the third preferred *claim.* A typical problem with a small sample size! The activity took us about an hour.

Overall, the business communication data is probably most similar to the findings for philosophy (except for the latter's use of *say*).

Note 14 (answer key for Task Twelve)

1. No problem. The folks in parentheses are examples of the *many researchers.*

2. (A) A problem: Did Braun make this observation, or was he or she an example of one of the very few studies? Needs editing.

3. Since there were "no studies" Braun must be a commentator.

4. (A) This is obscure. What does (*but see Braun 1999*) imply? Again, needs rewording.

5. No problem. The work dated 1932 is clearly "classic."

Note 15

The excerpt is from the following source.

Smith, T. W., J. P. Limon, L. C. Gall, and L. Q. Ngu. 1996. Interpersonal control and cardiovascular reactivity: Goals, behavioral expression, and the moderating effects of sex. *Journal of Personality and Social Psychology* 70:1012–24.

So it turns out that Adler and Matthews is a review article and in fact provides a generalization that will be developed in the rest of the paragraph. On the other hand, Smith and Christensen is revealed as an experimental paper. The ambiguity in the latter could be clarified by some change, such as

> Smith & Christensen (1992) have also shown that the psychophysiological mechanisms described in psychosomatic models of CVR do not consistently occur in the interpersonal circumstances identified as risk factors.

Note 16 (sample responses for Task Thirteen)

Two of several possible solutions are the following.

The volume by Clement (1993) provides a broad investigation into the causes of illiteracy.

Much has recently been published on the relationship between culture and the successful treatment of hypertension (see Lee 1998 for a review).

Note 17 (sample responses for Task Fourteen)

There is wide room for disagreement of course on the Pradip and Rahim task, but we guess that most people would opt for something like the following.

1. I – P O
2. I O P O
3. I + P –
4. I – P O

Note 18 (sample responses for Task Fifteen)

Again possible responses to Task Fifteen are likely open to disagreement, especially because they are likely to be influenced by whether you work in a large field (organic chemistry) or a small one (the study of place-names in Sri Lanka). But from our perspective as applied linguists . . .

1. This makes sense to us.

2. The basic point seems right but *upsurge* is too strong.

3. Yes, but unnecessarily harshly put? The young and the cruel?

4. Certainly, this is one feature, but we do not think *impressive* is quite the right word; *interesting* might work better.

5. Not true from our perspective

Note 19 (sample responses for Task Sixteen)

For Task Sixteen we suggest

1. small   McWrath; Ahmed and Williams

2. large-scale   Sullivan

3. preliminary   Leon and Deng; Pradip and Rahim

4. early   McWrath

5. quantitative   Lo and Li

6. limited   Van Hoek; Scott; McWrath; Leon and Deng; Pradip and Rahim; Lo and Li

Note 20 (sample response for Task Eighteen)

Fulani will doubtless wish to highlight his own research. Equally important, however, his own study seems to suggest that there can be a downside to the introduction of communication skills courses for engineering students. His findings will need to be contrasted with those apparently producing more positive outcomes.

Unit Five
More Complex Literature Reviews

This is the second of two units devoted to the literature review. The case study in the previous unit was narrowly focused on a sub-area of Fulani's prospectus. The two case studies in this unit range rather more broadly but will result in less work for you!

The breakdown of this unit is as follows.

The unit also includes Language Focus sections on citation, tense, and reporting verbs and on the use of quotation marks.

5.1 Weaknesses in Literature Reviews

We begin this unit with some typical observations by professors and reviewers on the problems they most often find in the LRs they read. We decided to keep this section out of Unit Four—we did not want to further increase your anxiety levels!

Below are five comments from professors and others on draft literature reviews written by graduate students or junior researchers. They are compilations of large numbers of comments we have received over the years and are not necessarily verbatim (see Note 1). The last specifically refers to the multidisciplinary or interdisciplinary LR.

1. "Your draft literature review is basically little more than a list of previous research papers in the field. While it is clearly well researched, it doesn't give me a sense of what has been more significant and less significant. It is hard to know where you stand."

2. "You have given me a chronological account, which might be fine for an encyclopedia entry or a historical background section to a textbook, but it doesn't function well as a prefacing mechanism for your own research. Although I know what your research hypothesis is, I don't see it informing your characterization of the previous literature. Somehow we need to see the relevant themes and issues more clearly."

3. "The first part of your review deals with *theory*, often invoking big names from the past. The second half deals with *practice*—in other words, more contemporary empirical findings. I don't see at the moment these two parts in any kind of coherent relation. I know it's hard, but . . . "

4. "This draft literature review describes adequately each piece of relevant research but does so as a kind of anthology, piece by piece. It needs a higher pass, something that does more to evaluate and connect."

5. "Interdisciplinary reviews are hard, and I am basically sympathetic to your dilemma. However, what you have done is keep everything within its original disciplinary boundaries. To be innovative, you need to make more connections across disciplinary areas, so that we can see the new connections and relations that you will ultimately be able to establish. Good luck!"

(See Note 2.)

Task One

What is your self-assessment of your own attempts at writing an LR? Which of the above observations might apply to your own efforts: (a) before Unit Four and (b) after Unit Four?

Does the comment apply to your work?	Yes	No
1. Before Unit Four		
After Unit Four		
2. Before Unit Four		
After Unit Four		
3. Before Unit Four		
After Unit Four		
4. Before Unit Four		
After Unit Four		
5. Before Unit Four		
After Unit Four		

5.2 A First Case:
Reviewing the Concept of Discourse Community

Our first case deals with studies of an issue that in one way or another comes to the attention of everybody who spends time in a university (or a research institution for that matter). Ask yourself this question and consider the following four possible answers.

How can we best conceptualize a university?

a. A university is best thought of as a single separate community.

b. A university is best thought of as consisting of several communities made up of its various colleges.

c. A university is best thought of as a collection of departments that have their own disciplinary cultures and community lives.

d. University communities of like-minded people can only really be found in departmental or research subgroups.

If you had to choose one of these alternatives, which would you choose and why?

One vehicle for approaching this difficult issue (where most of the answers seem to be an unhelpful combination of "yes" and "no") has been the concept of *discourse community*. Let us assume that there are basically two kinds of community. One is the typical homogeneous community of speakers that you might find in a mountain village or a remote tribe and that is typically studied by anthropologists and sociolinguists. Such groupings, with their shared histories, family ties, and so on, are known as *speech communities*. The other kind of grouping is very different in that it consists of often very diverse people, frequently having, for instance, different native languages and countries of birth, who come together for some occupational or recreational purpose. These *discourse communities* may be researching high-energy physics, playing in an orchestra, maintaining fire-fighting services in a town, or devoting themselves to the preparation of future elementary school teachers in a school of education. As we all can easily recognize, such communities develop, in order to carry out their missions more effectively, special ways of talking and writing (such as community-specific acronyms [see Note 3] or abbreviations) and special genres or community-specific variations of such genres.

So far, so good. However, the concept of discourse community (DC) has had a rather troubled history since it first began to be used in the early 1980s. John, who wrote about the concept extensively in a 1990 book (see Note 4), decided as part of a major research project investigating academic discourse to revisit the concept. He first assembled a chronological list of all the people who had discussed the discourse community concept (or its close terminological relatives such as *disciplinary community*) in some detail. He wasn't interested in those who had simply used the concept. Here is his working chronological list.

Porter 1986	Porter 1992	Bex 1996
Cooper 1989	Olsen 1993	Grabe and Kaplan 1996
Harris 1989	Swales 1993	Hanks 1996
Swales 1990	Miller 1994	Devitt 1996
Lave and Wenger 1991	Van Nostrand 1994	Beaufort 1997
Bizzell 1992	Schryer 1994	Gunnarsson 1997
Lyon 1992	Casanave 1995	Johns 1997
Killingsworth and	Berkenkotter and	
Gilbertson 1992	Huckin 1995	Prior 1998

This then is the *publication* history; it is not, of course, an exact *genealogy* of the concept because many of the ideas were aired earlier at conferences and in circulated manuscripts.

His next stage was to characterize these 24 contributions to our understanding of the DC concept. For his own purposes, he eventually decided to categorize them in terms of the following.

1. Their base—in terms of the writer's country (*provenance*) (see Note 5)

2. The discipline the writer represented (rhetoric and composition—RC; applied linguistics—AL; technical communication—TC, etc.) (*field*)

3. The writer's attitude toward DCs (*stance*)

   in favor of (+);
   against (−);
   neutral or conflicted (=).

4. The type of publication—book or a shorter piece (article, etc.) (*Genre*)

The results of this stage are presented in table 5.1.

TABLE 5.1.   Categorization of the Contributions

Author/Date	Provenance	Field	Stance	Genre
Porter 1986	U.S.	RC	+	article
Cooper 1989	U.S.	RC	−	chapter
Harris 1989	U.S.	RC	−	article
Swales 1990	U.S.	AL	+	book
Lave and Wenger 1991	U.S	education	+	book
Bizzell 1992	U.S.	RC	=	chapter
Lyon 1992	U.S.	RC	−	article
Killingsworth and Gilbertson 1992	U.S.	TC	+	book
Porter 1992	U.S.	RC	+	book
Olsen 1993	U.S.	TC	+	article
Swales 1993	U.S.	AL	=	article
Miller 1994	U.S.	TC	=	article
Van Nostrand 1994	U.S.	TC	+	chapter
Schryer 1994	Canada	TC	=	article
Berkenkotter and Huckin 1995	U.S.	TC/AL	=	book
Casanave 1995	Japan	AL	−	chapter
Bex 1996	U.K.	AL	+	book
Grabe and Kaplan 1996	U.S.	AL	=	book
Hanks 1996	U.S.	anthropology	+	book
Devitt 1996	U.S.	RC	=	article
Beaufort 1997	U.S.	RC	+	article
Gunnarsson 1997	Sweden	Swedish studies	=	article
Johns 1997	U.S.	AL	=	book
Prior 1997	U.S.	RC	−	book

He then decided as an experiment to reorder the table according to stance and dropping the categories of provenance and genre. The results are shown in table 5.2.

TABLE 5.2. Stance of the Contributions

Stance	Author/Date	Field
–	Cooper 1989	RC
–	Harris 1989	RC
–	Lyon 1992	RC
–	Casanave 1995	AL
–	Prior 1997	RC
+	Porter 1986	RC
+	Swales 1990	AL
+	Lave andWenger 1991	education
+	Killingsworth and Gilbertson 1992	TC
+	Porter 1992	RC
+	Olsen 1993	TC
+	Van Nostrand 1994	TC
+	Bex 1996	AL
+	Hanks 1996	anthropology
+	Beaufort 1997	RC
=	Bizzell 1992	RC
=	Swales 1993	AL
=	Miller 1994	TC
=	Schryer 1994	TC
=	Berkenkotter and Huckin 1995	TC/AL
=	Grabe and Kaplan 1996	AL
=	Devitt 1996	RC
=	Gunnarsson 1997	Swedish studies
=	Johns 1997	AL

Task Two

What tendencies or trends might emerge from the two tables? What else could be learned? (See Note 6.)

We recommend this kind of matrix, or any kind of working chart, tree diagram, or table, as a useful preparatory device. Such displays have three advantages especially when we are confronted with the arduous task of putting together an LR with literature from different fields as a preface to describing our own work.

1. They allow us to "eyeball" the literature.

2. They encourage us to make connections.

3. But, most important of all, they persuade us to perhaps find enough common threads so that we can make a "high pass," or even better a series of high passes, over what is, in its descriptive detail, highly complex material. Thus, we avoid getting trapped in lower-level comparisons and, in so doing, we may even be able to see things that have not quite been seen before.

Task Three

The four categories that John chose for table 5.1 (and the two he kept for table 5.2) were very much those that he thought he needed for his own particular purposes. Other LRs, including those incorporating work from different fields, will need very different categories (apart perhaps from date of publication). Here are some possibilities.

- Methods used?
- Theory or theoretical model followed?
- A theoretical or an empirical study?
- Computer modeling/simulation used?
- Size of the sample/number of cases?
- Statistical treatment included?
- Practical applications stressed?
- Any ideological commitment made? If so, what kind?

What other categories occur to you?

Now prepare a sketch diagram of the categories you might choose for your own LRs (past, present, or future!). (See Note 7.)

Task Four

Here is a short write-up of the information that appears in the articles categorized in table 5.1. However, the short paragraphs are no longer in their original order. Read them carefully and attempt to reconstruct the text as it originally was by writing the numbers from 1 to 6 in the blanks provided. Is more than one order possible? Does the LR succeed at making a "high pass" over the material? Why or why not?

The Concept of Discourse Community: A Review of the Literature

___ A. Most of the strongest objections to the DC concept have come from the rhetorical community. As early as 1989, Harris complained that the concept was utopian, while Cooper argued that it took insufficient account of individual agency. Arguments along both of these lines continued to be made, but more recently, those who value the concept are further accused of being "structuralist" and of adopting a "strong text" approach that insufficiently recognizes the long moments of negotiation, revision, silence, and anxiety that preface the appearance of the final community directed document (Casanave 1995, Prior 1998).

___ B. Interest in the concept of discourse community (DC) is largely a North American phenomenon since the only detailed discussions from elsewhere have been provided by Casanave (1995) in Japan, Bex (1996) in Britain and Gunnarsson (1997) in Sweden. It would seem that leading Australian scholars in this field, such as Halliday and Martin, have focused attention on discoursal patterns per se, while their European counterparts (e.g., Van Dijk, Wodak) have been more involved with issues of discourse, ideology, and social justice. This North American interest clearly stems from English department involvement in rhetorical theory and its applications to the teaching of academic writing.

___ C. Rather few of the contributions to the literature have actually attempted to define what a discourse community is. This is rather odd because using the concept as a loose "term of art" can lead to circularity—that the discourse will be defined by the community and the community will be defined by its discourse. Of those who have attempted to be specific, the more detailed characterizations have been offered by Swales (1990), Killingsworth and Gilbertson (1992), Porter (1992), and Hanks (1996). Killingsworth and Gilbertson deserve particular credit for elaborating the differences between *local* and *global* discourse communities.

___ D. With both practitioner support and increased definitional clarity, we can once again begin to use it as a discriminating instrument. We might well need to bear in mind the distinction between local and global communities, even though this distinction is being fast eroded by electronic communications. We certainly should note that DCs do not have to be supportive or "close knit" (Bex, 1996), or "egalitarian" (Lave and Wenger, 1991), or even entirely free of gender, racial, and other kinds of prejudice. With these lessons from a rich literature, we are now in a better position to begin answering our research questions.

___ E. Porter (1992) offers a particularly neat solution to some of the complexities—that of the *forum*. A forum is a "concrete, local manifestation of the operation of a discourse community" (1992, 107). For Porter these fora can range from being a defined place of assembly, to being an occupational location, and on to being a vehicle for wider discourse community connection (cf. Killingsworth and Gilbertson, 1992), such as a conference and a journal. He then suggested that it is these forumlike discourse community "traces" (p. 108) that provide convenient points of entry for study and research (see also Schryer, 1994, and Berkenkotter and Huckin, 1995).

___ F. In contrast, the DC "supporter's club" is heavily populated by those that consider themselves in some sense as *practitioners*; these include applied linguists who tend to work with non-native speakers of English, as well as experts in technical and business communication who are interested in preparing students for writing in the workplace. Whatever residual doubts these groups may have about the concept, they see it as a valuable and practical framework for preparing people for specific upcoming writing tasks.

(See Note 8.)

Task Five

Now take a closer look at the following two versions of paragraph A, which deals with objections to the concept of discourse community. Can you see the differences? What are the consequences of the changes carried out in A2?

A1. Most of the strongest objections to the DC concept have come from the rhetorical community. As early as 1989, Harris *complained* that the concept was utopian, while Cooper *argued* that it took insufficient account of individual agency. Arguments along both of these lines continued to be made, but more recently, those who value the concept are further *accused of* being "structuralist" and of adopting a "strong text" approach that insufficiently recognizes the long moments of negotiation, revision, silence, and anxiety that preface the appearance of the final community directed document (Casanave 1995, Prior 1998).

A2. [1]Most of the strongest objections to the DC concept have come from the rhetorical community. [2]As early as 1989, Harris *stated* that the concept was Utopian, while Cooper *maintained* that it took insufficient account of individual agency. [3]Arguments along both of these lines continued to be made, but more recently, those who value the concept are further described as "structuralist" and adopting a "strong text" approach that insufficiently recognizes the long moments of negotiation, revision, silence, and anxiety that preface the appearance of the final community directed document (Casanave 1995, Prior 1998).

(See Note 9.)

Language Focus: Citation, Tense, and Reporting Verbs

We dealt with this topic in Unit Seven of *Academic Writing for Graduate Students;* here we take a second, briefer look. First, consider the subjects of the present perfect verbs in the write-up (now listed in their correct order of occurrence).

Paragraph	Subject	Present Perfect
1	the only detailed discussions	have been provided by
1	leading Australian scholars	have focused attention on
2	Most of the strongest objections	have come from
4	Rather few of the contributions	have actually attempted to
4	the more detailed characterizations	have been offered by

So we can learn two things from this display. First, the present perfect is closely associated with generalizations (often hedged or modified) about the literature. Second, these kinds of generalizations tend to cluster in the earlier paragraphs and/or at the beginnings of paragraphs.

However, as we said in *AWG*, tense choice when discussing previous work can also be subtle and strategic. For example, it will be clear from the concluding paragraph (D) that John continues to believe that the DC concept is useful; it only needs to be "rehabilitated." Thus, we see the use of the present perfect supported by adverbs such as *now* and *once again*.

Now consider this sentence (sentence 3 in A), which follows a summary of the views of two people who are against the concept of discourse community.

> Arguments along both of these lines *continued* to be made, . . .

Surely, you might well argue—especially in the light of the five examples in the chart above—that the present perfect should have been used here, as in

> Arguments along both of these lines *have continued* to be made . . .

Certainly, both of these are grammatically possible. Indeed, the present tense might be another option if such arguments were still being presented at the time of writing.

> Arguments along both of these lines *continue* to be made . . .

We can now see that the writer's actual choice of the past tense is motivated by his belief that such arguments are old, dated, no longer relevant; need not be taken so seriously today; and so on. His use of the past tense is thus quietly dismissive.

Task Six

Produce your own fragment of a multidisciplinary literature review, either from your previous work or something new. Add a brief commentary on your experience.

5.3 English in the Research World: A Further Perspective

We had a first look at this highly relevant issue in Unit One, Section 1.3; we now look at some further comment. Below you will find an abstract on a dental topic. Temporomandibular joint (TMJ) disorders affect the joint of the jaw located just in front of the ear canal and cause chronic, severe pain. In the United States 90 percent of the sufferers of TMJ pain are women. Read the abstract and then decide which of the following best captures the authors' main point.

a. Medical journalists should be careful when they report on research.

b. Dunn et al. have made an important discovery.

c. Researchers should check literature in languages other than English before publishing.

Media Hype: Musculus Sphenomandibularis

J.C. Türp, T. Cowley, C.S. Stohler

Abstract

The report of an allegedly so far unknown craniomandibular muscle ("the sphenomandibularis") in 1996 by Dunn and co-workers provided much comment in journals and newspapers. The authors' hypothesized role of the "m. sphenomandibularis" in temporomandibular disorders and headaches created hopes and expectations. The present article examines whether two detailed descriptions by Ramalho and co-workers [1978, in Portuguese] and by Zenker [1954, 1955, and 1956, in German] deal with the very same muscle. From a comparison of these descriptions it becomes evident that the "m. sphenomandibularis" is not a new muscle, but corresponds to the "medial portion" [Zenker], or "deep portion" [Ramalho et al.] of the temporalis muscle. Further directed search identified descriptions of the muscle in question back in the 19th century.

J. C. Türp, T. Cowley, and C. S. Stohler, Media Hype: *Musculus Sphenomandibularis*, *Acta Anatomica* 158 (1997): 150–54. Reproduced by permission.

(See Note 10.)

As it turned out, the authors decided not to include the "Concluding Remarks" in the manuscript that they submitted. Read the remarks and then answer the questions that follow.

> Irrespective of the outcome of the present research on the "spheno-mandibularis," there are some general lessons that can be learned from this "discovery."
>
> 1. In certain scientific fields, significant findings have been published in languages other than English. By solely relying on English or American textbooks and journals, important information may therefore be missed. This is not only true for anatomy—"the oldest medical science" [Lang, 1995] (p. v)—but also for other "classical" disciplines, such as dentistry. As Groscurth recently pointed out: "Times have changed. Whereas today the vast majority of research papers are published in English, this was not always the case—something we should remember when researching all fields but particularly those that were active so many years ago" [Groscurth, 1996] (p. 1163).
>
> 2. With very few exceptions, MEDLINE only includes articles that appeared after 1966. In addition, it should be noted that this database only considers a selection of all currently published medical and dental journals, thereby favoring journals that use the English language. Hence, if MEDLINE is the only source of a search on a specific topic, relevant articles written in a language different from English may not be found. Authors should also bear in mind that many excellent peer-reviewed journals are currently not listed in MEDLINE.[1]
>
> 3. As a result, there is a chance that a supposedly "new" observation, approach, technique, idea, or description of an anatomical structure or a medical syndrome may be just a re-discovery or re-description of something that had previously been reported elsewhere [Gorlin, 1996; Ring, 1980].
>
> 1. For example, peer-reviewed journals published in a language other than English and currently not being considered in MEDLINE are, among others, *Deutsche Zahnnärztliche Zeitschrift* (dentistry; Germany), *Stomatologie* (dentistry; Austria), and *Der Schmerz* (pain; Germany/Austria), as well as *Nederlandse Tijdschrift voor Tandheelkunde* (dentistry; Netherlands).

a. Do you know of comparable instances of "false" discoveries from your own field?

b. Did your native language use to be more important as a source of important scholarly and research information?

c. How often do you search for literature in your native language as opposed to English?

(See Note 11.)

Language Focus: Uses of Quotation Marks

In Unit Four, we looked at two basic quotation types: within sentence and block quote. As you know, quotation marks within a text can be used for a number of purposes.

1. To represent the exact words of something said or written by somebody else

2. To refer to a title

3. To indicate that what is written within the quotation marks is not to be taken literally. This is usually known today as the "scare-quotes" use since writers detach themselves (nervously?) from the truth of the quoted material or the appropriateness of using the quoted expression.

The 1969 edition of the famous *Chicago Manual of Style* is highly critical of this third practice: "Such use of quotation marks should always be regarded as a last resort, to be used when the irony might otherwise be lost" (144). However, although we know of no relevant research, we suspect that its use has both increased and become more "respectable" (and here of course we are using scare quotes ourselves) in these postmodern times. (The 14th edition of the *Chicago Manual of Style* still expresses reservations about this use, however.)

Task Seven

Look back at the two dental texts. Highlight all quoted material and categorize it as 1, 2, or 3 as listed above.

Are there some uses of quotations that seem to you to be ambiguous?

Are all the uses of scare quotes basically the same? Or do you think they might be subcategorized? And if so, how?

(See Note 12.)

5.4 A Second Literature Review Case

"The Nature of Academic Writing in an Interdisciplinary Field" (Betty T. R. Samraj, Ph.D. diss. in linguistics, the University of Michigan, 1995)

Task Eight

Consider the literature review problems facing Betty Samraj as she embarked upon her dissertation work in linguistics. Her working topic was graduate student writing in interdisciplinary contexts—as represented by the university's School of Natural Resources and the Environment (SNRE) (which is why we chose it as the second main activity in this section).

a. Indicate with a Y (yes) or N (no) which of the following areas she would need to cover in the literature of her dissertation proposal and later incorporate in her dissertation

b. For those areas you marked with a Y, would she need to be exhaustive (E) in her coverage, or could she get away with some briefer (B) acknowledgment of the literature out there?

Here are 10 possible areas.

	Should this be covered?	Should coverage be exhaustive or brief?
1. A history of the SNRE, which was chosen as the research site	—	—
2. General theories about interdisciplinarity and multidisciplinarity	—	—
3. Previous studies about the nature of academic writing	—	—
4. Previous studies on environmental discourse	—	—
5. The nature of interdisciplinarity in environmental studies	—	—

6. Previously demonstrated linguistic techniques for analyzing academic discourse   —   —

7. The content background to what her chosen students would be writing about   —   —

8. Educational literature on how graduate students learn to be graduate students   —   —

9. Previous research on how students acquire—or do not acquire—the ability to write interdisciplinary discourse in an SNRE setting   —   —

10. Previous studies of student writing   —   —

How many areas do you think she should include? (See Note 13.)

These first-level decisions about what and what not to include are hard enough. Even harder are those second-level decisions that relate to how to best organize these rather disparate bodies of literature. So let's consider how Betty might proceed. The first thing to note is that Betty found—to her considerable relief—no previous studies that had attempted to answer area 9. In that sense then, this finding gave her a green light to go ahead with her dissertation research.

Now suppose that Betty eventually decided (as in fact she did) that she had to say at least a little something about both areas 1 and 2. Here is what she might have started to write on each area.

Area 1

> In 1901, the university established a Department of Forestry, which in 1927 became a School of Forestry and Conservation. Primarily in response to changing job opportunities for its masters and doctoral students [citations omitted], the school was renamed in 1950 as the School of Natural Resources. The next major change occurred in 1966 when the Department of Landscape Architecture was transferred from the School of Architecture and Design. This move reflected a new concern to incorporate conservation practices and principles in landscape architecture, such as the preservation of native plant species [citations omitted]. Four

years later, the traditional departmental structure was abandoned in favor of broader-based "concentrations" in order to further interconnect ways of presenting and producing professional environmental knowledge. Finally, in 1992 the school was renamed once again, now becoming the School of Natural Resources and the Environment. All these changes, both in substance as well as in nomenclature, thus show the research site reacting to shifts in the administrative, occupational and legislative landscape.

Area 2

Klein (1990) makes an important distinction between *exogenous* interdisciplinarity, which originates outside of the academic world because of problems in society, and *endogenous* interdisciplinarity, which is intrinsically concerned with new ways of producing new knowledge. Klein goes on to note "the tension in the discourse between those who define interdisciplinarity as a philosophically conceived synopsis and those who believe interdisciplinarity is not a theoretical concept but a practical one . . . " (1990:42). Others have stressed the *local* nature of interdisciplinary activity [citations omitted] and its bridging role to practitioners [citations omitted], particularly in the field of environmental science [citations omitted]. It is also clear from this literature that interdisciplinary discourse is a hard-won achievement; Journet (1990) shows, for example, that it required the exceptional abilities of Luria and Sacks to "combine the analytical exposition of neurological data with psychological narrative and story" (p. 182) in order to forge several decades ago the new cross-disciplinary field of neuropsychiatry. Finally, Fuller (1995) importantly observes that we need to distinguish interdisciplinary discourse that simply reflects and ratifies a previously established interdisciplinary stance from discourse that actually creates it.

Task Nine

These two paragraphs are obviously very different. What are the differences between them? Would either of them make a good starting point for an LR for a linguistics prospectus/dissertation? And if not, why not? (See Note 14.)

More seriously, we can see that the very differences between these two paragraphs—for all their individual competence—are already pulling her literature review apart into "subchapters" that handle each topic in turn. The writer is thus faced with the probability that the "experts" (advisor, article reviewer, book manuscript reviewer) will make observations like the following.

> Okay, the author apparently knows the various literatures well enough, but the connections among them are missing. What are the connections, the *new* connections?

One initially attractive solution might be to combine areas 1 and 2 in some wonderful synopsis and synthesis. So let's consider how this might work out.

Areas 1 and 2

> What is now the university's *School of Natural Resources and the Environment* has renamed and reorganized itself several times since its origin as the Department of Forestry, first established in 1901. "Conservation" was added in 1927 as a gesture to the rise of concerns of an extra-economic nature and to the beginnings of the ecology movement [citations omitted]. By 1950 it had become redesignated as the School of Natural Resources in a further effort to move away from its tree-harvesting origination and to align itself both with the new job markets for its students and with a concern to relate faculty interests and practitioner preoccupations in the growing field of environmental science [citations omitted]. This interest in interdisciplinarity (Klein 1990) was underlined in 1970, when the old departments were replaced by four new "concentrations": resource ecology and management, resource policy and behavior, forestry, and landscape architecture (this last transferred from the architecture school in 1966) [citations omitted]. This then is Klein's endogenous interdisciplinarity (new academic formations for new academic knowledge), now added to the previously established exogenous (theory/practice) interdisciplinarity (Klein 1990). The discoursal implications of these developments (e.g., Journet 1990, Fuller 1995) will be discussed later.

Now here are some made-up e-mail comments by Betty's four committee members on her latest revision. Who do you agree and disagree with? And why?

Thanks, Betty, for the second draft. I really like the beginning now; I think you have integrated the two areas very well. I'm encouraged. Press on!

Chuck

Thanks for the revision, Betty. However, I have to say that as a member of the SNRE, I don't think your opening properly represents the history of the school. The real history, at least in my view, has been driven more by changes in the job market and by federal legislation than by changes in theoretical orientation. This perspective has been largely lost, to such an extent that your opening story is close to being misleading. Want to have another go? Sorry.

Sally

Hi, Betty

As you know, I spend a lot of time struggling with interdisciplinary issues, and I had little problem with your original synopsis. But now the real debates about the philosophical nature of interdisciplinarity have become lost within what is essentially a chronological narrative of ONE institution. I think we should meet ASAP.

Yours,
Carlos

I picked up your revised opening to the proposal a couple of days ago. Much of the later stuff I like, especially the more linguistic stuff. Well, you would've guessed that, wouldn't you? I don't know much about your opening topics, but your second draft strikes me as being rather "lifeless" in comparison to the first version. I really enjoyed your original SNRE story! Hope this helps and hope to see you at the colloquium tomorrow.

Pam

Task Eleven

Prepare Betty's e-mail response to her committee. Begin, "Thank you all very much for responding so promptly to my latest draft." (See Note 15.)

Below is a brief summary of what Betty eventually decided to do. The list in Task Eight is repeated here for your convenience. How effective do you consider her solutions to her problem? Grade each one "good" (✓+), "possibly OK" (✓), or "probably not" (✓–) in the space provided.

1. A history of the SNRE, which was chosen as the research site
2. General theories about interdisciplinarity and multidisciplinarity
3. Previous studies about the nature of academic writing
4. Previous studies on environmental discourse
5. The nature of interdisciplinarity in environmental studies
6. Previously demonstrated linguistic techniques for analyzing academic discourse
7. The content background to what her chosen students would be writing about
8. Educational literature on how graduate students learn to be graduate students
9. Previous research on how students acquire—or do not acquire—the ability to write interdisciplinary discourse in an SNRE setting
10. Previous studies of student writing

___ Area 1. She moved the history of SNRE to the introductory chapter.

___ Areas 2 and 5. She fed these theoretical discussions into the main LR account (see below) as and when opportunities arose.

___ Areas 3, 4, and 10. These areas became the central focus of the LR; in other words, the primary focus became writing, as seen from a multidisciplinary perspective.

___ Area 6. She postponed this technical area until the following data collection and methodology chapter.

___ Area 7. Discussion of SNRE course content and that in student term papers was also postponed, but this time until the results chapters.

___ Area 8. She was able to persuade her committee that she did not need to review the literature in this area in detail for a linguistics Ph.D.!

___ Area 9. As we have seen, she found nothing here (to her considerable relief!).

(See Note 16.)

Here is how Betty actually organized her literature review in her dissertation.

And now here is Betty's introduction to her 22-page LR (sentence numbers have been added).

[1]In the opening chapter I have attempted to outline and motivate my study of graduate student writing in a school of natural resources and environment. [2]The purpose of this chapter is to relate this study to previous scholarly attempts to describe, analyze and explain academic writing and the processes of its acquisition. [3]One purpose here is to establish what has been revealed in other academic contexts as a basis for the findings of my study. [4]Another purpose is to attempt a general critical evaluation of the research so far.

[5]The amount of potentially relevant literature is very large and comes from various sources: composition specialists, social constructionists, EAP/ESL (English for Academic Purposes/English as a Second Language) specialists, and discourse analysts. [6]For my purposes, I will concentrate on the studies in undergraduate writing tied to the writing-across-the-curriculum (WAC) movement, graduate student writing (produced both by native and non-native speakers of English) and disciplinary rhetoric, with special attention given to interdisciplinary and environmental discourses. (Samraj 1995, 28)

Task Twelve

Answer the following questions.

1. The passage opens with "In the opening chapter I have attempted to . . . " As you can see, the verb is in the present perfect. She could have written "In the opening chapter I attempted to . . . " What is her strategic motive for choosing the present perfect? (Obviously it is different than that discussed in Section 5.3.)

2. The remaining three sentences of the first paragraph open in a remarkably similar way.

   The purpose of this chapter is to relate . . .
   One purpose here is to establish . . .
   Another purpose is to attempt . . .

   What is the technical name for this kind of language?
   What might be the positive and negative aspects of such repetitions?

3. Consider a sentence like "The amount of potentially relevant literature is very large." Which of the following choices might you expect to follow such a sentence?

   a. ; therefore, this review will be rather long.
   b. ; therefore, it will be divided into a number of sections.
   c. ; therefore, I will principally focus on . . .

4. Sentence 6 opens with "For my purposes, . . . " In your view does this refer back to the purposes mentioned in the first paragraph? Or does it refer forward, as in "For the purposes of the arguments that I am going to make . . . "

(See Note 17.)

5.5 Using Metadiscourse

One way that writers can help readers to follow the development of their LR or any text is by using metadiscourse—discourse about discourse. As has been noted by many researchers, metadiscourse is writing about the evolving text rather than referring to the subject matter. Metadiscourse is an important part of our everyday language and "a major feature of the ways we communicate in a range of genres and settings" (Hyland 1998). (See Note 18.)

Metadiscoursal elements do not add propositional material (content); rather they are intended to help readers make their way through a text by revealing its organization, referring readers back to a part of the text, and providing definitions, among other things. For example:

Part I of this paper traces the development of section 4B of the Clayton Act. The negative aspects of recycling plastics *will be taken up in the next section.*

As you can see from these two examples, the metadiscourse phrases enable the author to intrude into his or her text (in a way to talk to the readers) in order to direct or engage the readers in some way. (See Note 19.)

One of the primary roles of metadiscourse is to reduce the cognitive load on our imagined readers. It aids communication, helps support a writer's position, and serves to build a relationship with an audience. As such, it is not surprising that the amount and kind of metadiscourse in English are influenced by a number of factors.

1. Other things being equal, there is likely to be proportionately more metadiscourse in longer rather than shorter texts. After all, longer texts (such as a dissertation) impose a greater memory load and are not likely to be read in one sitting. Thus, metadiscourse is particularly associated with books, dissertations, and theses.

2. There is some variation across disciplines in terms of the type and amount of metadiscourse used (Hyland 1998).

3. Metadiscourse is more often used to support complex rather than straightforward material. This is at least part of the reason why metadiscourse is particularly prevalent in philosophy.

4. Metadiscourse is common in extensive spoken monologues, such as lectures and colloquia, presumably again to reduce the cognitive and memory load.

5. Metadiscourse is more likely at the beginnings and ends of sections, chapters, papers, lectures, and so on.

Although metadiscourse may not play a major role when you write in your native language, as an NNS of English, you need to be aware of its importance in U.S. academic English for the following three reasons.

1. NNS texts may not be as clear to their readers as NS ones, and so metadiscourse might be particularly helpful in signposting what is going on.

2. As we have seen, American academic English seems today to value metadiscourse.

3. As we have also seen, NNS writers may come from academic traditions that, for one reason or another, may place lower value on metadiscourse.

Research has shown that, at least for native speakers of English, the right amount of metadiscourse gives readers the sense that a writer is fully aware of what he or she is doing, thus giving the impression of authority. (See Note 20.)

Scholars working in contrastive rhetoric and cross-cultural communication have shown that the use of metadiscourse in a text varies across a range of national and linguistic academic cultures. As a number of NNS scholars have noted, the value and virtue of metadiscourse remain unquestioned in the U.S. literature on academic writing. However, in other academic cultures heavy use of metadiscourse can be seen as indicating unnecessary promotion of one's own text (Finland, Sweden) or as reflecting an insultingly low assessment of the intelligence and attention of the reader (China, Japan).

There are also suggestions that the size and cohesiveness of the presumed audience may also be factors in deciding when or how to use metadiscoursal phrases. For instance, Swedish linguists writing in Swedish and Malaysian scientists writing in Malay use less metadiscourse than they do when writing in English. (See Note 21.)

A recent dissertation (Bunton 1999) (see Note 22) on dissertations points out that metadiscourse that refers to other parts of the dissertation can be described in terms of direction and level, which then can be further described in terms of scope and distance. Take, for instance, the following sentence.

> In the next section I present the results of a study that examined the influence of CO_2 and temperature on retranslocation during autumn senescence in sugar maple.

In this example, we see that the direction is forward; the scope is a section (e.g., rather than a chapter), and the section is one that is different from the current one.

Direction: preview   Scope: section   Distance: section different from
                                            the current one

The full range of options is given in table 5.3.

TABLE 5.3.   Metadiscourse in Dissertations: Linear Text References[a]

Direction	Level
Previews Look forward, anticipate, summarize, or refer to a later stage of the text **Reviews** Look back, repeat, summarize, refer to an earlier stage in the text **Overviews** Look in both directions and refer to the current stage of the text in overall terms	**Scope** of the segment being referred to 1. dissertation as a whole 2. chapter(s) 3. section(s) 4. paragraph(s) 5. sentence(s) **Distance** to the segment referred to 6. a different chapter 7. this chapter but another section within it 8. this section but a different part of it

[a]Linear Text References are explicit references to other parts of the linear text, further defined by the *direction* of the reference as well as by the *level*—in terms of both scope and distance.

Other forms of metadiscourse that can help guide your reader through your text include the following.

Nonlinear Text References

Explicit references to tables, charts, figures, plates, equations, or appendixes

> See table 1.

Intertext References

Explicit references to other texts, especially of other authors

> According to Aldini, . . .

Text Act Markers

Explicit markers of the discourse acts being performed in the text (as opposed to research acts done independently of the text)

> In summary, . . .

Text Connectors

Connectors that show relationships between different parts of the text

> First, I will discuss . . .

Text Glosses

Explicitly indicated explanations of what particular terms or symbols in the text mean.

> For the purposes of this discussion, *persistent* means . . .

Task Thirteen

Let's now examine two paragraphs from Betty's sections on graduate writing and on published writing. Can you find the linear text references? How would you describe them in terms of direction, scope, and distance, as presented in table 5.3?

Graduate Writing

In contrast to the extensive and growing amount of work in the area of undergraduate writing in the disciplines, there are only a handful of studies on graduate writing in the disciplines, especially by native speakers of English. Though few in number, these studies are valuable in the insights they provide into the context of graduate writing, the writing processes adopted by graduate writers and the acculturation process that graduate students also have to undergo to attain success in their fields of specialization. A number of studies have been conducted by EAP/ESL specialists directly involved in equipping non-native speaker graduate students for the academy [citation omitted]. These will be considered briefly before I discuss studies focusing mainly on native speakers of English.

Published Writing

Studies on the structure of published writing can be sub-categorized according to their primary focus. First, there are a number of studies that focus on disciplinary differences in textual structures. Some of these studies deal with writing in interdisciplinary fields and will be discussed separately. Naturally enough, I will pay particular attention to studies on writing in the interdisciplinary field of environmental science. Second, there are studies that focus more on the structure of different genres or on parts of a genre, such as the structure of the Materials and Methods sections in Biomedical journal articles. Research comparing the structures of two genres has also been conducted. The historical development of a particular genre has also been studied [citation omitted]. In addition, some scholars have paid particular attention to a specific linguistic aspect of a set of texts, such as topic sentences in research articles [citation omitted] or the use of metadiscourse in academic texts [citations omitted]. Finally studies on the structure of published material have also been concerned with contrastive rhetoric [citations omitted]. I will only be reviewing literature from the first subcategory as this has the most relevance to my study.

(See Note 23.)

Take a look at the final sentence of the paragraph on published writing. Do you think Betty has provided enough explanation for her omissions? Should she have perhaps justified her decision more strongly? (See Note 24.)

Task Fourteen

Here is a transition sentence Betty used in her section entitled "Writing in Interdisciplinary Fields" to introduce environmental discourse. How effectively does it link the two sections together?

Writing in Interdisciplinary Fields

Having discussed several studies on writing in interdisciplinary fields, I turn now to some studies on environmental discourse.

(See Note 25.)

Read through this part of Betty's section on undergraduate writing and answer the questions that follow.

Undergraduate Writing

[1]The issue of being initiated or acculturated into a disciplinary or discourse community [citation omitted] was mentioned earlier as an underlying reason for investigations into discursive practices of different disciplines. [2]However, when studies are not comparative in their methodology, there seems to be some real danger of equating linguistic and rhetorical features with a discipline when they could merely be the manifestation of formal discourse in any academic community. [3]The work of Drury and Webb (1991), for instance, is undertaken to explore the apprentice role of students. [4]Though the study examines only a few texts from the field of education, the conclusions reached are generalized to include all writing in the university situation. [5]It is said that the university situation "generally requires an analytical approach of either a factual or persuasive kind" (Drury and Webb 1991:215). [6]Though the authors state that they intend to show how a successful text meets the literacy requirements of the discipline area, their analysis in terms of a variety of textual features such as thematic choices and transitivity structures is unable to reveal what makes this text a successful *psychology* text. [7]Rather, their analysis appears to describe the features found in an argumentative rather than a personal text.

1. What does Betty's purpose seem to be? How successful is she at achieving it?
2. What sentences contain the chief criticisms? Highlight the evaluative language in the text.
3. What is the purpose of the first sentence?
4. How strong is the criticism in the text? Has it been softened in any way?
5. In what way do professionals in your field criticize the work of others? Do you know how to be critical of work in your own field? What does it take to develop a critical stance?

(See Note 26.)

5.6　What about Interdisciplinarity?

We have stopped short of claiming that either of the case studies presented in this unit is an example of multidisciplinary work. We have done so primarily because whether or how a multidisciplinary LR is different from a more straightforward one is not clear. Trying to clarify the differences would also require us to attempt making distinctions among the following four terms.

Interdisciplinary
Cross-disciplinary
Transdisciplinary
Multidisciplinary

We know that distinctions are sometimes made, especially between the "higher" concept of *interdisciplinary* and the "lower" concept of *multidisciplinary.* However, the working out of such a distinction can probably only be carried out in specific disciplinary settings. Attempting to do so is thus neither helpful nor necessary in a book on research English in general. For our purposes, though, to make sure that you have some understanding of what we mean by *interdisciplinarity* we offer the following. It is sometimes thought that *interdisciplinary* means simply borrowing information from other disciplines, which may or may not undergo a transformation in the process. However, interdisciplinarity can perhaps be thought of as a process of creating a new field of knowledge that is inextricably linked to its disciplinary roots. Students are often encouraged to pursue interdisciplinary work for a number of reasons. For instance, interdisciplinary research may help make them aware of research questions not usually asked in their own fields; or it may help them solve problems that are beyond the scope of a single discipline (e.g., environmental studies).

No doubt, interdisciplinarity is a difficult achievement, as revealed by the following two quotations.

> Of course we are not interdisciplinary ourselves; we make our grad students do that. We make them hop from one disciplinary island to another, acquiring different intellectual capital on each.
>
> —A professor of social history

> The hope is that students acquire knowledge from different disciplines while they are here, and they get some skills that let them function in a workplace that forces them to do some integration.
>
> —A professor in a school of natural resources

These quotations underline the point that much multidisciplinary work is an individual adventure. Graduate students in the United States may be pushed toward such adventures by cognate requirements, by cognate members on their committees, or by their advisors. But, as the first quote suggests, they tend to be *pushed*, rather than gently *led* by illustrious example! In the second, the speaker implies that pressures of postgraduation work may create the kind of integration that the university itself did not engender.

Of course in other situations, the nature of the chosen topic may create a demand to search beyond disciplinary boundaries for insights, for reassurances of the topic's originality, or for a range of methodologies. In such cases, as in biomedical engineering, there may be clearer precedents.

At the time of writing, interdisciplinary work has become very fashionable. In fact, at the time we were revising this unit, our own university issued the report of its Life Sciences Commission. Here is a brief extract.

> The fundamental approach of this initiative is the combination of empirical and theoretical approaches, and the use of information science and emerging technologies to better understand the complexity of life. An important emphasis is one translating the resulting knowledge to practical applications, which have implications for the treatment of human illness and the protection of other species, and of our shared environment. (Press release, February 12, 1999)

Because interdisciplinarity has such a high contemporary profile, it can become idealized, as we attempt to show in the next task.

Task Sixteen

Read the following fictional account and try to choose the correct answer to the question that follows. Work with a partner if possible.

**A Diary of Five Weeks in the Library,
One with a Tutor, and One at Home**

Week One

This week I start my multidisciplinary literature review. Off to the library I go! I am starting with the cultural history of the Middle Ages.

Week Two

Now I am on to studies of medieval Latin. Good thing I have some previous training here!

Week Three

This is the week for the early history of science, especially on Islamic influences on western Europe.

Week Four

Been busy this week learning the basics of astronomy.

Week Five

Whew! I've had a hard struggle all week trying to make sense of the relationships between religion and science in earlier times.

Week Six

My long-planned intensive daily tutorials with Emeritus Professor Manfred, the great expert on paleography, or old handwriting. Masses of homework looking at medieval manuscripts. Making good progress.

Week Seven

Home at last! Writing away every day on my Chapter Two.

Oh, you don't know the topic of my grandly multidisciplinary dissertation, do you? Well, as you might have guessed it's . . .

    a. The Influences of Arabic Script on Latin Science Manuscripts
    b. The Role of Astronomy in the Cultural History of the Middle Ages
    c. The Evolution of the Medieval Science Encyclopedia
    d. Religious and Scientific Medieval Latin: A Stylistic Comparison

(With thanks to Ana Montero)

(See Note 27.)

Task Seventeen

Be ready to discuss any multidisciplinary aspects of any of your research projects (past or present). What difficulties did you experience, and how did you solve them?

5.7 Notes and Comments for Unit Five

Note 1

Verbatim is a Latin term used by scholars to indicate that the exact words of the original writer or speaker have been used. As we said, this is not true in this case.

Note 2

Upon seeing the list of comments, a very senior and highly successful graduate student said, "Oh, all of those things have been said about my work at one time or another." Nor of course would we want to claim that our own scholarly writing is free of such criticisms. We also do not want to suggest that the criticism in 2 is entirely well founded. There is very often a chronological underpinning to sections of the LR. The point, we think, is that a simple and purely descriptive historical account will not help the writer's "positioning."

Note 3

Acronyms are "words" that are made up of the first letters of a longer noun phrase. Here are some examples.

LED	light emitting diode
ESL	English as a second language
SEM	scanning electron microscope
CIA	Central Intelligence Agency

Note that the article usage depends on how the acronym is pronounced, not on how it is spelled. We write and say, "*An* SEM" because it is pronounced as "S_E_M" and not "sem," rhyming with the word *hem*. If it were pronounced "sem" we would write and say "*A* SEM." What about LED? You might think it would be pronounced as "led," but in the United States, even though you can pronounce it, we say "L_E_D." Thus, it is "*An* LED."

Note 4

Swales, John M. 1990. *Genre analysis: English in academic and research settings.*
    Cambridge: Cambridge University Press.

Note 5

Provenance is a term used by archaeologists to indicate the place of origin.

Note 6 (sample responses for Task Two)

Here are some points from table 5.1 that you might like to make.

1. Most of the work seems to have been done in the United States.
2. The concept originated in rhetoric and composition and then spread.
3. A lot of books have been written in this area.
4. There have been supporters and critics of this concept through its short history.

    You could make the following points based on table 5.2.

1. Most of the critics come from rhetoric and composition.
2. Most of the supporters can be found in more practical areas such as technical
   communication and applied linguistics.

Note 7 (sample responses for Task Three)

Other categories that class participants have mentioned to us include the
following.

Hermeneutics
The length and nature of fieldwork
Cross-national data (or not)
Taxonomic revision (or not) in biology

Note 8 (sample responses for Task Four)

A 2
B 1
C 4
D 6
E 5
F 3

An alternative order might be B C E A F D.

In order for the alternative order to work, though, you would have to change the transition at the beginning of the last paragraph to something like

> With considerable practitioner support and increased definitional clarity . . .

Finally, we think that we have made a pretty good effort to make a "high pass" over this literature.

Note 9 (sample responses for Task Five)

As you can see, the reporting verbs have been changed here. The verbs in A1 seem adversarial, while those in A2 are more neutral. The force of the presentation seems to be diminished with the use of the more neutral verbs.

A more general point to note is that reporting verbs indicate *different strengths of claim* (e.g., *demonstrated* vs. *speculated*).

Note 10 (explanation of the main point of the "Media Hype" excerpt)

Although the piece is entitled "Media Hype," the main point of the piece is not statement a but statement c. There is much in the short text that is dismissive of Dunn et al. (statement b), such as the use of *allegedly* in the opening sentence and *the authors' hypothesized role* in the following one.

Note 11 (sample responses for the questions about the concluding remarks of the "Media Hype" excerpt)

a. Somewhat to our surprise, this kind of false discovery seems to be quite rare, at least according to our informants.

b. Yes, this seems to be the general trend.

c. Again, this would seem quite uncommon, except in fields like comparative literature and some areas of the humanities.

Note 12 (sample responses for Task Seven)

In the abstract

"the sphenomandibularis"	probably 3 but see below
"m. sphenomandibularis"	3
"medial portion"	1
"deep portion"	1

In the concluding remarks

"sphenomandibularis"	probably 3 but see below
"discovery"	3
"the oldest medical science"	1
"classical"	3?
"Times have changed . . ."	1
"new"	3

The first use of "sphenomandibularis" in the abstract is a little ambiguous. On the one hand, it is Dunn's term; on the other, the use of *allegedly* suggests a bit of irony and sarcasm. "Classical" looks like a fairly neutral scare quote, while "new" in the final sentence is clearly ironic.

Note 13 (sample responses for Task Eight)

There are no certain answers here. One possible response is as follows.

1.	YB	6.	N
2.	YB	7.	N
3.	YE	8.	YB
4.	YE	9.	YE
5.	YE	10.	YB

Note 14 (sample responses for Task Nine)

The area 1 paragraph is a local narrative, while the area 2 paragraph is a complex, philosophical exposition. Both approaches are probably a little off for a linguistics dissertation since neither language nor writing issues are included in either opening.

Note 15 (sample response for Task Eleven)

Betty is in a tough spot here. Only one member of her committee actually thinks the combined text is an improvement. The two responses that should be attended to most are Sally's and Carlos's. Here is one possible response.

> Thanks, everyone, for responding so promptly to my latest draft. In light of Pam's, Sally's, and Carlos's comments, it looks as though my attempt at integration was too ambitious, doesn't work, and is possibly misleading. I guess it's back to my drawing board. Carlos, I'll take you up on your offer of a meeting if I get stuck and need help.
>
> Betty

Note 16 (Task Eleven)

We think all of Betty's planning decisions are pretty good.

Note 17 (sample responses for Task Twelve)

1. Her strategy is to tie the two chapters together. The use of the present perfect gives her earlier work in Chapter One *present relevance* to the issues at hand.

2. These are highly repetitive structures, which are examples of metadiscourse. These kinds of repetitions are most common in genres like political speeches, while in research writing there is some expectation of lexical variation. Often such repetition can suggest that a writer is having difficulty moving a text along or is perhaps having trouble finding the right words. However, here the repetitions work well for Betty because they establish her presence in the text by demonstrating how firmly she is in control of her material.

3. The first option, a, is unlikely because of the earlier use of *potentially,* and a similar case can be made against b. Option c is the most likely continuation in our opinion.

4. This is a very difficult question. We think it actually refers forward to "For my dissertation . . . " We think that if Betty had meant to refer back, she would have written something like "For the purposes outlined above . . . " or "Given these purposes . . . "

Note 18

The reference here and to other citations of Hyland (1998) is as follows.

Hyland, K. 1998. *Hedging in scientific research articles.* Philadelphia: John Benjamins.

Note 19

Crismore, A., and R. Farnsworth. 1980. Metadiscourse in popular and professional scientific discourse. In *The writing scholar: Studies in academic discourse,* edited by W. Nash. Newbury Park, CA.: Sage.

Note 20

Mauranen, A. 1993. *Cultural differences in academic rhetoric: A textlinguistic study.* Frankfurt: Peter Lang.

Note 21

Fredrickson, K., and J. M. Swales. 1993. Competition and discourse community: Introductions from Nysvenska Studier. *ASLA* 6:9–22.
Ahmad, U. K. Scientific research articles in Malay: A situated discourse analysis. Ph.D. diss., the University of Michigan, 1997.

Note 22

Bunton, D. 1999. The use of higher level meta-text in Ph.D. theses. *English for Specific Purposes* 18:S41–S56.

Note 23 (sample analysis for Task Thirteen)

In the first paragraph

> These will be considered briefly before I discuss studies focusing mainly on native speakers of English. (preview, current chapter, next section perhaps)

In the second paragraph

> Some of these studies deal with writing in interdisciplinary fields and will be discussed separately. (preview, scope unknown, distance unknown)

> Naturally enough, I will pay particular attention to studies on writing in the interdisciplinary field of environmental science. (preview, scope unknown, current chapter)

> I will only be reviewing literature from the first subcategory as this has the most relevance to my study. (preview, scope unknown, distance unknown)

Note 24 (sample response regarding omissions in paragraph writing, Task Thirteen)

First, it is not entirely clear what the *first subcategory* actually refers to. Second, while it is OK to state that a particular body of literature *has the most relevance to my study*, this can actually be presumed.

Note 25 (sample responses for Task Fourteen)

This kind of section linking is often highly effective. Remember Hamilton's clever, if evasive, move in the "Misfits" subsection of Unit Four? It can also add a sense of drama and expectation.

Note 26 (sample responses for Task Fifteen)

Possible responses to the five questions.

1. The ostensible purpose is to show that results and conclusions in the area have to be made very carefully.

2. Sentences 3 through 6 contain the main criticisms. Examples of evaluative language include the following phrases.

   S2. *. . . there seems to be a real danger of . . . when they could merely be . . .*
   S4. *Though the study examines only a few texts . . . the conclusions reached are generalized to include all writing . . .*
   S6. *Though . . . , their analysis . . . is unable to reveal . . .*

3. Both to make a link with her previous discourse and to provide a rationale for her kind of investigation

4. The criticisms of Drury and Webb (sentences 3–6) are rather strong. For example, in sentence 6 we read "their analysis . . . is unable to reveal . . . " One small softening element is the use of *seems* in sentence 2.

5. Answers will vary.

Note 27 (answer key for Task Sixteen)

This, of course, is a fanciful story with no connection to reality. Interdisciplinary work is almost always much more a story of trial and error. Ana's dissertation topic is real, however. But which is it? It is almost certainly not option a—there just isn't enough about Arabic in the diary. Since astronomy is mentioned only once, option b is also unlikely. Her topic must then be either c or d, but d would not really justify the astronomy part. The answer then is c.

On the lighter side

We close this rather complicated unit with an amusing little story that suggests in its own way that wide academic knowledge is "power."

A famous British scholar in the early part of the twentieth century was Sir Maurice Bowra. He was president of an Oxford college and presided over the dinner every evening traditionally held with the other "fellows" in the college. At dinner, whatever the topic of learned discussion, Sir Maurice always dominated the conversation with his massive erudition. So in desperation, the younger fellows organized a plot to finally defeat their president. They decided to take a very obscure topic, secretly study it, and then unobtrusively introduce it at the dinner table. They chose thirteenth-century Iranian pottery. Finally they were ready, and the great day came. One young lecturer said something like "The thirteenth-century vase in the British Museum discussed in last week's *Times* was ascribed to Tehran, but from the decoration I suspect it probably was made in Isfahan." And so the conversation continued for about 20 minutes, with Sir Maurice remaining silent at the head of the table. "Got him at last," the plotters thought. Then Sir Maurice looked up and mildly observed, "I'm glad to notice, gentlemen, that you have been profiting from my unsigned article on medieval Iranian pottery in the *Encyclopedia Britannica*."

Unit Six
Further Steps and Stops on the Dissertation Road

V S Hixson

"Look, this time, my committee <u>has</u> to pass my dissertation. There's nothing left in it except the parts they put in themselves."

The previous four units (which discussed the conference abstract, the conference poster, and the literature review [two units]) have been designed to be gone through from their beginnings to their ends (leaving out whatever seems less relevant). In this unit, we return to the arrangement we used for the opening unit. In effect, we offer here some help on several aspects of the dissertation that are best turned to as and when needed.

The aspects of the dissertation dealt with in this unit include the following.

6.1. The Dissertation Abstract

6.2. Thesis and Dissertation Acknowledgments (See Note 1.)

6.3. Principled Narratives and Extensive Methods Sections

6.4. Dealing with Unexpected Results

6.5. The Problematic Final Chapter

6.6. Notes and Comments for Unit Six

6.1 The Dissertation Abstract

There are many kinds of abstracts that researchers have to write (see Unit Two). One rather special type is the dissertation abstract (DA). One reason for its special status is that at many U.S. research universities, it is a separately examined part of the dissertation. On a typical graduate school evaluation form there is a separate line for the abstract where committee members are asked to check off one of the following.

___ acceptable as submitted

___ acceptable after minor typographical corrections

___ acceptable after minor substantive revisions

___ acceptable after major substantive revisions

___ not acceptable

A second potential source of anxiety comes from the fact that Bell and Howell Information and Learning (formerly UMI) "publishes" in digital or microfilm format dissertations from many U.S. universities. As part of this service, the company requires a dissertation abstract of no more than 350 words. Given that dissertations represent large amounts of research and scholarship, getting the text down to the word limit can often be a frustrating task. As might be predicted, one common problem with early drafts is that too much space is taken up with the introductory matter and an outline of methods, leaving insufficient room to do justice to the findings and their implications.

At least in some fields, especially when the described work is interdisciplinary or multidisciplinary, there can also be a problem in making the abstract accessible (at least in part) to scholars (and even examiners) who might have a more marginal or incidental interest in the study. This aspect can be especially difficult for dissertation writers, who are, understandably, extremely closely involved in their research projects.

It is not surprising then that chairs, committee members, and friends often work with the candidate to finalize the abstract, frequently prior to, sometimes at, and sometimes after the oral defense.

In this section, we use two case studies to illustrate the complex processes of putting a dissertation abstract together. In the first case, we focus on the final product; in the second, we explore how a dissertation abstract slowly evolved toward its prefinal form.

Dissertation Abstract Number One

Below is a recent dissertation abstract in linguistics with which John was involved. It underwent the problems we have mentioned above. The end result was, however, found acceptable. Read the abstract and answer the questions that follow. Work with a partner if possible.

Abstract

Patterns and Variations in Contemporary Written Business Communications in Turkey: A Genre Study of Four Companies

by
Didar Akar

Co-chairs: Priscilla S. Rogers
John M. Swales

[1]This dissertation examines the discourse properties of contemporary Turkish commercial correspondence. [2]The primary data used consist of approximately 450 memoranda (internal correspondence) and fax messages (external correspondence) associated with four different Turkish companies selected to represent a range of sectors, sizes and management styles. [3]The text and discourse analyses are supported by text-based interviews with informants from these companies.

[4]The linguistic analysis is first framed within the socio-historical context of the emergence of the private sector in Turkey, and then within recent linguistic and literacy trends, and finally within the context of corporate cultures. [5]These frames of contextualization reveal how corporate culture can affect certain aspects of communicative practice, while also indicating that certain other aspects are inherently Turkish. [6]One particularly strong general influence in the memoranda came from public sector bureaucratic styles.

[7]The rhetorical analysis focuses mainly on requests in both memoranda and fax messages. [8]Requests in Turkish are shown to be highly impersonal and relatively indirect. [9]Although the particular strategies preferred for internal or external communication vary, politeness strategies typically depersonalize the requests by avoiding reference to the receiver's agent status; as a result, the company emerges as a discourse participant which is, at times, more prominent than the sender or receiver. [10]On a syntactic level, one consequence is the heavy use made of

passivization, nominalization, and particles such as {-DIr}. [11]On a discoursal level, postponement of a message's main communicative purpose following extensive groundwork appears as a common rhetorical pattern. [12]Emerging differences evolving away from the traditional arrangements and styles of business communication were found in fax messages, especially in the smaller companies, due to factors such as audience, means of delivery and types of intertextuality. [13]The dissertation closes by exploring the implications of this study for genre theory, and for teaching business communication courses in Turkish universities and corporate settings.

Task One

Here are now the questions.

1. The title took (as usual!) a long time to finalize. As far as the committee was aware, this was the first real study of Turkish business language. Didar wanted to appeal to three groups with her title: First, specialists in the Turkish language; second, experts in (cross-cultural) business communications; and third, linguists concerned with discourse. For this last group, she was particularly interested in getting the word *genre* into the title, partly because it is currently in theoretical fashion and partly because she thought she had an important theoretical point to make. The use of the word *genre* would also help link her specialized and "off-center" study to the wider field.

   Do you think Didar succeeded in making an appeal to her three groups?

2. Sentence 1 is a short, simple opening sentence that offers a summary of the dissertation. It could have started otherwise of course, such as

   > Little is known about Turkish business language.
   > Turkey is a growing economic power straddling Europe and Asia.

   Do you think Didar chose the right opening? And if so, why?

   The sentence in fact opens with a piece of metadiscourse (*This dissertation*); the first verb is in the present tense (*examines*), and, as you will have noted, this tense predominates.

   Do you approve of these decisions?

3. In sentence 2 we find *The primary data used consist of . . .*

   Do you think any of these variants are better than the original?

   a. The primary data consist of . . .
   b. The primary data used in this study consist of . . .
   c. The primary data used consists of . . .

4. In earlier drafts sentence 2 provided the exact number of memoranda and faxes, but this was replaced by an approximation.

   What are the advantages and disadvantages of this decision?

5. Sentence 2 states that *four different Turkish companies [were] selected to represent a range of sectors, sizes and management styles.* This statement is in fact one of those post hoc (after the fact) rationalizations. In reality, the "selection" of companies was opportunistic in that Didar relied on personal contacts. It just happened that the people she knew worked in different kinds of companies.

   Should she have expressed this differently? Perhaps more true to fact?

6. Sentence 3 is all that remains of an earlier paragraph that described the various methods of analysis. These methods are now referred to one by one in the third paragraph (rhetorical, syntactic, discoursal, etc.) within the context of *results.*

   Would you have preferred more on methods?

7. Notice sentence 5 opens with *These frames of contextualization . . .*

   What term would you use to characterize this phrase?

8. In sentence 6 we find the first use of a past tense. Why?

9. In sentence 8 the finding is expressed pretty strongly (*Requests . . . are shown to be . . .* as opposed to, say, *Requests tend to be . . .*). Why?

   (*Hint:* What might be the expected form of written American business requests?)

10. Notice that sentences 10 and 11 respectively open with *On a syntactic level . . .* and *On a discoursal level . . .*

    What do we call this rhetorical device?

11. Just as the abstract opened with a metadiscoursal reference to itself, so the final sentence begins with the same tactic. Note this time, however, that the demonstrative *this* has been replaced by the definite article *the*.

Is this clever?

(See Note 2.)

Task Two

Mark any parts of the abstract that remain unclear to you (and to your partner, if you are working with one). This should indicate how comprehensible it is to a wider audience. What would you conclude?

Task Three

Find and photocopy a dissertation abstract from your own field. Rhetorically and organizationally, how is it similar to or different from the one discussed above? If there are major differences, what explanations would you have?

Task Four

If relevant to your situation, write a draft abstract for your Ph.D. dissertation or thesis. If you are outside the United States, follow your local rules for length, layout, and so on.

Dissertation Abstract Number Two

The second case explores the story of the dissertation abstract of Feng-en Chen (a pseudonym). Feng-en was a doctoral candidate from Taiwan in ergonomics, and she was writing her abstract in April–May 1999 while also attending Chris and John's dissertation writing class for non-native speakers of English. During this period, she wrote essentially four versions of her abstract with the following word counts: 367, 345, 358, and 350. Here is Version 2.

Effects of Keyboards, Armrests, and Alternating Work Positions on Subjective Discomfort and Equipment Preference in VDT (Video Display Terminal) Workplaces

by
Feng-en Chen

Chair: Charles J. Woodward

The expanding utilization of computers in the workplace has made the VDT-related musculoskeletal disorders a growing concern. This dissertation investigates the effects of three kinds of possible intervention (involving keyboards, armrests, and alternating work positions) on subjective discomfort and equipment preference. The investigation focused on data entry operators in their workplaces, rather than in a laboratory setting.

In the 6-week keyboard study, a total of 84 workers were used to test two types of keyboard (KB2, straight with a spring key action; KB3, fixed-split, lateral inclined) against their original keyboard (KB1, straight with a soft key action). After five weeks of use, KB2 and KB3 were preferred over KB1; they also produced greatly reduced overall upper body discomfort.

In the 14-week armrest study, a total of 157 workers were used to examine keying with two types of armrest (AA, CA) against the original work equipment with no armrest. AA could be clamped onto the edge of the workstation, while CA attached to both sides of a chair. Only AA could move freely with the forearms during keying. After 13 weeks of use, AA and CA were reported as preferable over the no armrest condition; they also resulted in considerably reduced overall upper body discomfort; they were used for 90% and 75% of the keying time, respectively.

In the third 14-week experiment, a total of 78 workers were used to test keying in alternating positions (between sitting and standing) with two types of modified workstation (ALT1, ALT2) against the sit-only position of the original workstation. ALT1 allowed keying in both sitting and standing positions, while ALT2 allowed only a standing position, original workstations were needed for sitting. At the end of the study, keying in alternating positions with either modified workstation greatly decreased overall whole body discomfort and was reported as significantly more desirable. On average, subjects in each group stood for 14% of the keying time.

Based on the findings of this dissertation, all the three interventions could be recommended to effectively improve the quality of work life among data entry operators.

(minor editing)

Task Five

Make a short list of your immediate reactions to this abstract, keeping in mind your assessment of Didar's abstract and of the one from your own field that you found and photocopied for Task Three.

As it happened, we agreed that Feng-en should e-mail this version of the abstract to the 20 members of the dissertation writing class for discussion the following week.

Task Six

In the lively discussion in class, these were some of the suggestions that were made. Assess these contributions as one of the following.

Y = Yes, this is a good suggestion that should be taken seriously.
N = No, this is probably not really relevant.
? = Well, this might be nice with more space but probably can't be done.

Second, how do you think Feng-en responded to these suggestions?

___ 1. The abstract is mostly clear about what happened but doesn't seem to be very well integrated in the literature. We don't quite know what is new here.

___ 2. I don't think the use of all those abbreviations (KB1, KB2, etc.) actually helps; in fact, they mostly get in the way. Are they relevant to your intended audience?

___ 3. Shouldn't you be saying something about the cost savings of your experimental improvements?

___ 4. The way it is written, there is a single paragraph for each of the three studies (paragraphs 2, 3, and 4). Although this is clear, it fails to show how the three studies are interrelated.

___ 5. What does "original workstations were needed for sitting" in paragraph 4 mean?

___ 6. Don't you think you should tell us a little bit more about "their workplaces," as mentioned in paragraph 1?

___ 7. The main descriptive paragraphs (2, 3, and 4) all open in basically the same way. Could something be done about this? And are the numbers of workers that important?

___ 8. The final one-sentence paragraph could be expanded, especially if the descriptive paragraphs could be integrated and so reduced. Would this be possible?

___ 9. Do you make it clear enough that you seem to be relying on self-report data of discomfort and preference?

___ 10. At the end of the penultimate paragraph, you use the word *significantly*. Are you using this in a statistical sense? Could you be clearer here?

(See Note 3.)

Here now are Feng-en's reactions to these suggestions, either in class or in follow-up e-mail discussion.

1. Yes, I agree. I can now see that the whole thing is rather flat and too much like an experimental report.

2. Well, they are used throughout the dissertation, and as in the second half of paragraph 2 they allow me to save some words. I think my advisor would want me to keep them. Even if they may not be particularly helpful to an outside reader, I think I will keep them in for the time being.

3. We didn't collect data on that. I think it will be discussed in the dissertation a bit, but probably not here.

4. I will look into this. (Later, after she had integrated the three studies, she continued to have doubts. She sent the following e-mail.)

> However, I am not sure how my chair will like this because I omitted lots of detail for each study because I kind of lumped them together. (It is not possible to fit into 350 words without lumping them.) It is very

likely that he considers this as a messy way of presenting the study design. He usually wants readers to be very clear about the distinction between test conditions.

5. Okay, I will fix this.

6. The research contract required that the location be kept confidential. Sorry, nothing can be done about this.

7. I think I will try to integrate. The numbers and length of the studies are important because most other work has been much smaller scale. I will try to work this point in.

8. I will try. I agree that the last paragraph needs to be expanded to provide a more positive impression of the study's results.

9. I think it is clear to people in my field.

10. Yes, I was using *significantly* in a statistical sense.

A week later Feng-en Chen was ready with Version 4. Here it is.

Effects of Keyboards, Armrests, and Workstation Positions on Subjective Discomfort and Equipment Preference among Computer Users

by
Feng-en Chen

Chair: Charles J. Woodward

The expanding utilization of computer technology in the workplace has made VDT-related musculoskeletal disorders one of the fastest growing concerns in the field of occupational health. Although much previous research has focused on minimizing adverse health effects among VDT workers, very few studies have been undertaken "on-site" and with satisfactory sample sizes over a multi-week period. Previous findings suggested that improved comfort can be achieved through keying with: 1) enhanced key feedback or more neutral wrist posture, 2) supported forearms, and 3) increased physical movement. This dissertation thus investigates the effects of three related interventions—involving keyboards, armrests, and alternating work positions—on body discomfort and equipment preference with three groups of data entry operators at their workplace for a period of six or fourteen weeks. Each selected intervention aimed at testing one proposed hypothesis.

The first study tested three types of keyboard (KB1, KB2, KB3); the second study examined three conditions of arm support (no armrest, articulating armrest (AA), chair armrest (CA)); and the last study investigated two working positions: sit-only and alternating between sitting and standing positions using two types of modified workstation (ALT1, ALT2). In all test conditions, KB1 (straight, soft touch), keying without armrest, and keying in a sit-only position were the original work conditions. Eighty-four, 157 and 78 participants were recruited for studies #1, #2 and #3, respectively. Results from the three studies showed that all the newly introduced interventions produced reduced body discomfort and were preferred over their corresponding original conditions. Reasons for preference could be attributed to: enhanced feedback through spring key action (KB2); fixed-split, lateral-inclined geometry (KB3); excellent upper limb support, adjustability, and movement (AA); and opportunity for keying in alternating positions (ALT1, ALT2).

Based on the findings of this dissertation, each newly introduced equipment and work position can be recommended as effective measures in reducing or preventing musculoskeletal disorders associated with VDT operation. Given the ever-increasing number of workers who are being exposed to computers, such ergonomic modifications can make a contribution to workplace health (and potentially help reduce costs associated with related disorders).

Task Seven

Suppose you were asked to lead a discussion on Version 4 and how it differed from Version 2. What would you focus on? What has been gained in the revision, and what has been lost? Make a short list of observations that you would like to offer to the group. (See Note 4.)

By early May Feng-en had heard from her advisor. He had only two suggestions. First, he suggested deleting all abbreviations of the equipment tested in the study (all those KB1s and KB2s). He also rewrote the first sentence of the final paragraph, offering instead

> Study results demonstrate that discomfort associated with intensive keying is sensitive to workstation design. These interventions were specifically targeted to reduce posture stresses and static exertions associated with repetitive keyboard operation.

(Although this looks like a happy end to the story, unfortunately it was not. There were further comments and revisions from other committee members, and the chair himself eventually wanted a higher profiling of the results and less attention to the previous literature. A dissertation abstract writer's work can seem never to be done!)

Task Eight

If you wrote an abstract for Task Four, now revise it in the light of the Feng-en story. If you did not, try to find somebody else's draft that you can work on.

6.2 Thesis and Dissertation Acknowledgments

Acknowledgments, for obvious reasons, are not an examinable part of a master's thesis or doctoral dissertation in the United States. What is written is entirely at the discretion of the writer. Indeed, there is a rumor that there exists a dissertation acknowledgments section that closes as follows.

> Finally, I would like to thank my chair, Professor XXXX, without whose excessive "help" and meticulous attention to detail, this dissertation would have been finished months ago.

There lies a danger, especially for the non-native speaker, in the unexamined nature of acknowledgments. Since the acknowledgments come at the beginning of a thesis or dissertation, mistakes and infelicities in them can cause a very unfortunate first impression. Clearly, then, it is important for you to have your acknowledgments reviewed by a friend or colleague before it is too late!

In our experience, master's thesis acknowledgments in the United States tend to be quite short, while those prefacing dissertations can be quite long, especially those written by Americans. There are usually many people and several organizations to be thanked, and it is important to find a range of ways of expressing gratitude (see the Language Focus on pp. 204–5).

Task Nine

Here now is a draft of the acknowledgments for a master's thesis. Some of the verbs have been left out; which of the choices below would you recommend?

Acknowledgments

First and foremost, I would like to 1. _____ my profound gratitude to the Royal Thai Government, specifically to the Ministry of Foreign Affairs, for granting me support to 2. _____ my graduate studies. The support has given me not only a future career, but also opportunities to 3. _____ to higher education abroad, to work on a project I am interested in, and to prepare myself to better serve my country and society.

There are two people whom I would like to 4. _____ individually. First, I am deeply grateful to Professor XXXX, my thesis advisor, for her encouragement, and careful and wise guidance of my project. Secondly, I 5. _____ a great deal to Professor YYYY, my second reader, whose supervision and advice 6. _____ substantially to my study.

Finally, I 7. _____ thank all my friends in Ann Arbor who have always supported me during the long process of 8. _____ this project.

—Luejit (minor editing)

1. communicate / express / offer
2. pursue / obtain / follow
3. be open / be confronted / be exposed
4. introduce / cite / acknowledge
5. have / owe / offer
6. have devoted / have helped / have contributed
7. want to/ need to / would like to
8. working on / completing / undertaking

(See Note 5.)

Task Ten

Below are three extracts from acknowledgments that in their different ways we think are a little bit "off." Can you identify the problems we believe we have found?

1. The author wishes to express his deep and sincere appreciation to the co-chairpersons of his doctoral committee, Professor XXXX and Professor YYYY, not only for their valuable advice and unfailing guidance but also for providing oral support and encouragement during a frustrating period. The author is deeply and forever grateful to both of them.

2. I am enormously grateful to the Institute and to its then director, XXXX. Even more significant was the field research fellowship awarded to me by the YYYY. I cannot put into words my appreciation for the many facilities put at my disposal by the director—Dr. ZZZZ. The office's staff members received me with open arms and . . .

3. Writing this dissertation has given me opportunities not only for strengthening my academic achievement but also for understanding American people and culture. Thus, it has been exciting and challenging for me to carry out research on small-town America's neighborhood quality of life.

(See Note 6.)

Now we will look at the extensive and complex acknowledgments section at the beginning of a Ph.D. dissertation written by an American student of linguistics, Rita Simpson. Read it carefully and undertake the tasks that follow.

Acknowledgments

___ I owe a debt of gratitude to many people whose help has been crucial to my success in completing this dissertation. First of all, I have been privileged to have the direction and guidance of two excellent mentors, my co-chairs Rosina Lippi Green and Lesley Milroy. From the inception of this project, Rosina has been generous with her time and has provided eminently helpful advice on everything from the methodological design to the writing process. Her faith in me and her ability to bring me back on track at difficult times have been a godsend. Lesley has likewise made invaluable contributions to the development of my ideas and the organization of the analysis. She has always motivated me to do my best work, offering timely feedback on each chapter and keen insight into the significance of my research. My other committee members, Peter Hook and Tom Hudak, have also contributed insightful and critical comments and suggestions. Tom's command of Thai and his familiarity with the complexities and subtleties of Thai culture have been reassuring and stimulating. I would also like to thank David Solnit for his help during the pilot project that led to this dissertation.

My heartfelt appreciation goes out to all the Thai people who have helped me over the years, especially the teachers and students of Phalangraat Phitthayasan School in Mukdahan and the Peace Corps teachers and trainers who first introduced me to the Thai language and culture ten years ago. My understanding and love of Thai owe much to their warmth and generosity. Many people in Chiang Mai helped me during my fieldwork: The professors and students of the Thai Department at Chiang Mai University sponsored me as a visiting researcher and welcomed me as part of the university community. Professor Panit Boonyavatana of the English Department was extremely generous with her time and provided invaluable assistance and enthusiasm. I am grateful to Bill Galloway for stimulating conversation that reassured me of the significance of my research, helped me to focus some of the theoretical ideas, and provided me encouragement at a crucial time. Finally, to the others at Chiang Mai University who assisted in various ways—as informants, research assistants, transcribers or friends—I am extremely appreciative.

I am grateful to the U.S. Department of Education for financial support during my fieldwork in the form of a Fulbright-Hays Doctoral Dissertation Research Abroad Fellowship, and to the Center for South and Southeast Asian Studies of the University of Michigan for Foreign Language and Area Studies fellowships during the first two years of my program. In addition, the Program in Linguistics, the English Language Institute, and the Horace H. Rackham Graduate School of the University of Michigan have all supported me financially in various ways throughout the past five years.

I have enjoyed the camaraderie of Ummul Ahmad, Alicia Beckford, Peggy Goetz, Ruth Goetz, Matt Gordon, Joseph Pimentel, and Sarah Shin. I have benefited much from discussions with each of them at various times and places, and in particular from the participation of the members of the sociolinguistics support group headed by Lesley and Rosina. My esteemed colleague and dear friend Joseph provided just the right amount of everything I needed from a friend to get through this process and not lose perspective—most memorably, the waltzes and other dance escapes. Thanks also to John Swales and the members of his dissertation support group for taking me in for a summer and cracking the whip at the right times, and to the faculty and staff of the English Language Institute, who have been a source of much encouragement.

＿   Many other people have helped me weather the emotional storms and stress of graduate school, some of whom deserve special mention. Linda Kurtz provided editorial assistance and helped me to relax and smile during the final stages of writing and revising. To my O'Keefe family in Ann Arbor—especially Graciela Cabana, Saeedeh Malekoltojari, and Lynn Noellert—I am grateful for the companionship, diversions, and nourishment of body and soul. Thanks to the wonderful Simpson clan far and near for their constant support of my efforts, especially all the Ohio folks who provided a refuge for me in their homes at holidays or whenever I needed an escape. My brother and sisters and their families have always offered me their support, sympathy, and admiration—especially Becky, faithful e-mail correspondent and in many ways my number one fan.

＿   Finally, I owe much to my parents for always believing in me and encouraging me to achieve my goals. My father, to whom this dissertation is dedicated, provided me with rare opportunities as a child to learn foreign languages and to expand my horizons. He, more than anyone, nurtured my intellectual curiosity and fostered my love of language, and I regret that he could not see the fruits of this labor. My mother has always been there for me, and has never failed to do what she could to further my progress. Her compassion, generosity, and steadfast emotional support have been invaluable in helping me to focus on my academic pursuits. She forever inspires me with her infinite capacity for love, joy, and faith.

Task Eleven

1. Number the six paragraphs from 1 to 6. Now give the "topic" of each paragraph (what group is being thanked) and enter your conclusions below.

Paragraph 1: _____

Paragraph 2: _____

Paragraph 3: _____

Paragraph 4: _____

Paragraph 5: _____

Paragraph 6: _____

2. What design do you now see in Rita's acknowledgments? How is it different from the organization of Luejit's (Task Nine)? What would be your own preference?

(See Note 7.)

As we have seen, Rita wrote a pretty long acknowledgments section for her Ph.D. dissertation. We have good reason to believe that in most other countries, the acknowledgments section will be shorter. What would be your preferred length? Are there groups of people whom you might not acknowledge?

Task Twelve

1. Highlight all the names in Rita's text (the "O'Keefe family" refers to the name of the housing co-operative where she lived; ignore this one). As you know, there are several ways of rendering names on paper.

   a. Professor Smith
   b. Professor E. A. Smith
   c. Professor Elizabeth A. Smith
   d. Professor Elizabeth Smith
   e. Professor Liz Smith
   f. Elizabeth Smith
   g. Liz Smith
   h. Elizabeth
   i. Liz

   What is Rita's preferred form? What exceptions can you find? How might you account for these exceptions? How does Luejit's practice differ? What is your preferred option?

2. Highlight all the adjectives in the first paragraph. What kinds of adjectives predominate? What can we learn from this?

(See Note 8.)

Rita's Story

On more than one occasion, Rita has visited our classes to talk about the story behind her acknowledgments. This story has both its expected and unexpected aspects. In terms of the former, she said things like, "This was the funnest part of the whole dissertation for me"; "I wanted it to be personal and not at all dry"; and "It was the one place where I could be my own person."

Unexpectedly, at least to most of her audience, we discovered that she started her acknowledgments almost as soon as she started writing her dissertation—over a year before its completion. She often returned to the acknowledgments when she found herself stuck with the "real" research, although many of the details were not completed until the very end of the dissertation process. She regularly thought about which names to leave in and which to leave out and sometimes discussed this with her friend Joseph. She knew she had a lot of people to acknowledge and, to help her with the language for this, she ran thesaurus searches for the words *gratitude* and *encouragement.*

If there is a useful lesson to be drawn from Rita's story, it would be that the acknowledgments section can be a safe, even a therapeutic, place for the stressed dissertation writer to spend some time in.

Language Focus: Expressions of Gratitude

There is a restricted range of phrases for expressing gratitude and appreciation. We have divided these into *primary* and *secondary* expressions of gratitude.

Primary

I am very thankful to X for Y.
I am deeply grateful to X for Y.
I would like to offer my sincere thanks to X for Y.

I would like to express my deep gratitude to X for Y.
I have greatly appreciated the X of Y.
I am deeply indebted to X for Y.
I owe a great deal to X for Y.
I owe a debt of gratitude to X for Y.
I am pleased to acknowledge the support of X for Y.

Secondary

Special gratitude is also extended to X for Y.
Many thanks are also due to X for Y.
My heartfelt appreciation also goes out to X for Y.

Notice that there are a limited number of adjectives that can be used in these phrases. It is not necessary to always use one of these intensifying adjectives. Not every case can be "special"! (See Note 9.)

Some writers try to avoid the repetition of these phrases by opting for a list format. Here is a good example.

> I would like to offer my sincerest thanks to my committee members: to the chair, WWWW, for his wise counsel and direction; to XXXX, who has for many years supported and encouraged me; to YYYY for always answering my inquiries so promptly; and to ZZZZ for his time and help in working out certain technical problems.

We dare say that the acknowledgments writer's nightmare is to inadvertently leave somebody out who ought to have been included. Some writers try to avoid possible offense by offering a generalized statement of thanks at the outset. Here are two examples.

1. It would be difficult to acknowledge everyone who has in some way or another contributed to the research reported in this dissertation.
2. During the year and a half it took me to write this dissertation, I have been helped and encouraged by many people in ways both small and large. However, there are several people whom I would like to single out for special thanks: A, B, C, and D.

Task Thirteen

If appropriate to your situation, write a draft acknowledgments section for a thesis, dissertation, or monograph.

6.3 Principled Narratives and Extensive Methods Sections

Methods sections in dissertations tend to be much longer and more detailed than in journal articles. Indeed, it is our understanding that research groups in science, medicine, and engineering sometimes buy dissertations from elsewhere because only there can they find the detailed information they need regarding how a particular experimental procedure was carried out. We also believe that these descriptions of methods tend to be particularly careful and extensive in experimental social science research using human subjects. This kind of research can occur in a wide range of fields, including education, social work, psychology, and the health sciences.

In *Academic Writing for Graduate Students,* we introduced the concept of "speed" to get at this variability in method descriptions. Methods sections may be "fast" if they either use gapping (see Unit Three) or rely on citations or standards, as in the following.

1. The samples were microtomed, placed in solution, centrifuged, and stored.

2. Occurrences were noted, scanned into the computer, and sorted into frequency categories.

3. Methods of collection were essentially those of Huang and Jones (1984).

4. Standard AOAC methods were used for the determination of total solids.

Note that so far we have no explanatory detail. But now consider the following.

5. Quantitative image comparison was conducted by calculating the cross-correlation value between the experimental micrographs and the simulated images using different specimen thicknesses and defocus values.

6. Etch rate was obtained from the evolution of the etch depth as a function of etching time, the slope of this thickness-time evolution yielding the etch rate.

In a final and even "slower" type of method, explanatory elements can take on a tone of justification.

7. When participants had completed the first half of the battery of questionnaires, the experimenter collected the completed measures (which included the attitude functions measures), ostensibly to give them more room to work on the remaining materials. This allowed the researcher to unobtrusively score the attitude functions measures so as to determine which message the participant would view. It also ensured that participants would continue to work on several other questionnaires, decreasing the likelihood that they would focus solely on the attitude functions measures and be influenced by their availability or salience (Clary et al. 1994, 1134).

This last extract is thus the kind of principled narrative that is the topic of this section. And note here that the authors in 7 provide a complex series of four justifications for their procedure.

ostensibly to give them more room . . .
allowed the researcher to unobtrusively score . . .
ensured that participants would continue . . .
decreasing the likelihood that . . .

The contrast, we think, between the kind of language used in 1–4 and in 7 is obvious enough.

While extensive descriptions of methods are usually thought of as being relatively easy to write, they can also be relatively unexciting to read. One way of enlivening these sections is to use some *left dislocations.* Left dislocations occur when material (in left-to-right scripts) is placed to the left of the grammatical subject. Some left dislocations in English are perfectly normal, as when a subordinate time clause or phrase opens a sentence.

8. Before the participants began the task, they were instructed to . . .

9. After cooling for 24 hours, the solution was then . . .

10. In the first series of experiments, the original material was found to be unsuitable for . . .

However, a more unusual and hence *marked* kind of left dislocation occurs with purpose statements. Here are some examples taken from a paper entitled "A Whiff of Reality: Empirical Evidence concerning the Effects of Pleasant Fragrances on Work-Related Behavior" (R. A. Baron and M. A. Bronfen, *Journal of Applied Social Psychology* 24 [1994]:1179–1203).

11. In order to assess the possibility that pleasant fragrances would mitigate the adverse effects of stress on task performance, participants in the present research performed a word instruction task . . .

12. To counteract sensory adaptation to the fragrances, the study was conducted in two parts.

13. Because of the lingering quality of both fragrances employed, it was necessary to conduct the no-fragrance and fragrance conditions on different days.

14. As an additional check on the effectiveness of the fragrance manipulation, participants were asked whether they detected any odor in the experimental rooms, and if they did, to rate it in terms of pleasantness.

Task Fourteen

Reflect upon the stylistic and discoursal effects of placing the purpose statements first in 11–14. What impression does the left dislocation make? (See Note 10.)

Task Fifteen

Rewrite example 7 with left-dislocated purpose statements. Beware: this is a more complicated and extensive piece of rewriting than might appear at first sight! (See Note 11.)

Another interesting type of left dislocation is to break up a standard *of* noun phrase. Compare the following two sets of statements.

A total of 150 hospitalized patients volunteered to take part in the study. Forty-seven percent of these volunteers were male and 53% were female.

A total of 150 hospitalized patients volunteered to take part in the study. Of these volunteers, 47% were male and 53% female.

Task Sixteen

Left dislocate the following.

1. Michael Jordan proved to be the best known across all age groups of the 12 public figures rated.

2. Eighty-one percent of those who returned the questionnaire stated that they were currently employed full-time.

3. Only two of the six measures investigated produced statistically significant results.

4. Nearly 21% of the devices fabricated using this experimental method functioned as predicted.

5. Most of those who failed to respond to treatment turned out to suffer from some form of diabetes.

(See Note 12.)

Language Focus: Dangling Modifiers

One common kind of "normal" left dislocation is an initial nonfinite clause, as in the following.

1. After completing the interview, each participant received $20.

2. After reading a description of the research, all subjects signed a consent form.

3. Before starting the experimental regime, each patient was assessed for abnormal heart conditions.

4. Being over a hundred years old, the specimen was handled with particular care.

But now consider these variants.

1a. After completing the interview, we paid each participant $20.

2a. After reading a description of the research, we asked all subjects to sign a consent form.

3a. Before starting the experimental regime, we assessed each patient for abnormal heart conditions.

4a. Being over a hundred years old, the biologist handled the specimen with particular care.

The above four sentences all contain a "dangling" modifier. This is because the *implied* subject of the nonfinite clause is presumably not the same as that given in the main clause. Perhaps this is clearest in 4a, where it is obviously the specimen and not the biologist that is over a hundred years old!

When using opening nonfinite clauses (without subjects), always make sure that their implied subjects are the same as those in the main clauses (as in 1–4).

Language Focus: The Use and Position of "Bare" Participles

Final chapters (and other types of discussions) attempt to summarize and "place" the research that has been undertaken. We can occasionally find here (as well as elsewhere) the use of a single (hence "bare") participle *following* the noun. The following examples (some modified) are taken from final chapters of dissertations.

1. The results *obtained* thus confirm three of the four hypotheses.

2. Although the assumptions *made* have an intrinsic appeal, they were shown to be somewhat suspect in one regard.

3. The first approach *adopted* had to be abandoned because . . .

4. However, because of the restricted number of events *studied* and the nature of the research questions *posed*, no quantitative data has been provided.

Corpus research on written academic English shows that close to 90 percent of single, bare participles occur before the noun (as in *increased temperature* or *proposed solution*). Here then we are concerned with the remaining 10 percent or so that occur after.

First, we need to recognize that in English, the *adjective-before-the-noun* rule is very robust and powerful, the main exceptions being

a. in poetry ("poetic license"), for example, "Little Boy Blue";

b. in some old expressions of French origin, for instance, "Courts martial" versus "military courts";

c. after words like *something* and *anybody,* for example, "Something unusual"; and

d. after (sometimes) a few special adjectives such as *available* ("on the data available").

We would expect then that participles that come after the noun (i.e., postposed ones) would be the exceptions. Some of these exceptions can be accounted for by the fact that certain participles have somewhat different meanings when preposed or postposed. Compare the following statements.

a. Most graduate students in the United States buy used cars.
b. According to police reports, the car used was a Ford.

Task Seventeen

Can you complete these statements in some suitable way? (Remember that for the sake of this exercise the postposed participles are supposed to be "bare," so do not follow them by prepositional phrases, such as *The syringes used in hospitals are now disposable.*)

1. The used syringes _____

2. The syringes used _____

3. This involved case _____

4. For two of the cases involved_____

5. The concerned physician   _____

6. The physicians concerned _____

7. Any given result _____

8. The result given _____

9. The spoken language _____

10. The language spoken _____

(See Note 13.)

Now let us consider some data from Hyland's corpus of 80 research articles (see Note 9, Unit Four). Table 6.1 lists the most common single participles for each position.

TABLE 6.1. **Participles in Each Position**

Preposed		Postposed	
given	129	used	20
increased	72	described	16
chosen	70	presented	15
proposed	66	reported	12
fixed	61	given	11
measured	61	obtained	10
projected	57	discussed	8
perceived	55	chosen	7
shared	43	examined	7
required	35	tested	6
written	35	considered	5
expected	33	identified	5

Source: Data from K. Hyland, "Academic attribution: Citation and the construction of disciplinary knowledge," *Applied Linguistics* 20 (1999): 341–67.

(See Note 14.)

Task Eighteen

Which participles occur in both columns? Reflect upon your own usage. Which of the single postposed participles in the right column can you recollect using? Are there others that you remember using? If you like, look through one of your recent papers for instances. (See Note 15.)

A next clue to participle placement is that most postposed participles turn out to be definite rather than indefinite. Compare the following statements.

Natural laws describe *observed* phenomena.
The phenomena *observed* could not be accounted for.
The vapor pressure of a *given* substance changes with temperature.
While not all of the figures *given* are reliable, some are.

In the Hyland data, all seven instances of postposed *chosen* were definite, as in *Second, the particular mall chosen is the largest mall in the city.* However, we have to be careful here, because a majority of the 70 preposed examples were also definite!

We can next note that bare participles quite often have a metadiscoursal function (i.e., to—typically—refer back to earlier material in the text). Many of these will be definite and will tend to occur in post-position.

1. The curve shown . . .
2. However, even the few facts presented . . .
3. All three of the cases discussed . . .
4. The values listed . . .
5. The findings reported above . . .
6. The data given . . .
7. The literature cited . . .
8. The works referred to . . .

Consider again example 5. There are a number of "textual adverbs" that can co-occur, as in the following.

1. The results reported above . . .
2. The arguments discussed earlier . . .
3. The data presented below . . .
4. The position taken here . . .

It is very doubtful if these uses could be moved to pre-position.

1a. ??The above-reported results . . .
2a. ??The earlier-discussed arguments . . .
3a. ??The below-presented data . . .
4a. ??The here-taken position . . .

But note that this restriction does *not* apply to *previously,* where we can find both.

5. The hypothesis previously mentioned . . .
5a. The previously mentioned hypothesis . . .

Also note that the old-fashioned *aforementioned* (although there are four occurrences in the Hyland corpus) probably has to take pre-position.

So this brings us to Bolinger's original 1967 hypothesis (and that of some later distinguished grammarians). (See Note 16.) The pre-position is associated with a concept that has permanence and that often takes on the form of a characteristic; the post-position is associated with temporariness and action. In a way then, pre-positions are more "adjectival," and post-positions are more "verbal." So we could talk about "a lost book" but not about "a found book," since loss is more or less permanent but finding is not. On the other hand, we could say, "Any books found should be handed in to the office."

Task Nineteen

Now consider these pairs. How can you account for the differences in participle position?

1a. The reaction is dangerous because the hydrogen *evolved* may catch fire.
1b. This occurs because the *dissolved* air becomes less soluble at higher temperatures.

2a. The taxonomy *employed here* diverges from that of Thompson and Ye in that . . .
2b. The *usually employed* taxonomy is that of Thompson and Ye, which . . .

3a. The literature *cited* has been quite extensive.
3b. The *cited* literature is quite extensive.

4a. The following is the *proposed* mechanism.
4b. The following is the mechanism *proposed.*

(See Note 17.)

With luck, we can now see that shifting a simple participle to the post-position is a tricky maneuver that involves issues of definiteness, temporality, novelty, and reference to your own text rather than to those of others.

Having said all this, it remains the case that we sometimes reach the limits of currently available grammatical explanations. In some cases, we may have to concede that there may actually be a free choice as to where to place certain bare participles in certain contexts. Individual stylistic preferences certainly play some part.

Task Twenty

Consider the position of *obtained* in these excerpts from the Hyland data. Can you make any sense of the data? Good luck!

1. Measuring recall immediately after exposure clearly inflates the scores *obtained* and may explain why the expected differences between the users and nonusers were not as large as predicted.

2. In fact, the shapes *obtained* are comparable to those of the IR ones.

3. It was noted that none of the values *obtained* exceeded the values determined using the Code expression for C2 given in equation 10 above.

4. Not only is the approach considered to be too subjective to interpret, but it also does not seem to be validated by the experimental data *obtained*.

5. The results *obtained* suggest that the algorithm provides a solution in an acceptable resolution time.

6. In other words, we can determine the slope of the moderating independent variable (i.e., Z = satisfaction) based on the first derivative of the *obtained* regression equations.

7. The actual data of NGL were correlated (Figures 1 and 2), and the *obtained* correlations, with fit coefficients of 0.59 and 0.94, are given in Eqs. (5) and (6).

8. . . . , and the *obtained* correlation (with the fit coefficient of 0.975) for making future projections is given in Eq. (11).

(See Note 18.)

Task Twenty-one

Do one of the following.

a. Look at one of your own methods sections. What would you say about its "speed"? Highlight all left dislocations. Any conclusions? Any dangling modifiers?

b. If you are one of those who need to write principled narrative descriptions of procedures, submit a sample of your work to your instructor.

6.4 Dealing with Unexpected Results

Methods sections can be further slowed by a discussion of methods tried and abandoned. Read through the following extract from a dissertation in electrical engineering and the interview with the author that comes after it. The goal of the work was to produce a GaAlAs/GaAs laser that would be suitable for short-distance fiber communication as well as integrated optics. This excerpt comes from Chapter Three, which describes the fabrication of the laser device, particularly the making of the ridge shown in the diagram.

Task Twenty-two

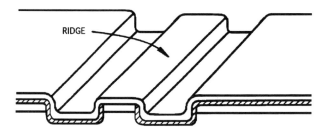

The Ridge

[1]The 2.50 and 3.75 μm ridges were formed by etching 5–6 μm wide channels on either side. Originally this was attempted using standard photolithography[a] and wet-chemical etching. [2]However, the etchants[b] used in this process posed several problems.

[3]First, the etchants available, in this case $H_2SO_4:H_2O_2:H_2O$ (1:8:1), with an etch rate between 2 and 3 µm/min at 2–3°C, and $CH_3OH:H_2O_2:H_3PO_4$ (3:1:1) with an etch rate of 1.7 (µm/min. at 20°C, were highly temperature dependent, thus limiting our ability to control the etch depth to 5 percent, as required to reliably produce proper index guiding.[c] [4]Secondly, they are isotropic etches which produce sloping sidewalls. [5]While this facilitates contacting the ridge, it does not allow very tight optical or current confinement at the base of the ridge. [6]For example, for a 2.5 µm wide contact on the top of the ridge, and an etch depth of 1.5 µm, the base of the ridge is 3.5 µm or more. [7]Thirdly, the wet etches tried undercut the mask, and many had some degree of GaAlAs/GaAs selectivity, making the fabrication of precise ridge widths difficult and complicating the formation of continuous contacts to the ridge. [8]Finally, the wet-chemical etchants tended to etch p+ material very quickly, and were therefore incompatible with the Zn diffusion step to improve contacting. [9]When the Zn diffusion was carried out first, the mask was totally undercut before the proper depth was reached. [10]If carried out after the etch, even with proper masking, rapid diffusion down the ridge wall to the active region occurred. [11]Some devices were fabricated with wet-chemical etching, but because of the reasons just cited, they were not as reproducible, and their thresholds were three times as high.[d]

[12]Chemically assisted ion beam etching (CAIBE), on the other hand, solves all of the aforementioned problems. [13]This process was carried out by . . .

a. A procedure that allows placement of a pattern on a semiconductor material or a pattern of another material on a semiconductor
b. A mixture of chemicals that etch or erode a material
c. Proper guidance of light
d. The light was not being guided that well.

(See Note 19.)

CF: Why did you include the discussion of the problems with the etchants and wet-chemical etching, rather than simply discussing the more successful chemically assisted ion beam etching?

GF: Well, I wanted to give a complete picture of what I did and why I did it that way. If I'd left it out, someone might think that I didn't even try wet-chemical etching before trying CAIBE. Or they might think that wet-chemical etching would be a good thing to try.

CF: Your description makes it sound like CAIBE was the logical next step. But, what's the real story?

GF: Believe it or not, when I started on this project I wasn't planning on trying CAIBE, so I guess I'm leaving out some detail here. What happened was some technicians in the Submicron facility had just come up with this new way of etching material but didn't have any applications for it. I saw what they were doing and thought maybe it would work for laser fabrication. No one had ever actually done that before.

CF: Do you think it is generally a good idea to discuss methods problems encountered in your research?

GF: Yeah, well, sure, depending on what it is you're writing. I mean you can't put the stuff that didn't work into a typical published research paper. There's just not enough space. But in your dissertation or thesis, it makes sense. It makes you look like you've covered all the bases; like you're careful and thoughtful. Also, if another group looks at my dissertation, it will help them avoid some of the problems I had. You don't want everyone reinventing the wheel.

CF: How did you decide which problems should be discussed and which not?

GF: For the dissertation I didn't put in all the dead ends and failures. That would have been ridiculous. I mean, how far back do you go? All sorts of things go wrong when you're first starting out. Anyway, I focused on the sorts of things that would be useful for others in the field.

1. In your current work (thesis, dissertation, or research paper), how important is it for you to discuss "dead ends and failures"?

2. To what extent should your thesis or dissertation be directed at others in your field doing similar work?

6.5 The Problematic Final Chapter

The main reasons why the final chapters of many dissertations turn out to be problematic are essentially two: lack of creative energy and shortage of time. By this stage, after arduous labor extending over many months, the dissertation writer typically just wants to "be done." The thought of having to rise to a further occasion in the final chapter by finding something fresh and interesting to say is not one that the dissertation writer typically anticipates with any kind of excitement. Indeed, sometimes dissertation writers at this late stage hardly care what the wider significance of their work might be!

Second, there may often be extreme time pressure as the time for the scheduled defense approaches. Because of such factors, the final chapter of a dissertation tends to be a rather bland summary of what has gone before and little else. It is partly for this reason that most U.S. dissertations do not easily transfer into scholarly books (in those fields that still expect a scholarly monograph from a reputable press for tenure).

Some of the observations we made about discussion sections in research articles in *AWG* also apply to dissertation final chapters (in particular b, c, and d below). What at the minimum the committee hopes to see in the concluding chapter are the following.

a. a restatement of what the dissertation has attempted to do and why;

b. a "higher and broader pass" over the main or most significant findings;

c. some discussion of the limitations of the study; and

d. some suggestions for further research and why it would be worthwhile (although this last may be omitted in highly sensitive or competitive areas).

So what do we mean by a "higher and broader pass" (Move 2)?

We mean a review of the material that

a. handles most of the main findings at a fairly abstract level of generality;

b. identifies one or two key findings for more detailed treatment;

c. situates the findings on the current research front;

d. highlights any theoretical contributions and implications;

e. considers in detail practical applications and implementations.

As it happens, one of the few final chapters that John remembers fondly was that written by Didar Akar, whose dissertation abstract we saw in Section 6.1. Since we have some familiarity with her study of Turkish business communications, we focus on this.

Didar produced a solid 25-page chapter entitled "Theoretical Implications and Practical Applications." It is divided into three main sections.

5.1. The Factors Affecting Business Texts (183–91)

5.2. The Genre Approach to Business Correspondence (191–95)

5.3. Teaching Business Communications in Turkey (195–207)

Here is her opening paragraph, followed by some observations.

> [1]The main findings of the preceding chapters have shown that a number of factors have influenced the form and function of the written business texts in my data set. [2]However, it is important to note that none of the factors is an independent variable; instead, they are all intertwined in many complex ways. [3]Starting from the most general, there are ostensible influences that come from national, cultural ways of conducting business, even if these today are themselves being affected by globalization and subglobalization trends. [4]Another crucially influential factor is the corporate culture, in particular the size and the industry sector of the company. [5]A third factor which has a highly visible influence is the Turkish bureaucratic tradition, that is, official writing. [6]A fourth factor is the communication medium; as has been discussed in Chapter Four, the fax machine has impacted certain texts in certain nontrivial ways. [7]In this section, I will comment on each of these factors and relate the findings of this study to those found in the literature.

1. The paragraph opens with a nice piece of metadiscourse that summarizes what has been accomplished in the preceding chapters.

2. Note that in formal academic English *none* takes the singular (*none of these factors is . . .*). In academic speech *none of* often takes a plural (*none of these factors are independent*). In the MICASE data *none* is followed by a plural six times more often than it is by a singular form of the verb.

3. Didar then lists these factors *starting from the most general,* thus maintaining a general to specific arrangement of her material. Each of her four factors is then given its own subsection.

4. In sentence 6, note the use of *impact* as a verb; see the earlier discussion in Note 8, Unit Two.

5. The final sentence of the paragraph offers some forward looking metadiscourse and also promises to fulfill the committee's expectations that the candidate will situate her findings on the research front.

In the second section of her final chapter, Didar discusses what her study might have to offer in terms of its theoretical contribution to discourse analysis. She argues for an approach that combines several perspectives. The final two sentences are presented in Task Twenty-three.

Task Twenty-three

We have italicized certain elements in this short text. We believe that these elements contribute to what is a powerful and successful close to her theory section. What do you think we are getting at here?

> *If* we so combine these elements, we have *not only* Miller's centering on the "action [a genre] is used to accomplish," but *additionally, and importantly,* on the tangibilities of how that action is accomplished (urgently by fax, in a more leisurely manner by letter, widely by a heavily cc'ed memo, and so on). *In effect,* we can *now* perceive of business genres, as Beebe (1994) does for both literary and popular culture texts, in terms of their "use value," *a more broadly contextual vision* that *additionally underpins the instrumentality* of the types of text discussed in this dissertation.

(See Note 20.)

6.6 Notes and Comments for Unit Six

Note 1

There are two possible spellings: "acknowledgments" and "acknowledgements." The former may be becoming standard in American English, perhaps largely because of spell-checkers on word processing programs; the latter is more British English.

Note 2 (sample responses for Task One)

1. Yes, we think so. After all, she now has a tenure-track job in a linguistics department in Istanbul and teaches part-time at an American-style business school in the city.

2. All three opening sentences are indeed possible. Her choice is probably the best if only because this was a linguistics dissertation. We approve of the decisions regarding the use of metadiscourse and tense.

3. There is much uncertainty as to whether *data* is a plural noun (as it is in Latin) or has become uncountable (like *information*). It may be "safer" to keep it plural for the time being (as opposed to singular, as in choice c). The use of *used* shows clearly that something has been done with the data; *used in this study* strikes us as a little redundant.

4. Approximations have the advantage of giving a clearer overall picture; they have the disadvantage of giving an impression of vagueness.

5. We think this is just about OK for a 350-word abstract; in the dissertation itself of course some further clarifications will be necessary.

6. If the methods are described in more detail, this would have the effect of making the abstract less comprehensible to nonlinguists. On the other hand, . . .

7. An interpretive summary phrase

8. Because this is a historical claim about cause and effect

9. This is a major finding. The business communications literature (largely based in the United States) argues that requests are more successful when they are expressed personally and relatively directly.

10. Parallelism

11. Yes, at least the co-chair thinks so.

Note 3 (sample responses for Task Six)

Our own judgments—for what they are worth—would be as follows.

Y: 1, 4, 5, 6, 7, 8
N: 9, 10
?: 2, 3

Note 4 (sample responses for Task Seven)

Possible Points

- Congratulations on a comprehensive revision!

- The rationale and importance of the research now come through well in paragraph 1.

- The three studies are now integrated well in paragraph 2, although we have in the process lost some useful information about the details of the results.

- The third paragraph now "places" the study better in its wider context.

Note 5 (sample responses for Task Nine)

We suggest the following as the better choices.

1. express   2. pursue   3. be exposed   4. acknowledge   5. owe
6. have contributed   7. would like to   8. working on

Note 6 (sample responses for Task Ten)

1. Although the acknowledgments will be written in a largely academic style, they do not need to be written impersonally. As far as we are aware, *I* is always acceptable for acknowledgments, even if it may not be acceptable for the dissertation itself.

2. The acknowledgments section should be positive in its expression of gratitude. One thing to keep in mind is that it does not need to be continuously ecstatic.

3. The acknowledgments should be precisely that: primarily thanking other people rather than discussing the personal benefits gained during the dissertation process.

Note 7 (sample responses for Task Eleven)

Paragraph 1—Her committee
Paragraph 2—People in Thailand/fieldwork
Paragraph 3—Units that provided financial support (sponsors)
Paragraph 4—Her fellow linguistics students (and a few others)
Paragraph 5—Other special friends and relatives
Paragraph 6—Her father and mother

Rita moves from the dissertation itself, to help with data collection and learning Thai, to financial support, and then in the last three paragraphs to more social and personal support from fellow students, other friends and family, and finally her parents. In effect, she goes from the narrow to the broad both in space and time. Luejit, as a Thai civil servant, felt she had to show allegiance to her government first. Some of our students have also pointed out that their cultures might require them to acknowledge their immediate families first.

Note 8 (sample responses for Task Twelve)

1. Rita's preferred mode of address is (f) (Elizabeth Smith) for first mention, although she may move to (h) (Elizabeth) for later references. She seems to be variable in her use of short forms of first names, typically choosing the form

by which individuals are most usually known. The only title used was for the Thai professor in paragraph 2; Rita said she did this because she felt this individual was "somewhat removed in time and space."

Luejit, on the other hand, referes to professors and others she wishes to thank using a more formal tone. She expresses gratitude to Professor XXXX and Professor YYYY using their titles (a, b, c, or d). Luejit acknowledges her social support network only briefly, listing no individuals by name, and makes no mention of her family.

2. crucial, excellent, generous, (eminently) helpful, invaluable, timely, keen, privileged, difficult, best, pilot, insightful, critical, reassuring, stimulating

Most of the adjectives are (highly) positive; they are the kind of adjectives that could likely be found in recommendation letters.

Note 9

D. S. Giannoni (1998), in a paper entitled "The genre of journal acknowledgements: Findings of a cross-disciplinary investigation" (*Linguistica e Filologia* 6:61–84, University of Bergamo), includes some quantitative data on lexical choices. The verb *thank* occurred 32 times, *be grateful to* 11, and *be indebted to* 4. There were only 3 instances of the verb *acknowledge,* which he describes as "colder." The most common adjective was *helpful* (15 instances), followed by smaller numbers of *valuable, useful,* and *excellent.*

Note 10 (sample response for Task Fourteen)

There are two principal effects, both of rhetorical significance. First, the initial purpose statement can operate to prevent doubts arising in the reader's mind about the particular procedure being described. Second, the early placement seems to suggest that the reason and justification for the particular procedural element were already all worked out in advance, while, in fact, we often know that the justification can be an afterthought.

Note 11 (sample response for Task Fifteen)

Here is one version of this difficult task.

In order to (ostensibly) give participants more room to work on the remaining materials, the experimenter collected the completed measures (including the attitude functions measures) after the first half of the battery of questionnaires had been completed. However, an underlying motive for this was that the researcher could now unobtrusively score the attitude functions measures so as to determine which message the participant would view. Finally, to decrease the likelihood that participants would focus on the attitude functions measures, and thus be influenced by their availability and salience, this procedure encouraged them to continue work on several other questionnaires.

Note 12 (sample responses for Task Sixteen)

1. Of the 12 public figures rated, Michael Jordan proved to be the best known across all age groups.
2. Of those who returned the questionnaire, 81% stated they were currently in full-time employment.
3. Of the six measures investigated, only two produced statistically significant results.
4. Of the devices fabricated using this experimental method, nearly 21% functioned as predicted.
5. Of those who failed to respond to treatment, most turned out to suffer from some form of diabetes.

And notice (as in 2), this kind of left dislocation can help you avoid having to start a sentence with a number of some sort.

Note 13 (sample responses for Task Seventeen)

1. The used syringes must be disposed of properly. (already used once or more)
2. The syringes used in the study were retrieved from landfills. (employed)
3. This involved case has perplexed researchers for years. (complicated)
4. For two of the cases involved environmentalists have been very active. (connected, under consideration)
5. The concerned physician contemplated a second transplant. (anxious, worried)
6. The physicians concerned were co-authors of the controversial paper. (involved)
7. Any given result could be suitable. (within a certain range)
8. The result given must be interpreted carefully. (provided)
9. The spoken language can be quite difficult to learn. (as opposed to the written language)
10. The language spoken is related to Finnish. (the language used in a certain area)

Note 14

Postposed participles are much more restricted in the MICASE data. Most are verbalizations of mathematical expressions (x^2—x squared—is congruent to . . . ; $L/2\pi^3$—L over 2π cubed). Aside from these and the use of certain names such as that of the magazine *Sports Illustrated,* there are only 17 examples of postposed participles in the first 350,000 words in the corpus. Only the word *involved* occurs more than once (4 times).

Note 15 (sample response for Task Eighteen)

John looked through 20 pages he had written and found only one example of a bare postposed participle: *the structure tested was . . .*

Note 16

Bolinger, D. L. 1967. Adjectives in English: Attribution or predication? *Lingua* 18:1–34.

Note 17 (sample responses for Task Nineteen)

1a/1b. If there is an explanation here, it might be that in a the reaction is quick and temporary, while in b the process is more long term. The first sentence looks like *action,* and the second looks like *state.*

2a/2b. The first is again more particular and more innovative. As for b, we have some small preference for the pre-position because it depicts a stable condition (Bolinger's "characteristic"), although we recognize that the post-position is also possible.

3a/3b. The first suggests that literature has just been cited (as in a talk) or read about (as in an article or a dissertation) and is being referred back to, while the second suggests this is the literature that is typically cited by those in the field.

4a/4b. The difference between these two does not seem as clear as in the previous examples. However, a gives the impression that the writer was building to the point of suggesting a mechanism and will now propose or has just proposed the mechanism. Once the mechanism has been proposed, b can be used to refer back to it.

Note 18 (sample response for Task Twenty)

These examples seem to suggest that you have a choice as to whether to place *obtain* in pre- or post-position, but *obtain* appears to be more frequently found in post-position since the act of obtaining is temporary.

Note 19

The source for the excerpt is the following.

Feak, G. B. Low threshold ridge waveguide single quantum well lasers. Ph.D. diss., Cornell University, 1987.

(Task Twenty-two Teaching Hint: The two questions raised at the end of Task Twenty-two make for interesting discussion. You might want to try addressing the questions through a panel discussion with four or five representatives from the hard or soft sciences discussing their views. Students from fields where such issues may not arise can be the audience and can be encouraged to ask the panel members questions.)

Note 20

The *if* suggests that this combination is somehow late-breaking news; if *when* had been used instead, the reader might conclude that such combining is common practice.

a. Miller's centering we can assume to be the current standard position, so we *not only* have that, but also *additionally, and importantly,* some kind of addition. This language, plus the extensive exemplification in the parentheses, allows Didar to indicate a clear sense of cumulative development.

b. *In effect* then suggests a coming reinterpretation as a consequence, powerfully indicated by the little word *now*—only now (never before) can we have a new perception.

c. Finally, the movement forward is recast as a broader *vision,* but not one that is hopelessly abstract, because it *additionally underpins the instrumentality* of Didar's business texts.

And as a final thought on this matter, please note that we have chosen for this last task one of the high points of Didar's final chapter. A committee will also accept more "ordinary" writing for the most part. Do not be discouraged.

Unit Seven
Academic Communications in Support of the Research Process

DREAMS OF ACADEMIC GLORY

"Dear Mr. Singh:
We would be delighted to publish your paper. Not only that,
but we have decided that your beautifully written submission
letter is publishable as well."

So far in this volume we have focused mainly on the constructing of research publications. In this unit we move to a number of genres that support the research publication process but are not themselves part of the research record. In Unit Eight we cover applications of various kinds, recommendations, and the curriculum vitae (CV). This latter group functions more as *academic communications in support of a career.* (As we said in the introduction, we have decided not to include a section on proposals for research funding since this is one area that is comprehensively covered in books, manuals, workshops, and the like.)

Unlike research articles, conference posters, and dissertations, genres such as requests, submission letters, reminders, and reviewers' and editors' reports are largely "out of sight." On the one hand, they are documents that typically remain on file; on the other, they are rarely part of the public record (except for the minority of journals that publish reviewers' reports as appendixes to the articles themselves). These "hidden" genres are written for specific or small-group audiences and yet may be full of demonstrated scholarship and be organized so as to present the people who write them as fair, wise, and insightful professionals in their own field.

There are several consequences of these characteristics.

1. Relative newcomers may have difficulties in matching the expectations of their targeted audiences.

2. Many of these expectations will be more shaped by local cultural values and national academic traditions than is the case with more technical writing. (There is, e.g., good evidence [see Unit Eight, Section 8.4] to support the view that what counts as a "good" recommendation varies considerably from one academic culture to another.)

3. Maier (1992) (see Note 1) has shown that negative reactions to examples of these genres tend to come more from inappropriate phraseology than from problems with organization or from unexpected content. Similar results were also obtained by Chang and Hsu (1998) (see Note 1).

As a result of all this, junior NNS scholars may experience particular difficulties with these genres. Comments from our classes strongly support this view.

This unit will deal with the following.

7.1. Requests

7.2. Reminders and Responses

7.3. Disclaimers and Apologies

7.1 Requests

Academic and research requests can be of many types, but one of the most common is the simple request for a copy of a paper. Requests for copies of papers can themselves take various forms and in an increasing number of cases may not be needed at all because research papers may be downloaded from the author's home page. Even so, the traditional postcard-type *reprint request* still survives and has long proved successful—with average response rates of around 70 percent. Here is a typical example.

Southwest University

School of Public Health

Dept. of Family Health

Bennerville, TX 55555 USA

Dear Colleague:

I would greatly appreciate a copy of your article/paper entitled:

_____

from/at   _____

if available. Thank you for your courtesy.

Signed _____

More likely today, however, requests of various kinds will come via e-mail and will often be expressed in today's e-mail mixture of formal and more informal elements.

Task One

You (and your partner) are assistants to Professor Gardener. He forwards you the following five e-mail messages, accompanied by this one from him.

Guys, these just in. They never seem to stop. What should be
our priorities here? Could you sort them out in rank order,
with the most urgent or important at the top? Then at the
weekly lab meeting we can decide what to do—or not to do!
Thanks for doing this for me.

Rank order the requests. What are your reasons for your choices? What do you think the decisions will be at next week's lab meeting?

Message One

```
From: martino@unimolf.it
To: Gardener@xxx.edu
Subject: Request
```

Dear Sir,

I am a researcher at a small local university here near
Palermo, and am carrying out research in your area of materials science. I would like to visit your department as an
observer researcher for a short time (about three months) in
order to get ideas about my thesis.

As I am a native speaker of Italian, I would be delighted to
help your students learn Italian in your modern languages
department, or I could collaborate in any other way that you
can suggest.

If you accept, I could come during the next academic term.
Please let me know your answer as soon as possible since I
need to apply for a travel grant. Looking forward to hearing
from you.

Yours faithfully,

Message Two

Dear Professor,

I am currently working on a master's thesis on the processes
of metallic-ceramic fusion, and I have recently read a recent and highly relevant paper by your group in _Materials
Science Digest_ (20XX, Vol. 45, pp. 345-57). I am wondering

if there are similar papers on this topic that you could refer me to or let me have copies of? (The library here isn't very good.)

My advisor here is Ana Augusto, who sends her regards. She met you at the Caracas conference in 1999.

Rosinda de Souza
Rua Campo Verde, 174—apto. 12
Bela Colina—MG
CEP 12340-187
Brasil

Message Three

Dear Professor Gardener,

First let me introduce myself. I have recently returned to Malaysia, having completed a Ph.D. at Desert University with Dr. William D. Jones as advisor, who has recently retired. On return, I was asked to start a small research group on materials science in our research institute. On Dr. Jones's suggestion, I am asking whether you might be willing to act as an informal and unofficial advisor to my group. I know you are a very busy and important man, but if you happened to be in this part of the world (we know you sometimes go to Australia), my colleagues and I would greatly appreciate a visit of a few days or so. Unfortunately, we have no funds for international travel, but we can cover regional travel and all local expenses.

Dr. Ali Osman
Materials Science Research Group
Sarawak Science Research Institute

Message Four

Dear Professor Gardener,

This is a preliminary inquiry as to whether you might be in principle willing to act as external examiner for a Ph.D. thesis from here on metallic-ceramic fusion. The thesis is expected to be completed next month, and the defense will need to take place within two months of the submission date.

We would expect a 2 to 3 page evaluation. There is no need for you to be present in Hong Kong for the defense itself. The university is able to pay a small fee for this important service. If you would like any further information, please do not hesitate to ask.

If you would be able to accept (and I can imagine how busy you must be), I will forward your name to the central administration, which will then take up the administrative details.

With best wishes,

Henry Liu
Head, Department of Materials Science
Shatin University
Hong Kong

Message Five

Dear Professor Gardener,

I am writing to you on the recommendation of Professor Grossman here in Vienna, where I am his research assistant and working part-time on my dissertation, which has the provisional title "Ceramic-Metallic Fusion Properties at Extremely High Temperatures." I understand from Professor Grossman that you have done a lot of work in this area. Since I would certainly like to base my work on the latest results and methods, I really need your help! I am especially interested in your publications, latest experiments and their results. I would also be grateful if you have any suggestions about my dissertation topic and for any further bibliographic references that would aid me in my research. I thank you very much in advance and only hope that it won't require too much of an effort for you to help me. Looking forward to hearing from you soon!

Yours sincerely,

Annika Graf

(See Note 2.)

Task Two

Complete the chart below and be ready to discuss your "findings."

	Message One	Message Two	Message Three	Message Four	Message Five
1. Presumed first language of author					
2. Status of requester					
3. Type of help requested					
4. Place in text where main request occurs					
5. Phrases you like					
6. Phrases you dislike					

(See Note 3.)

Language Focus: The Position of the Request Statement

There is some evidence that different cultures have different preferences as to where to place the main request. Discuss the following abstract from a paper entitled "Information Sequencing in Mandarin Letters of Request" by Andy Kirkpatrick of the Australian National University. (See Note 4.)

> Native speakers of Chinese prefer to place requests toward the end of interactions or messages. Such requests generally conform to the following schema: salutation, preamble (facework), reasons, and then the request itself. This article analyzes requests that appear in letters written by Mainland Chinese to the China Section of Radio Australia.

1. Here are the two main possibilities for where to place the request: (1) Request + Reasons/justifications; (2) Reasons + Request (Kirkpatrick 1991). Does your culture have a general preference? If so, can you think of any explanations for the preferred choice?

2. What about yourself? Do you have a preference?

3. Or do you think it all depends on the circumstances? For example, simple requests can be direct and "up front," while major and imposing requests will need considerable preparation.

(See Note 5.)

Task Three

Consider the e-mail request from Task One that you ranked in lowest position. Suppose the writer had come to you with the request as a draft—what suggestions for changes would you make? Rewrite the request to reflect your suggestions. (See Note 6.)

Task Four

In your own field what sorts of things are easy to request and what are hard? Write a request for one of the hard things.

Language Focus: *to* + VERB + *-ing* Patterns

Perhaps the classic instance of this pattern is the closing phrase we have seen in two of the requests: *looking forward* to hearing *from you.* For many nonnative speakers of English this pattern is counterintuitive since they have been typically taught in schools that verbs can be followed by either VERB + infinitive *(She hopes to improve)* or VERB + participle *(She hates revising).* *To* + VERB + *-ing* seems to break these straightforward rules. However, in this case, the *to* is in fact a preposition that just happens to come before the participle. This structure can occur after a number of grammatical items.

A. *To* + VERB + *-ing* following verbs. Here are some of the more common ones.

I am looking forward *to receiving* further information.
He is committed *to teaching* all kinds of students.
Her experience is not limited *to teaching* in the United States.
She is used *to running* complex statistical tests.
She objected *to having* to redo the assignment.
Certain groups are often subjected *to being* searched on entry.
They admitted *to failing* to follow the safety procedures.

(Some other more informal patterns occur largely in speech, such as *When he* gets around to running *the experiment, we may finally see some results* or *All this* boils down to saying *that it won't work.*)

B. *To* + VERB + *-ing* following some complex prepositions

In addition *to working* on his dissertation, he is also teaching a class.
Prior *to entering* the Ph.D. program, she worked in industry.
With a view *to increasing* enrollment, the department developed an
    interactive Web site.

C. *To* + VERB + *-ing* following certain adjectives

She is close *to completing* her grant proposal.
This is crucial *to understanding* the nature of the problem.
The director may be open *to rescheduling* the meeting.

He is resistant *to being* relocated.

This is tantamount *to saying* that there is probably no difference.

D. *To* + VERB + *-ing* following certain nouns

There is no alternative *to replicating* the experiment.

She had several objections *to being* labeled a "radical feminist."

This is a useful guide *to constructing* similar computer programs.

His approach *to understanding* society is more psychological than
sociological.

There was considerable resistance *to implementing* the curriculum
reform.

Task Five

Complete the following with a suitable VERB + *-ing*.

1. I am looking forward to _____ your presentation at next month's conference.

2. The director is not accustomed to _____ his
decisions questioned.

3. The student admitted to _____ the term paper
from the Web.

4. The tax reform is being introduced with a view to _____
_____ benefits for the poor.

5. There can be drawbacks to _____on probabilistic measures.

6. She is averse to _____ her dissertation abstract
for a sixth time.

(See Note 7.)

7.2 Reminders and Responses

It happens to all of us that some of our best-crafted and most reasonable requests are met with silence. If the matter is still important, we may now need to send a reminder.

Task Six

How would you characterize the following strategies? Which one do you prefer and why?

And how might you further improve your preferred choice?

Reminder A

> Dear Professor Wilson,
>
> You may remember that several weeks ago I messaged asking if you could write a recommendation for me in support of my application for a doctoral fellowship. You may also recall that you agreed to do this. According to the graduate secretary of my department, the department has yet (as of yesterday) to receive a letter from you. I am wondering therefore if I could remind you about this? Of course, please ignore this message if you have already written.

Reminder B

> Dear Professor Wilson,
>
> I am resending my request for a letter (April 24, 200X) in case you have overlooked it. I know how busy you are at this time of year, but I would be very grateful if you could manage something.

Reminder C

> Dear Professor Wilson,
>
> Completed applications for next year's doctoral fellowships are due at the central administration by 4 P.M. this Friday. My application is complete except for the letter you agreed

```
to write for me some weeks ago. It is now too late for me to
approach another professor about a letter. Can I therefore
ask you to do this by noon on Friday? Without all of the
necessary documents, my application will be automatically
rejected and my academic future compromised. I would be very
willing to pick up a letter from your department on Friday
and take it across campus. If you need to contact me in the
next 24 hours I can be most easily reached at 234-5678.
```

(See Note 8.)

Task Seven

Compose a reminder for one of these contexts.

1. You wrote to your country's national archives requesting three reports relevant to your research, sending a check to cover copying and mailing costs (as agreed on the telephone). They replied two months ago that they were processing your request but to date you have received nothing.

2. Six weeks ago you sent a copy of your research proposal for comment to a professor at your previous university, who was your first mentor and advisor. Your ex-professor said she would gladly read your proposal and make some suggestions but she hasn't yet got back to you.

3. Your writing instructor/tutor said that she would lend you one of her copies of the *BBI Combinatory Dictionary* a couple of weeks ago. Remind her of this promise.

4. You sent a letter some time ago to a well-known researcher in your field in Los Angeles saying that since you would be there next week for personal reasons, you would like an opportunity to make a brief visit and hopefully talk to him or to one of his colleagues. You heard nothing and sent a reminder. Send a second e-mail reminder of your request.

Apart from reminders, there are various other kinds of responses. Very often the way these are handled affects how you are perceived and thus is highly relevant to your positioning as a junior scholar. After all, you may want or need to contact a particular researcher again, and certainly you might like him or her to remember who you are in a favorable way.

Task Eight

Below is a very professional-looking letter. Read it and answer the questions that follow.

> Dr. J. L. Green
> Complex Systems Institute
> 3034 Ideas Building
> Midwest State University
> Midville, MO 45308
>
> Dear Dr. Green,
>
> Further to our recent exchange of e-mails, may I now confirm the following arrangements.
>
> 1. I have an appointment with you on June 2nd at 10:00 A.M. in your office (Ideas Building 3034).
> 2. I will be arriving on June 1st in the afternoon on Midwest flight 0245 at 3:30 P.M. I will be met by a friend, with whom I will be staying. In case you might need it, my friend's home phone number is 555–5555.
> 3. At your suggestion, I will be bringing the new software program along in order to demonstrate it at an informal "brown bag" at noon on June 2nd.
> 4. I have arranged to leave on June 3rd in the early morning on Midwest Flight 2249. I will be making my own arrangements to get to the airport.
>
> Let me close by saying that I am very grateful for the opportunity to discuss my work and ideas with you. I look forward to meeting you on June 2nd.
>
> Sincerely,
>
> H. J. Park

1. Delete any information that you consider unnecessary and add any information (make up suitable details) that you think should be included.

2. Are there any phrases you particularly like or dislike? What do you think about the style and tone of the communication?

3. Do you think the letter is too "writer oriented" (look at all those *I*s)? Should it be turned more toward the reader?

4. Assume that the visit was successful. What should Ms. Park do by way of a follow-up communication?

(See Note 9.)

7.3 Disclaimers and Apologies

As we saw in Unit Six, acknowledgments are fundamentally concerned with thanking individuals and institutions for *assistance rendered* (note the postposed participle; this is probably a fixed phrase). A very different kind of accounting occurs when it is *we* who have not done something, or not done it right, or might not have it right. One rather specialized occasion for this is the *published disclaimer*. (We deal with this here rather than in Unit Six because these disclaimers seem very rare in dissertation acknowledgments.)

Language Focus: Article Disclaimers

The first element in these consists of the standard language as displayed in the Language Focus in Unit Six.

1. We would like to thank _____ and _____ for their assistance.

2. I am grateful to _____ and _____ for their comments on an earlier draft of this paper.

Typical expressions of the *disclaiming* part of individual acknowledgments are the following.

a. However, any remaining errors are our own.
b. However, they are in no way responsible for any remaining errors.
c. I alone am responsible for the opinions expressed here.

A slightly different formula tends to operate with official sponsors. Again the opening is standard.

3. We gratefully acknowledge the financial support of the _____ Foundation. However, the foundation is not responsible for the opinions expressed here.

4. I am extremely appreciative of this support. However, I am of course ultimately responsible for the writing that has emerged from that research and any views this writing might express.

5. The research for this article was supported under the Educational Research and Development Center Program Grant No. 876/23/99. The findings and opinions expressed in this report do not reflect the position or policies of the Office of Educational Research and Improvement or the United States Department of Education.

(See Note 10.)

Written apologies are typically e-mail messages these days. One very common situation is an apology for a delay in response. These apologies can vary greatly in formality, largely depending on

1. the relationship between the correspondents;
2. the topic of the delayed response;
3. the length of the delay;
4. the reason or excuse for the delay.

Task Nine

Below are six e-mail messages sent to a professor. With a partner, if you have one, mark each one as

FF (very formal), F (quite formal), I (quite informal), II (very informal)

After indicating the level of formality, try to guess the relationship between sender and receiver.

___ 1. I am sorry I have taken so long to get back to you on this. Maybe we could get together for lunch one day. If you could suggest two or three days that work for you, Kathy and I can select one and firm up arrangements.

___ 2. Groveling apologies for being so slow. I've been snowed under with a zillion things. Here, finally is what you wanted.

___ 3. Please accept my apologies about the delay in notifying you concerning your application. At its meeting, the committee learned that the space we had anticipated will not be available for a further year. On the basis of this news, the committee has decided to suspend this first round of competition and reopen it again next year when we have a better picture of resources and space.

___ 4. I am, I know, slow in acknowledging receipt of the items sent by your research assistant. I am at fault for not noticing the time periods on the data before this time. If it isn't too much trouble, I could use your further help by additionally having the data for the six months following.

___ 5. I apologize for being slow to respond to your proposal. This was reviewed by the Evaluation Board. The discussion was pretty rich and complex, and it was, after the meeting, difficult to discern the actual instruction given me in how to respond to you. I have since checked back with the chair, and I now forward her message to you.

___ 6. Please forgive the delay, caused in the first instance by a faulty fax, from which it was difficult to extract your message. So let me confirm that the delay certainly does not signify a lack of interest in your project on my part.

What linguistic cues helped you do the task? (See Note 11.)

7.4 Submission Letters

Let us hope that your previous academic communications have helped you assemble a paper for possible publication. You have selected a journal and now need to write a submission letter (also known as a "cover letter" or a "letter of transmittal") to the editor of that journal.

Remember that a submission letter (SL) is what an editor reads first. While it is very likely that the appropriateness of the SL has no impact on the eventual editorial decision regarding the enclosed paper, first impressions can have lasting effects. It does no harm to make a professional first appearance.

Task Ten

Below are two submission letters. Read them, discuss them with a partner (if possible), and be prepared to comment or offer advice.

Letter A

> Dear Dr. Carduner,
>
> First of all, let me introduce myself to you. My name is _____, Associate Professor of Finance, working at _____ University, a leading institution in my country. I have written several articles on microfinancing, and I would now like to contribute the enclosed paper to your distinguished journal. I hope you will be able to include it in a forthcoming issue. Please make any corrections you think necessary.
>
> I look forward to an early reply,
>
> Sincerely,

Letter B

> Dear Dr. Carduner,
>
> I would like to submit to your journal for possible publication the enclosed paper entitled "Microfinancing in Rural Bangladesh: Causes of Microenterprise Success and Failure." The specific subject of this paper has not been submitted for publication elsewhere; it is based upon research performed for the completion of my Ph.D. thesis.

As per your journal's instructions, I am enclosing three copies of my paper and also include a 50-word biographical statement.

I would be pleased to give you any further information that you might request.

Sincerely yours,

(See Note 12.)

John (1996) analyzed 65 submission letters to a journal he used to co-edit. He found—in his field—that basically 10 topics (or elements) occurred. These were, in alphabetical order, as follows.

1. Address/mail issues. ("As the university mail is unreliable, please use my home address for correspondence.")
2. Advocacy for paper. ("I believe the paper is relevant to readers of your journal because . . . ")
3. Bio-data. ("I am an assistant professor at _____ and obtained my doctorate from _____.")
4. Commentary on paper. ("An earlier version of this paper was presented in May at the _____ Conference.")
5. Editor invited to revise. ("Please make any corrections you think necessary.")
6. Networking. ("It was Professor Hiroke Kobayashi who strongly suggested that I submit this paper to your journal.")
7. No other publication plans. ("The enclosed paper is not being considered by any other journal.")
8. Offer by author to revise. ("I will be happy to make any changes that you or your reviewers might like to suggest.")
9. Request for response. ("I look forward to hearing from you in due course.")
10. Submission. ("Please find enclosed three copies of . . .")

Task Eleven

Which three elements do you think were the most frequent and which three the least frequent? And why? (See Note 13.)

Observations on the Ten Elements

1. Address/mail issues. If you live in a part of the world where the mail is indeed unreliable, it is perfectly appropriate to make suggestions to lessen the problem.

2. Advocacy for paper. This is usually unnecessary, unless the author justifiably feels that, at first sight, the paper might indeed be considered unsuitable for the particular journal.

3. Bio-data. Mention of position, years of experience, number of degrees, and so on is not relevant to the quality of the submitted paper. Therefore, usually there is no good reason to include bio-data. One possible exception might be if this is the author's first attempt at publication in a refereed journal; in this case the SL could mention this in the hopes of attracting the editor's sympathy!

4. Commentary on paper. This kind of commentary can be helpful, but please avoid writing things like: *The submission is Chapter Three of my dissertation.* Shape it first to the requirements of the selected journal.

5. Editor invited to revise. No!

6. Networking. Probably not, unless the person referred to is a member of the editorial board!

7. No other publication plans. Some journals welcome this. If there are any complications about prior or pending publication, the SL should explain this background clearly.

8. Offer by author to revise. SL writers have nothing to gain by offering to revise; in 99 percent of cases this is going to happen anyway!

9. Request for response. This is fine if some neutral phrase like *in due course* is used. Do not use pressure tactics, as in *Expecting a response at your earliest convenience.*

10. Submission. This is essential; it is also very important to include the title of your paper. It is not unknown in editorial offices for the SL to become separated from the manuscript!

Other fields may have other expectations for submission letters. Would you expect to have to say something about any of the following? Use Y (yes) or N (no) to mark your responses.

___ 1. Multiple co-authorship?

___ 2. Page charges? (Especially in science, engineering, and medicine, authors may be expected to pay a substantial sum for each printed page. A typical sum might be $50 dollars a page; however, the current cost for a page containing a color graphic in *Nature* is 500 pounds sterling.)

___ 3. The treatment of human or animal subjects?

___ 4. Illustrations and/or photographs?

___ 5. The use of proprietary (or commercial) material?

Anything else?

Task Twelve

Draft an appropriate submission letter to accompany one of your manuscripts.

7.5 Further Correspondence with Editors

Most journals acknowledge safe receipt of manuscripts within a few days of their arrival. After that, there is likely to be a considerable delay while the manuscript is sent out for review, reviewers' reports are received, and editors ponder their decisions and write their letters or e-mails.

Task Thirteen

How many months is a reasonable time to wait for you? After that time is up, it may be time to contact the editors. Which of the following communications do you prefer and why?

Letter A

> Dear Dr. Green,
>
> Six months ago I submitted my manuscript ("Nutritional Values of Vine-Ripened Tomatoes") to your journal, receipt of which was swiftly acknowledged. Given this considerable time, I am now wondering when you will be in a position to report on this manuscript. I can be most easily contacted at marcosf@puel.telmex.net.
>
> With best wishes,

Letter B

> Dear Dr. Green,
>
> I sent you a manuscript six months ago, and I have been waiting anxiously for your response for the last three months. Since I am currently on the job market, it is very important to me to have as strong a list of publications as possible. Can you do anything to help me in this difficult situation, especially as it would strengthen my job prospects if I were to have an article "forthcoming" in your distinguished journal?
>
> Hoping for an early reply,

(See Note 14.)

Eventually you receive the editor's letter and the reviewers' reports. Here is one such letter, which, unfortunately, is not atypical!

> Dear _____,
>
> Thank you for choosing our journal for your manuscript entitled "Nutritional Values Of Vine-Ripened Tomatoes," and my apologies for being a little slow in responding. As you will see from the enclosed reviews, this has not been exactly an easy case. Reviewer 1 feels that the basic research is adequate but is insufficiently informed by the most recent literature, particularly that coming from Holland. Although this

literature may be difficult for you to access in Mexico, his criticisms are certainly something you should take seriously. Reviewer 2, on the other hand, has no comments to make on the literature but does question certain aspects of your methodology and seems particularly unhappy at your choice of statistical measures. She also feels, however, that the topic is of importance for food science given the considerable public interest (and some increasing skepticism) in this type of commercial tomato production.

My own judgment is that the observations of both reviewers have merit. So this is a case where we are asking you to "revise and resubmit" with no guarantee as yet of final acceptance. It is also my view that there are places where your manuscript could be tightened up, and I have indicated some of these on the returned photocopied pages.

If you are willing to consider this route, it would help if I could receive the revised manuscript by the end of the year, accompanied by a letter that clearly explains how you have responded to the reviewers' comments. And please make sure in your revision that you do not exceed the word limit of 4,000 words.

Yours in Science,

XXXXXX, co-editor

Task Fourteen

Your colleague comes to you with the editor's letter and asks for your advice. Which of the following would you be most likely to say?

Response 1

Look, this isn't going to work. If I were you, I would try to get it published virtually unchanged in our own *College Science Annual Research Report*—what the Americans call working papers. That should be easy, and then you can move on to the next stage of your research.

Response 2

> Well, the reviewers' reports and the editor's comments are pretty standard for this level of journal. They are not as negative as you think. After all, everybody has to revise. Although the two reviewers have different opinions, they are not actually contradictory—which is a big help. I think you should sweat it out and basically do what they want. This would help your career most.

Response 3

> In my opinion, Reviewer 1 is basically unfair. What's this *Gröningen Journal of Commercial Crop Developments*? I have never heard of it. I would suggest you write back to the editor and say that you can do what Reviewer 2 wants but from here in Puebla you can't do much about Reviewer 1's critique, unless the journal can help out with references.

Response 4

> My guess is that the editor is essentially if indirectly telling you to go away. So don't bother with that "revise and resubmit with no guarantee." Instead, take the comments of everybody very seriously, rework your paper as best you can and submit it to *another* journal—a good one but perhaps not quite on the level of your first choice. That way you could turn probable defeat into probable victory.

Response 5

> (Any other suggestions that you might have)

(See Note 15.)

7.6 Notes and Comments for Unit Seven

Note 1

Maier, P. 1992. Politeness strategies in business letters by native and nonnative English speakers. *English for Specific Purposes* 11:189–206.

Chang, Y. Y., and Y. Hsu. 1998. Requests on e-mail: A cross-cultural comparison. *RELC Journal* 29:121–51.

Note 2 (sample responses for Task One)

Our students, colleagues, and ourselves can legitimately disagree about this, but one preferred order is as follows.

1. Message Two. Well-written, clear, professional, easy to implement.

2. Message Three. Easy to say in principle "yes," as nothing seems likely to happen in the immediate future; also good to support new developments in his own field.

3. Message Four. This is a reasonable request. Senior professors should provide this service if they can. There is also the prospect of good contacts.

4. Message One. This does not come across very well. The research area is underdefined; the offer of teaching Italian (presumably for pay) seems a little far fetched. The best course might be to ask for a more specific request.

5. Message Five. Does the writer know Dr. Gardener's work? Why does she ask for everything? And in a rather insistent manner? Is there any way this request can reasonably be met? Send a couple of offprints?

Note 3 (sample responses for Task Two)

	Message One	Message Two	Message Three	Message Four	Message Five
1. Presumed first language of author	Italian	Portuguese	Bahasa Melayu	Cantonese	German
2. Status of requester	researcher	master's student	assistant professor?	head of department	doctoral student
3. Type of help requested	short-term visiting scholar	research literature	consultancy	external examiner	everything!
4. Place in text where main request occurs	second sentence	second sentence	fourth sentence/ middle	first sentence	second half

	Message One	Message Two	Message Three	Message Four	Message Five
5. Phrases you like	none?	*I am wondering if there are similar papers on this topic that you could refer me to or let me have copies of?*	*On Dr. Jones's suggestion, I am asking whether you might be willing . . .*	all?	*I am writing to you on the recommendation of . . .*
6. Phrases you dislike	*. . . in order to get ideas about my thesis.* *Please let me know your answer as soon as possible . . .*	none?	none?	none?	*I am especially interested in your publications, latest experiments and their results.*

Note 4

Kirkpatrick, A. 1991. Information sequencing in Mandarin letters of request. *Anthropological Linguistics* 33:183–203.

Note 5 (sample responses for Language Focus questions)

Remarks by our classes suggest that there may well be general preferences regarding Reasons + Request versus Request + Reasons, with most cultures favoring the former and the latter often being thought to be "American business style." However, we also agree with our participants that "obvious" requests can be presented more directly and that "imposing" requests probably need more preparatory work in nearly all cultures.

Note 6 (sample response for Task Three)

Message Five

First sentence as is. Then:

> I am therefore particularly interested in any recent work you and your colleagues may have done on this kind of fusion at elevated temperatures. Access to any work in this area "in press" would be particularly valuable since I am in the process of fine-tuning my dissertation project. In return I would be happy to send you a copy of a forthcoming paper by Professor Grossman and myself.

Note 7 (sample responses for Task Five)

1. attending / hearing
2. having
3. downloading / plagiarizing
4. increasing / enhancing / protecting
5. relying
6. rewriting / revising

Note 8 (sample responses for Task Six)

Reminder A is written "more in sorrow than in anger." It is polite and tentative and gives the full background. The last sentence provides a kind of "escape clause." It should work pretty well if Professor Wilson is a fairly responsible individual.

Reminder B is even more tentative; really nothing more than a "nudge." Notice that "manage something" may not produce a strong letter, although the "re-sending" is a useful strategy.

Reminder C may well achieve the action required. These indeed are pressure tactics of a high order. But is there a cost? Will Professor Wilson perhaps resent being "bullied" in this way?

Most people opt for Reminder A as the best starting point. Most suggest that the second sentence could be incorporated into the first to make it appear more "congenial" and that something should be said about the time frame. Here is one possible reworking.

```
Dear Professor Wilson,

You may remember that several weeks ago you agreed to write
a recommendation for me in support of my application for a
doctoral fellowship. However, according to the graduate sec-
retary, the department has yet (as of yesterday) to receive
a letter from you, and the deadline is this coming Friday
afternoon. I am wondering therefore if I could remind you
about this? Of course, please ignore this message if you
have already written.
```

One of our class groups came up with a neat alternative solution. They suggested the following for S2 and S3.

```
In my request, I probably forgot to inform you that the
deadline for this letter is this Friday. Anyway, it seems
that the department has yet to receive a letter.
```

Note 9 (sample responses for Task Eight)

1. We don't think we need the information about the flights since Dr. Green and his group will not be involved in travel arrangements. On the other hand, we would anticipate that some advance information about the technical require-ments for the software demonstration might avoid yet another of those tech-nological disasters! And perhaps a reminder about the details of the "software program" would be helpful so that Dr. Green can circulate this information to others. No title for the brown bag? No wish to meet anybody else?

2. We think the language is basically fine. The tone strikes us as "positioning" Ms. Park as somebody who knows what she is doing.

3. We also think, however, that the message is rather "egocentric." Perhaps sentence 1 could be better expressed as

    (1.) Thank you for agreeing to see me in your office on June 2nd at 10:00 A.M.

4. A follow-up message to confirm safe arrival home and pleasure at making professional contact. Plus perhaps an expressed wish to talk with Dr. Green again at some future conference or professional meeting. And let Ms. Park not forget to send anything she promised to send. In our view, successful academics are both generous and committed to following through on any such offers.

Note 10

Perhaps you might like to ask yourself whether you need to offer such a disclaimer. We think you are only *required* to do so if the sponsoring organization has such disclaimers as part of their research contract. Have you seen other phrases that cover this situation in your readings in your field?

Note 11 (sample responses for Task Nine)

Once again there is room for different opinions here, but we think most people might conclude the following.

1. I (a senior colleague, perhaps in another part of the university)
2. II (close academic friend)
3. FF (outsider with a responsible position)
4. I (colleague in the field but not known well?)
5. F (administrator not known to the recipient?)
6. F (a distant colleague?) At a recent session, this last item gave rise to a lively discussion. Some argued that it was really FF, but others said that it only looked like that because it was "so British"—which it is!

Linguistic cues that could help you decide the level of formality include the following: complete sentences or not, first person usage, formal or informal academic vocabulary, slang, contractions or not, imperatives.

Note 12 (sample responses for Task Ten)

Letter A is supposed to represent how *not* to write an SL; Letter B is supposed to represent a model that can be usefully adapted. Most of the points to be made are already covered in the "Observations on the Ten Elements" listing that follows in the text.

Note 13 (sample responses for Task Eleven)

In the applied language studies field, the three elements found most frequently in the 65 SLs and the three elements found least frequently were as follows.

Submission	63
Commentary on paper	30
Request for response	27
Address/mail issues	10
Offer by author to revise	7
Editor invited to revise	5

The first element almost self-selects. The second element doubtless reflects the authors' heavy investment of time and effort in their papers and their wish to say *something* about their enclosed manuscripts. Requests for response are a typical, perhaps formulaic, closure.

The dispreferred elements are somewhat more associated with non-native speakers in this particular study. There are indeed problems with mail in many countries. The revision offers and requests largely reflect the understandable anxieties of academics in particularly isolated situations.

Note 14 (sample responses for Task Thirteen)

The time varies according to journal and, especially, according to field; from two weeks (?) for *Physics Letters* to more than nine months in some humanities journals. Academic clocks move at different speeds in different parts of the academy!

Letter A is clearly superior to Letter B. It is clear, it mentions the title of the paper (see 10 in the "Observations on the Ten Elements" listing in the text), it is not too "pushy," and it makes it easy for the editor to provide a quick update. None of these things are true of Letter B.

Note 15 (sample responses for Task Fourteen)

There are clearly no hard and fast answers here. There is, we believe, merit in all four responses! Response 4 gives rise to an anecdote. As you know, it is part of academic etiquette never to submit the same article to two different journals at the same time. Anyway, the editors of the two best applied linguistics journals once received the same manuscript at about the same time. (They learned this because they sent the manuscripts to the same reviewer, who then contacted them!) The journal editors decided to send a strong letter of complaint to the offending author. However, the author was not at all ashamed of his "crime." He replied, "Well, I never really submitted the article to your two distinguished journals, because I never thought that either of you would accept my article. What I was looking for was your customary excellent reviews, which would then allow me to undertake a thorough revision and which would then allow me to publish my paper in a second-rank journal." But do not try this yourself!

Unit Eight
Academic Communications in Support of a Research Career

"I don't think your vitae looks so bad. I think that writing 5,383 multiple-choice questions is a contribution to the research literature."

The focus of this final unit is on a variety of written genres whose purpose is to conduct the business of the academic community. These genres are primarily designed to get the "right" academic people in the "right" positions. Most we write in support of our own careers—hence the title of this unit. But one group, recommendations, is texts that we write in support of other people. All the texts presented in this unit are typically longer, more formal, and more carefully constructed and revised than those in Unit Seven.

For several of the genres, exemplars are widely available in numerous manuals and on many Web sites. One important exception is the academic recommendation letter, to which we give special attention here. In general, we focus on difficulties and anxieties of particular relevance to nonnative speakers.

As we have seen in Unit One, Section 1.2., and elsewhere, these genres form systems, or networks. In the diagram below, genres in parentheses may not always come into play. The sequence shown below is a "good news" story, or one with a happy ending; naturally and unfortunately for the applicant, this staged process can come to a stop at various points!

Posted Academic Position
↓
Application Package (letter, CV, references, etc.)
↓
(invitation to conference interview)
↓
Invitation to campus
↓
(dry run of job talk)
↓
Campus Visit
↓
Job Offer
↓
(negotiation)
↓
Acceptance

With this in mind, the main topics covered in this unit are the following.

8.1. The Curriculum Vitae

8.2. Fellowship Applications

8.3. Job and Position Applications

8.4. Letters of Recommendation

8.5. Notes and Comments for Unit Eight

8.1 The Curriculum Vitae

A curriculum vitae (CV), Latin for *course of life,* is an account in note form of your education and career. (Note that in British English the abbreviation "c.v." is often used.) Your CV is a "living" document in that it continues to change and grow along with your experiences. Senior researchers may have CVs extending over many pages, while junior researchers will need fewer pages. As with other genres presented in this unit, CVs will exhibit some cultural variation, which you may want to take into account as you prepare or update your vitae or revise it for a specific job application.

Task One

Discuss the following points with a partner (if you have one), assuming a U.S. audience for your CV. Mark the points as follows.

+ = We both agree.
– = We both disagree.
? = We are not sure or we don't agree with each other.

___ 1. A résumé and a CV are the same genre.

___ 2. You should include your date of birth, sex, nationality, and marital status.

___ 3. Your CV should include both your home and departmental addresses.

___ 4. It is best to use reverse chronological order throughout (i.e., put the most recent things first).

___ 5. The longer your CV, the better.

___ 6. Under the section for current education, give the working title of your dissertation and the name of your advisor (if you are at the dissertation writing stage).

___ 7. Provide some information about your high school.

___ 8. List only advanced or special courses you have taken.

___ 9. When describing your teaching experience, highlight the classes for which you had sole responsibility.

___ 10. List computer skills or expertise in using special equipment.

___ 11. List all languages that you know and how well you know them.

___ 12. List submitted or forthcoming articles after the articles that have already been published.

___ 13. The font for your name at the top should not be very much larger than the font of the rest of your CV.

___ 14. You should use capital letters for headings and subheadings.

___ 15. Provide your references at the end of your CV.

___ 16. You should not try to "translate" degrees that have no exact equivalent in the United States (Diplom in Germany, D.E.A in France, M.Phil. in Britain).

(See Note 1.)

Task Two

Here is a typical CV written by an American citizen for a U.S. audience. What do you like and dislike about it? What suggestions might you make to Robin Lee?

Robin S. Lee

Department of Biology
3039 Watson Hall
Central State University
Centerville, OH 12345-6789

e-mail: rsl@morch.emap.edu
URL: http://www.pers.morc.emap.~js/
(555) 555-0000

Education

2000–present	Doctoral candidate in Molecular Biology Central State University, Centerville, OH (Degree expected summer 200X)
1997	MS in Biology Southeastern State University Ithaca, NY Thesis: Protein Folding of Alcohol Dehydrogenase
1995	BS in Biology Eastern State University, Buffalo, NY (GPA 3.7)

Research Experience

Fall 1999–present	Research assistant: DNA isolation from fungal specimens with Dr. R. Anderson
Fall 1998–summer 1999	Research assistant: Electron microscopy of dried mycological specimens. PI, Dr. F. Guzman.
Summer 1996	Field assistant: Southeastern State University Biological Station

Teaching Experience	
Fall 1998	Laboratory instructor for Introductory Biology, Central State University Full teaching responsibilities for one undergraduate section of 18 students
Winter 1997	Teaching assistant for Anatomy and Physiology: Southeastern State University Full teaching responsibilities for one undergraduate section of 26 students
Fall 1997	Lab assistant for Physiology and Development: Southeastern State University Assisted students with weekly lab projects and answered student questions
Publications	F. Guzman and R. S. Lee. *Morchella asci* Ultrastructure. *Mycologia* (in press).
Conference Presentations	
Summer 1996	R. S. Lee and F. Guzman. Ultrastructure of *Morchella asci.* Poster presentation at AIBS, Baltimore, MD.
Honors and Awards	
1997	*Journal of Cell Science* Travel Award
1996	Southeastern State University Research Foundation Fellowship

Task Three

If the writer of this CV wanted to submit it to a university or a research institution in your country, what changes would you recommend? (See Note 2.)

As demonstrated in the CV above, information for a U.S. audience is usually presented in reverse chronological order. However, if your academic and/or employment history has noticeable gaps (which may exist for any number of reasons) you may have more success with a *functional* CV—one that groups your skills and achievements into sections, thus highlighting your skills rather than focusing on specific work titles and dates. For example, you may have subsections that focus on laboratory skills or equipment that you can use, presented in reverse chronological sequence of activities and achievements. (See Note 3.)

Language Focus: Gapping in CVs

As discussed in Unit Three, gapping is the deletion of certain linguistic elements. While gapping is often used to achieve smoothness in different kinds of texts, in a CV gapped phrases may be preferred over full sentences so that information is conveyed using the smallest number of words necessary.

The elements most likely to be gapped in CVs are first person pronouns, auxiliary verbs, articles, relative clause elements, and certain prepositional phrases. Thus, gapped phrases such as the following are common in CVs.

1. Fluent in Mandarin
2. Taught advanced-level calculus
3. Coordinated and implemented research efforts
4. Conducted data analysis
5. Designed Web pages for Introduction to Psychology (1997–99)
6. Duties included maintaining lab equipment
7. Accompanied students on 1998 geology field trip
8. Helped construct interactive database
9. Coded transcripts using Resourcer program
10. Programming expertise (LINOL, Access)
11. Languages spoken: Spanish, English, Portuguese
12. Courses taught: Latin American History, Mexico Today
13. Grants received: 2000–2001, Rivera Grant ($12,000) for archival research

Notice that in the last three cases, the participle follows the subject. This is because the gapped elements include *active* auxiliary verbs and relative clause elements. The full forms would be

11a. Languages that I can speak / have spoken:
12a. Courses that I have taught: . . .
13a. Grants that I have received: . . .

Placing the participle in pre-position could result in some confusion. For instance, a reader might think that *taught courses* (compare to 12 above) are *courses that were taught to you.*

Finally, note that gapping not only reduces the number of words but also makes your CV more readable. The elimination of all those first person references makes the CV appear less "egocentric," and the use of verbs makes your life story more achievement and action oriented. (Compare *Instructor for advanced-level calculus* with *Taught advanced-level calculus*.)

Task Four

Take the following short text that focuses on teaching experience and rewrite it so that it would be suitable for a CV. Be sure to make up a subheading, too.

> My first year (1996) in the Chemistry Department as a beginning grad student I worked in the Chemistry Tutorial Center, a center that provided one-on-one help to students in any Chemistry class. As a tutor I helped students from Introduction to Chemistry (Chem 100) as well as those from senior level Organic Chemistry (Chem 415). I have been a teaching assistant for the Department of Chemistry for the last four years. During that time I have taught a number of courses, including General and Inorganic Chemistry (Chem 125), General Chemistry (Chem 130), and Structure and Reactivity (Chem 210). I have been fully responsible for my own section of 210 each semester for the last year. I have really enjoyed my experiences as a teacher of chemistry and would like to continue teaching after I graduate.

(See Note 4.)

Task Five

Prepare or revise your own CV.

There are always lots of questions about what to include on a CV and how to include it. Here are some about presentations and publications that have occurred in our classes.

Task Six

How would you handle the following (if at all)? Work in pairs if possible.

1. A professor asks you to give a talk based on your research to her class. She asks you to fill the full 50-minute period.

   If you decide to do so, how would you enter it on the CV?

2. The same situation, but this time the professor asks for only a 20-minute talk.

   How might this be entered on the CV, if at all?

3. In the third case, the professor does not ask you to speak about your research but to talk about your academic experiences as a citizen of your home country.

   Does this change of topic affect your decision?

4. The final session of your advanced class is a poster session consisting of posters showcasing everybody's work. Friends and colleagues are also invited to attend.

   Is this a publication? If so, how will you cite it?

5. The 200-word abstract of your conference presentation appears in the glossy conference program.

   Is this another publication? And if so, how will you cite it?

6. Your 200-word abstract, but not your prepared and submitted paper, is published in the conference "proceedings."

   If you suggest including this as a publication, how will you cite it?

7. A 500-word report of the research you presented at a conference appears in the *New York Times*.

   How will you deal with this, if at all?

8. A reporter from the local newspaper visits the lab where you work and includes a summary of your research project in her article.

   How will you deal with this, if at all?

9. You translate one of your published papers into your own language for a journal in your home country. In so doing, you make a few small changes to make it more accessible for your "home market."

Is this a separate publication? What advice would you offer here?

10. You and your advisor produce an annotated list of 40 entries as part of the annual bibliography of your field, which is published every year by a leading journal.

How will you deal with this?

(See Note 5.)

8.2 Fellowship Applications

These days there is a wide range of scholarships, fellowships, and grants available for junior scholars and researchers. Often the application packets are quite specific and thus quite helpful with regard to what should and should not be included in the application. It therefore pays to carefully read the guidelines given. For example, if the instructions state that application letters should be no longer than two double-spaced pages, do not write half a page or three single-spaced pages. Take a look at this invented fellowship announcement and then do Task Seven.

VSHixson

"Here's an interesting letter of application. It says, 'Offer me the tenure track position, and I will bring with me my one-million-dollar research grant.'"

Applications are invited for Miller Fellowships 200X–200Y

Miller Fellowships are available each year to support Asian female graduate students from Turkey to Japan to facilitate field research in Asia. The scholarships award a full six months' support including tuition, travel, living expenses, health insurance, and related research expenses. Up to five scholarships will be offered for the coming year.

Applicants should provide a recent CV, the names of two referees, transcripts, and proof of Asian nationality (such as a photocopy of a valid passport). Applications should also be accompanied by a statement of purpose of no more than 250 words explaining how a Miller Fellowship would contribute to the applicant's further academic development. In this statement applicants must also clearly indicate how their work will further the position of Asian women in their country upon their return home. Applications are due in the Miller Scholarship Offices by December 15. Awards will be announced on February 1.

Task Seven

Your acquaintance from Korea, Ji-Young Kim, is in dire need of financial support to conduct her research. She has written three versions of her statement of purpose for the Miller Fellowship so far. She now needs your advice as to which one to submit and regarding whether the best of the set needs further work. Read through her drafts and decide which would likely be the most successful. What are the strong and weak points of each? What further advice would you give Ji-Young?

Version A

[1]My name is Ji-Young Kim, and I am a beginning second-year female master's student of Korean nationality in the School of Social Work. [2]As you can see from my transcript, my grades for my first year's coursework are very encouraging. [3]This year I really need a Miller Fellowship so that I can go back to Korea to collect data for my thesis. [4]My main area of interest is in gerontology, particularly in long term care provisions for elderly widows. [5]I could base my thesis on United States data and experiences, but both my advisor and I think it would be more useful for me

to collect Korean data, especially since this issue has been little addressed by Korean social work researchers. [6]My own family experience demonstrates how real the problem is. [7]I have two elderly aunts (both now in their 80s and widowed) who live in rural areas quite a long way from their relatives and who are virtual "shut-ins." [8]They are visited by an untrained church volunteer only once a week and by their families only once or twice a year. [9]As demonstrated by my aunts, this is a serious problem, and when I return to Korea I would like to be able to do more for them and for other elderly women in similar situations.

[10]This is why a Miller Fellowship is very important for my future.

Version B

[1]As can be seen from my supporting documentation, I am beginning my second year in the master's program in social work. [2]I plan to complete my degree in July 200Y after I have written and defended my master's thesis. [3]My primary professional interest is in the interface between social work and gerontology, more specifically in the care of elderly women whose husbands have died and who are not cared for by their family members. [4]Recent demographic data show that this at-risk group is growing rapidly in many parts of the world, including Korea. [5]My advisor, Dr. S. Grant, has suggested that, since I plan to return to Korea on completing my degree, it would be advantageous if I could base my thesis on Korean data. [6]Unfortunately, little information is available in this country, which is why I am applying for a Miller Fellowship. [7]If I am successful, I plan to spend three months in Korea in my hometown of Kunsan. [8]There I will interview a stratified sample of 40 elderly widows in order to develop a profile of how well the municipality is coping with this growing problem. [9]Without a Miller Fellowship I will not be able to carry out my plan. [10]Thank you for your consideration.

Version C

[1]Rising life expectancies, especially for women, are creating increasing social problems in many parts of the world. [2]The latest available Korean government census data show that 53% of Korean women in their 80s are either widowed or have never been married; of these nearly 30% are living alone and are rarely visited by their family members. [3]Current Korean social policy toward the elderly is at least partly premised on the

traditional Asian concept of filial piety, i.e., that younger family members will take care of their elderly relatives, but as the above statistics show, this tradition is not as strong as it once was. [4]Discussions with Sally Grant, my advisor, have convinced me that an appropriate topic for my upcoming thesis would be an onsite investigation of the medical, financial, and emotional status of elderly widows in my hometown of Kunsan, Korea. [5]If this investigation works as planned, Dr. Grant and I plan to submit a joint article comparing United States and Korean approaches to this problem. [6]If I am awarded a Miller Fellowship, I plan to carry out the case-study phase of the research from February to April as well as work on preliminary analyses of the findings. [7]I would then return to the university to write up my thesis and then hopefully defend in June. [7]I will then return to Korea and look for a position in the social work field.

(See Note 6.)

Task Eight

Do one of the following.

1. Rewrite Ji-Young's application for her, starting from your preferred version.

2. Prepare your own draft application for a fellowship or scholarship or grant that you might be applying for at some time in the future.

For those of you applying for dissertation fellowships and the like, a particularly helpful Web site is maintained by Harvard University's Graduate School of Arts and Sciences at http://www.gsas.harvard.edu/academic/fellowships/essays.html.

8.3 Job and Position Applications

Most final year Ph.D. students are "on the job market," looking for research positions in industry, postdocs, or academic positions as assistant professors (both tenure track and visiting).

Task Nine

In your field, which of the following would you expect to include in your application for an assistant professor position? (Y = Yes, N = No, ? = perhaps or sometimes.)

__ 1. A single-authored writing sample

__ 2. Samples of co-authored publications

__ 3. A short (half-page) cover letter

__ 4. A long (two-page) job application letter

__ 5. A statement of research interests

__ 6. A statement of your teaching philosophy

__ 7. A syllabus that you have designed

__ 8. A sample lesson plan

__ 9. A transcript (official copy)

__ 10. Copies of Likert-scale teaching evaluations

(See Note 7.)

Task Ten

Below is a sample job application letter for a beginning position at a small liberal arts college. We have numbered the paragraphs for ease of reference. Please read it and answer the questions that follow.

> (home address)
> (date)
> Dr. Mary Gordon
> Chair, Search Committee
> Department of Communication Sciences
> Sylvan College
> Sylvan, NY 22222
>
> Dear Dr. Gordon,
>
> 1. I am writing to apply for the position of Assistant Professor of Psychology, as advertised in the *APA Monitor*. I am currently a doctoral

candidate in psychology at Central State University and plan to defend my dissertation in April or May next year. I am especially interested in this position because my primary teaching interests parallel those described in your advertisement.

2. As you can see from my vitae, I have had considerable teaching experience in a variety of areas. In fact, at this university I have taught courses in three departments: Psychology, Linguistics, and English. Last winter term, I was a teaching assistant for Developmental Psychology (Psych 268). My duties included designing the syllabus and assignments for my discussion sections, leading discussions, grading, and assisting student groups in their joint research projects. In the Department of Linguistics, I was first a TA for the introductory survey course (Linguistics 101), and then last summer I was given an opportunity to design and have full responsibility for a second-level introductory course in psycholinguistics, my principal area of specialization. More than half of the 27 students in this class were elementary school teachers in training and so I gave special attention to child language acquisition. Finally, I have on three occasions taught writing-in-the-curriculum composition courses for the English Department, all three times focusing on writing in the social sciences. This last experience has helped me to rethink the role of writing in social science education and how this connects with ways of developing students' critical thinking and argumentation skills.

3. I therefore believe that I could satisfy your department's teaching needs in a number of areas. Indeed, I would welcome an opportunity to teach introductory courses in developmental and cognitive psychology and other courses in language acquisition, psycholinguistics, and bilingualism. I also believe that my experiences in teaching social science writing and advising students on their projects will be valuable for your team-taught "Research Lab in Communication Sciences."

4. My research interests are described more fully elsewhere, so I will only offer some highlights here. I am primarily interested in what children's conversations tell us about their thinking processes and about their beliefs about other people's thoughts (both children and adults). More specifically, I have focused on 8 to 10 year olds and how they justify, condemn, or explain the actions and behaviors of their peers.

I use experimental techniques for this involving pairs of children watching videotaped episodes of other children's verbal explanations. In my dissertation, this data is then used to construct what we might call a 10 year old's "theory of mind." I argue that how far this "theory" is developed in this age group predicts their level of social adjustment and maturation. As the CV shows, I have already begun to present and publish my work in this area.

5. My future research interests lie in expanding my dissertation in several directions. I am very interested in comparing the verbal justifications of my current research cohort with those of children of kindergarten age. Like many I am also acutely aware that the United States is becoming a more multicultural society, and I therefore want to examine the verbal explanations of bilingual children and whether this group has a more or less evolved "theory of mind" than their monolingual counterparts. These research projects could very easily involve undergraduates who are interested in children's cognitive and linguistic development.

6. I am enclosing a curriculum vitae and a summary of my dissertation for your consideration. I also enclose a separate sheet with the names of four people I have asked to supply letters of reference. If you need further information, I can be most easily reached at (123) 456–7890 or by e-mail (*sandrap@qcsu.edu*). I thank you for your consideration and look forward to hearing from you.

Sincerely,

Sandra J. Pomona

1. Sandra's letter contains the moves (see Unit Two) typical for a cover letter. Can you identify them?

2. What is the pattern of organization that Sandra has chosen for her middle four paragraphs (2–5)?

3. Sandra chose to use her home—rather than her departmental—address for her letter. What are the advantages and disadvantages of this?

4. In paragraph 1 Sandra mentions when she plans to defend her dissertation. Is this important? And if so, why?

5. What do you think about the last sentence in paragraph 2?

6. Highlight any words or phrases that you see as "promoting" or helping to "sell" Sandra.

7. What do you think of the phrase in paragraph 3 *satisfy your department's teaching needs?* What do you think of these alternatives?

   a. I believe I can contribute to your exciting curriculum in a number of ways.
   b. I am confident that I can add to your teaching strength in a number of areas.
   c. I would like to develop your curriculum in a number of areas.

8. In paragraph 4 Sandra is "light" on methodology. Might she have reasons for this? Should she say more?

9. One question often asked about assistant professors is whether there are signs of a coherent research agenda following the Ph.D. How well do you think Sandra has laid these concerns to rest?

10. In paragraph 6 she writes *the names of four people I have asked to supply letters of reference.* In formal English this might well have been *the names of four people* whom *I have asked to supply letters of reference.* Do you think she might be criticized for not using *whom* (bad grammar) or in fact for using it (pretentious and overly formal)?

(See Note 8.)

Task Eleven

Sandra is also applying for two other positions. Position B is an assistant professor of psychology position at a major research university which is well known for its large and influential psychology department. Position C is a postdoc position in an institute for child development. Sandra comes to you and asks, "For Position B can I just send my original letter?

For Position C, can I just leave out the teaching stuff? And, if not, what changes should I make?" What advice would you give Sandra? Write up your advice in the form of an e-mail message. (See Note 9.)

Write a cover letter for a position that you are or might later be interested in. If you do not have a position in mind, go to the employment section of a relevant journal in your field or to the *Chronicle of Higher Education* and find a position to "apply" for.

8.4 Letters of Recommendation

At some point in your academic career you will likely be asked to write a letter of recommendation for a student or colleague, such as for under-graduates or more junior graduates you have worked with. Moreover, in the United States, for instance, graduate students may be asked to write letters for assistant professors in their department being considered for tenure. Letters of recommendation are one of those genres that often bear the stamp of the academic culture in which they were written. Indeed recent research by Precht (see Note 10) on letters of recommendation for a graduate program in law revealed cross-cultural differences in terms of the type of support given, the inclusion of criticism, and the presence of a personal appeal to the reader.

The patterns of organization of the letters in her study varied from chronological to topical, and the type of support ranged from a factual list of achievements to anecdotes about a candidate.

Read through the following letter of recommendation for an undergraduate student applying to a graduate program in art history and answer the questions that follow.

February 24, 200X

To Whom It May Concern

I am pleased to be writing this letter of recommendation for Kristen Matthews, who was one of my students in fall term 200X. While she was my student she was very hard-working, punctual, and well mannered in class. She worked well with others in class and always turned in solid work. Her final project was exceptionally well-designed and creative. She is very honest, mature, and self-motivated. Her outgoing personality made her a pleasure to have in class.

While assisting Ms. Matthews with her papers during my office hours, I really got to know her quite well. As it turns out, she has an excellent background in art, having spent two summers as a docent at the American Museum of Art. As a docent she was responsible for giving tours to small groups, which ranged from children to adults, and demonstrated her ability to discuss art with the novice as well as the more experienced visitor to the museum. Ms. Matthews is also somewhat of an artist herself and has had some of her watercolors displayed in various locations in Ann Arbor. Currently some of her work may be viewed at the University of Michigan Hospitals. Ms. Matthews would like to pursue a career related to art, most likely as an art museum staff member, and therefore graduate school is the logical next step after she graduates. Given her performance in my class I am quite sure she will succeed as she pursues a graduate degree in art history.

Sincerely,

1. What do you think of beginning with *To Whom it May Concern?*

2. Note that the letter writer referred to the applicant as "Ms. Matthews" throughout. Could or should he or she also have used her first name?

3. Is the relationship between the letter writer and Ms. Matthews clear?

4. How well does the letter address concerns of potential interest to the reader?

5. What adjectives are used to describe Ms. Matthews? Are these effective?

6. Is there useful supporting detail?

(See Note 11.)

Language Focus: Positive and Less Positive Language in Recommendations

Take a look at the following list of adjectives and adverbs. Could any of them perhaps carry negative connotations without the addition of supporting evidence?

Place a check mark (✓) next to the adjectives you think an applicant for an academic position (such as yourself) might like to see in a letter of recommendation.

__ articulate	__ creative	__ observant
__ nice	__ imaginative	__ confident
__ dependable	__ satisfactory	__ eager
__ effective	__ assertive	__ adequate
__ pleasant	__ efficient	__ cheerful
__ good	__ innovative	__ cooperative
__ mature	__ steady	__ reasonable

(See Note 12.)

Task Fourteen

Now examine the following pairs of sentences. Put a check mark (✓) next to the one in each pair that in your view makes the stronger statement. If you see no difference put a question mark next to both.

__ 1a. Tatyana worked with us on an image processing project.

__ 1b. Tatyana collaborated with us on an image processing project.

___ 2a. Cristina wrote two papers with members of the group.
___ 2b. Cristina co-authored two papers with members of the group.

___ 3a. Eduard stimulated changes in laboratory procedures.
___ 3b. Eduard suggested changes in laboratory procedures.

___ 4a. Yun made good changes to the calculus curriculum.
___ 4b. Yun revitalized the calculus curriculum.

___ 5a. Ricardo found novel solutions to old problems.
___ 5b. Ricardo implemented novel solutions to old problems.

___ 6a. Soo-Mi participated in discussions of new protocols.
___ 6b. Soo-Mi facilitated discussions of new protocols.

___ 7a. Liam showed a unique ability to learn new concepts.
___ 7b. Liam exhibited a unique ability to learn new concepts.

___ 8a. Viktor coordinated the efforts of his research group.
___ 8b. Viktor was in charge of his research group.

___ 9a. Gustavo is second to none in his ability to interview and take notes.
___ 9b. Gustavo is the best interviewer and notetaker I have seen.

___ 10a. Maya's project turned out to be successful.
___ 10b. Maya's project turned out to be not unsuccessful.

(See Note 13.)

As seen in the recommendation letter in Task Thirteen, a letter that is short on relevant and "winning" details may do very little to help a candidate. More often than not, students in general are described as outstanding, creative, and in the top 20 percent of their class. Thus, in order to distinguish a candidate, it is important to provide examples that demonstrate how a candidate is exemplary or worthy of recognition. Also bear in mind that a vague letter of recommendation—one that is general and lacks specific examples—may be viewed as a relatively weak recommendation, as the reader tries to second-guess why the letter lacks detail. (The writer cannot remember much about the applicant? The writer's experience of the applicant is limited?)

Now notice how the following section from a letter of recommendation provides the detail necessary to really support the candidate. The letter was part of an extensive file for a graduate student being (successfully) nominated for the Outstanding Graduate Student Instructor Award. It was written by a senior faculty member very experienced in writing (and reading) such letters.

> I can more explicitly address Jasmine's teaching abilities by describing her contributions to our Graduate Student Instructor (GSI) Training course last term. First, I should point out that Jasmine was chosen as the program's Graduate Student Mentor this year based on a combination of her breadth of experience with our courses and her highly regarded teaching style. In the past the GSI training course met for one hour per week, but in our meetings before the term, Jasmine suggested that we instead have four 4.5 hour class meetings in order to facilitate interactions and discussions. Throughout, she had an integral role in the course design and execution, and throughout I was delighted with her creativity. For example, Jasmine organized the videotaping of selected discussion sections from Botany courses being taught for use in the seminar. She then developed role-playing office hours or sample homework exercises around appropriate portions of the videotapes. As a specific instance, in one snippet of videotape from a section of "Introduction to Botany" a bright undergraduate student asked an excellent question about hybridization and the identification problems it creates. The discussion leader followed up briefly, but it was clear that the student was not quite satisfied with the answer. The follow-up role play involved the undergraduate (played by Jasmine or me) coming to an office hour of the discussion leader (played by a seminar student) to mercilessly pursue this point. One of Jasmine's greatest inspirations was to have students take a "multi-headed" approach to role playing. For example, in the office hour just described, rather than put a single student on the spot in the role of discussion leader, Jasmine decided to "freeze frame" the office hour, during which time the target seminar student consulted with the other students before unfreezing the scenario and returning to the office hour attendee. This worked beautifully, not only setting the students at ease, but also stimulating creative, thoughtful solutions.

Would you agree that the "telling details" make a big difference?

Task Fifteen

What type of support could be offered to justify the following unsupported statements made in various recommendations. Don't just say "give examples." Be creative and come up with those examples.

1. Desiree has obtained one of the best grade point averages in our program, and she has done magnificent work in the materials laboratory.
2. Throughout her studies, Maria demonstrated good performance in classroom activities as well as in extracurricular activities.
3. Sergei is a very responsible person.
4. Mitsuyo is an excellent communicator.
5. Over the years it has become clear that Antonia is a very motivated student who sets high goals for herself.

(See Note 14.)

These days, especially in the United States, it seems letters of recommendation say little that is negative. However, occasionally you may think it necessary to discuss something negative regarding a candidate, not as a form of criticism but more as a pre-emptive strike. In other words, if you are concerned that the candidate might not make a good impression if interviewed or has something in his or her background that needs explaining, then you may want to discuss this in the letter and offer some explanation.

Task Sixteen

Read through this short section from the final paragraph of a recommendation letter written for a graduate student applying for a junior faculty position. Consider the questions that follow.

> Melissa Jones has an abundance of talent, energy, and knowledge. But let me end by confessing to a small anxiety. I have already said that she can sometimes be "quiet" and "shy" in more social occasions, although at other times she can be vibrant and entertaining. My anxiety is that she can still underperform in an interview or a professional conversation,

especially if she feels (rightly or wrongly) under pressure. I only mention this because any such reticences do not represent Melissa as she really is.

Please let me know if I can be of further assistance.

1. The writer is obviously concerned about the impression the candidate might make and wants to reassure the reader that the candidate is really a good catch. Do you think he dealt with his concerns fairly? Do you think he has helped the candidate?

2. Do you think the end of the letter was the best place to discuss his concerns?

(See Note 15.)

Sometimes we think so highly of a candidate that we write a letter of recommendation that makes the candidate seem too good to be true. If a very strong, positive letter is justified, then it is important to reassure the reader that the candidate is as good as you have described him or her to be.

Task Seventeen

What do you think of the following qualifications that could be included as a form of reassurance to a reader that the candidate is truly outstanding?

1. I know this letter describes a person that seems too good to be true, but I can assure you that Manju is truly exceptional.

2. I realize that this letter is extremely positive and enthusiastic, but in my many years of teaching, I have seen only one other student as outstanding as Anand.

3. I have seen Vadim evolve over the years into a creative, self-motivated researcher who took on a leadership role in our department. My words of praise are well deserved. I can foresee how this young scholar can someday be a major contributor to his chosen area of study.

4. There have been few students for whom I could write such a glowing letter of recommendation. I am pleased to be able to support Marie in her pursuit of a graduate career.

5. Although it is not my custom to write wholly positive and glowing letters, I am making an exception in this remarkable case.

(See Note 16.)

On the Lighter Side: Double Meanings in Recommendations

In the United States these days lawsuits and grievances are quite common. The noted anthropologist Clifford Geertz of Princeton once told the following tale. A factory has a problem. If it is a Japanese company, they hire a hundred engineers to fix it; if it is an American company, they hire a hundred lawyers to fix it. One effect of this has been a "chilling" effect on making negative comments in written reviews, evaluations, and letters of recommendation.

Task Eighteen

As a lighthearted exercise, study the following ambiguous recommendation statements, which from time to time have been circulated on the Web and in other places.

Can you figure out the two meanings, one positive and one negative, that can be attached to each of these?

1. You will be lucky if you can get this person to work for you.
2. I am pleased to say this candidate is a former colleague of mine.
3. I would urge you to waste no time in making this candidate an offer.
4. This candidate is an unbelievable worker.
5. I most enthusiastically recommend this candidate with no qualifications whatsoever.
6. I can assure you that no person would be better for the job.

(See Note 17.)

Here now is a further example of an ambiguous recommendation.

What follows is our modernized version of a famous letter of recommendation written originally in French by the famous French statesman Cardinal Richelieu (1585–1642) to the French ambassador in Rome.

To Whom It May Concern

1. I am writing this letter for Mr. Charles Green,
2. a colleague at this institution,
3. who has asked for one. Mr. Green is the most
4. intelligent, talented and least
5. difficult of all my past and present colleagues.
6. He impresses everybody he meets.
7. I have often written supportive letters for him,
8. because of my high regard for him, not
9. because he has put me under pressure to do so.
10. We would be very sorry to lose him.
11. I think it is my responsibility to suggest to you
12. in your own best long-term interests
13. to pay very serious attention to Charles Green,
14. for then will emerge talent rather than
15. a person unworthy of a senior position with you.
16. I could offer more praise, but
17. I believe I have communicated my true opinion.

Honestly yours,
Eileen Over

Now that you have read the letter, read it again, reading only the odd-numbered lines to reveal the true recommendation. Is this kind of letter possible in your own first language? (See Note 18.)

Joking aside, a letter of recommendation can be viewed as a "legal" document that reflects both you and the applicant. Thus, care needs to be taken when writing them. If you do need to say something negative about the person you are writing about, make sure you back it up with support.

Task Nineteen

Your supervisor has asked you to help him with this draft letter of recommendation for a student applying to graduate school. What advice can you give?

This is the final of more than a hundred "tasks" in *English in Today's Research World*. We hope that by this stage—and after long exposure to our attempts to increase your capacity to reflect upon academic language—you will find the task relatively easy.

Dear selection committee:

In spite of not knowing engineer Dos Santos when he was a student, I have no doubt that he was a real good one. This judgement is made on the basis about the things I've seen. For example his dedication, his responsibility, and the time he expends on his work duties. As a direct supervisor of him, I can say that all the things and work he does, they seem to be done with a lot of quality and I also believe he enjoys it.

About his ability to pursue and complete with success a program of graduate school, in my opinion, engineer Dos Santos has the enough knowledge and **motivation** (let me highlight this word) to carry on advanced study and research successfully.

When I said "motivation," I highlighted that word, because engineer Dos Santos has two permanent job offers of the two main branches of Polygon. Our company has a good fame for well paying; therefore, he is quitting a comfortable future that the most common citizen would like, for going to do his graduate work.

I have heard and also have seen his grades when he was an undergrad. During his career he achieved very good grades in all subjects, and also I realized that he likes to explain and to teach to his workmates.

I am also a materials scientist, and I recognize that he has a very scientific point of view, and I think his favorite topic is the concrete and his components.

Finally I don't have to know him for more time, and I strongly recommend him for all his plans about his graduate studies. Also . . . sorry about my bad English. I hope that this brief letter could give you an idea of the candidate and his goals.

With no more comments for this time and you can contact me for further information.

Your friend,

Finally, good luck with your academic or research career! And if you have comments, suggestions, or criticisms, we would be glad to receive them at jmswales@umich.edu or cfeak@umich.edu. We are always interested in improving our materials.

8.5 Notes and Comments for Unit Eight

Note 1 (sample responses for Task One)

1. A résumé (pronounced "resumay") is usually a very short vitae (sometimes only one page) with an opening that describes the position sought or the writer's career objective.

2. Not in the United States. In fact, employers in the United States are not permitted by law to ask for such information.

3. Your choice here, we think. A home address can certainly help in the later stages of job searches.

4. Probably reverse chronology is best, but see Note 3.

5. Unnecessary "padding" will do you no good. It's quality, not quantity, that counts. On the other hand, you want to present yourself in your full glory! Graduate master's students should aim for a CV of at least two pages and Ph.D. candidates for ones covering three to five pages.

6. Yes, both of these can be helpful. On the matter of mentioning the advisor, many of our participants point out that this may depend on how well known the advisor happens to be.

7. Probably not

8. Probably this is a good idea, at least in some fields.

9. Yes

10. Yes, if relevant

11. Certainly in some fields this can be very helpful.

12. Certainly list all forthcoming articles. If you already have several publica-

tions, put them at the end. If only one or two, you may consider putting them first. If your published list is rather thin, you may want to add "articles in preparation."

13. Yes, you don't want to shout your name out too loudly. Slightly larger font and bold?

14. This may depend on the format you choose, but it may be better to use bolded lower case. Look for good samples from others in your department.

15. This depends on whether you include them in your application letter, but they're often found at the end.

16. This is a tricky one. If you think the people whom you are hoping to work with will be able to interpret them, probably not. If not, you could try to translate them or provide a translation in your cover letter. But remember that attempts at explanation might be offensive to members of search committees who already know about degrees from your country; such members might believe that you are assuming that they will be ignorant!

Note 2 (sample responses for Task Three)

Obviously, we can offer only observations here. We note that *Robin* could be either a man or a woman and that there is no information about nationality, age, or marital status (which some countries require by law). *U.S.A.* should be added to the address, we presume. *Teaching assistant* might need explaining. As Robin is applying for an overseas position, we would think travel experiences and languages would also be helpful. Headings should be made more prominent, and maybe a list of references should be added.

Note 3 (sample functional CV)

The downside of a functional CV is that it can be much harder to prepare than a traditional CV and may be less familiar to your audience. Indeed functional CVs are not as common. Even so, if you have changed fields, have dropped out of academia, or have had a patchwork of academic experiences, this organizational approach may be right for you.

Here is a simple example.

Education

Over the last 15 years, I have obtained an MA in art history from San Diego State University and a Certificate in Restoration from UC—Riverside and plan to finish my current MA in museum practice in the next few months. My undergraduate major was in cultural history.

Note 4 (sample response for Task Four)

There are several options. Here is one.

> *Teaching Experience*
>
> 2001–2002   Teaching assistant for Structure and Reactivity (Chem 210)
>   Full responsibility for syllabus, assignments, etc., in my section
> 1997–2001   Teaching assistant for General and Inorganic Chemistry (Chem 125 and Chem 130)
>   Discussion section instructor and grader
> 1996–1997   Tutor in Chemistry Tutorial Center

Note 5 (sample responses for Task Six)

1. A majority of our informants believe that this should be entered under "Guest Lectures."

2. The length does not matter very much; the same solution as above.

3. Responses are very mixed here: some argue that such a guest lecture should be included; others argue against this because it doesn't deal with the speaker's research. Perhaps the response should depend on the type of position being considered.

4. The majority opinion seems to be that this activity should not be counted as a publication.

5. Not a publication; only cite the presentation.

6. Yes, this is a publication, but make sure that you also mention that it is an abstract; otherwise it will look like a one-page paper—which is worse!

7. After you list your presentation, mention the details of the newspaper report.

8. How about something in "Honors, Awards, etc.," like

   > The research project on . . . was included in a discussion on the research lab published in the A . . . News on 12/14/200X.

9. Not a separate publication. After the citation, mention that a translation in such-and-such a journal appeared.

10. Perhaps something like contributor to the *Annual Bibliography 2000 (Journal Title)* 43:342–454.

Note 6 (sample responses for Task Seven)

Task Seven is a complex and difficult assignment, not least because each version has its strengths and weaknesses.

Version A certainly makes the most direct appeal to the selection committee, invoking some direct personal experience and stressing her "need" for the scholarship; the draft seems very narrowly centered on the writer. (Bhatia [1993] discusses how job applications in the subcontinent appeal to "pity." See V. K. Bhatia, *Analysing Genre* [London: Longman, 1993].) Ji-Young also seems committed to helping Asian women, but the broader implications of her work are not clear. The research project seems underdescribed, and the mention of good grades is probably unnecessary. One participant quickly dismissed this version as a begging letter.

Version B seems much more professional in both style and substance. The rationale for the research project is adequately described and the reference to the advisor is helpful. Sufficient detail is included about the fieldwork. However, there is no mention of Ji-Young's postgraduation plans, and this will almost certainly lower her rating with the selection committee. The last two sentences add little to her case. Notice that this version (like Version A) begins with statements about the applicant.

Version C goes further than B in providing the theoretical background to her master's project, revealing that she has likely already done some work on her topic. Notice that this version is the only one to forefront the research at the outset. And Ji-Young, in the middle of her application, is able to suggest a close working relationship with her advisor (which A and B largely failed to do). The timescale in S6 also adds credibility. If there is a weakness, it is Ji-Young's vagueness about her future plans (*a position in the social work field*).

We would advise Ji-Young to revise, using Version C as the starting text and trying to say something more concrete about her plans when she returns home.

Note 7 (sample responses for Task Nine)

This will depend on the type of institution being applied to, ranging from a major research university to a community college. Even so, in general

1. Probably

2. Less probably

3. No. A half page is not sufficient.

4. Yes

5. This is probably needed at research institutions; it may do you harm at teaching institutions.

6. If required

7. Only for positions at small teaching colleges

8. The same as above

9. Yes

10. Only if requested

Note 8 (sample responses for Task Ten)

1. In this case, we can easily align a move with each paragraph.

   1. Brief introduction of self
   2. Teaching qualifications and experience
   3. Demonstration of a good teaching "match"
   4. Brief account of research interests
   5. Future research interests and how they are a good "match"
   6. Enclosures / references / contact information

2. Teaching past and present → teaching future → research present → research future

3. Has she distanced herself from her department? Does she want to keep her applications confidential? As a dissertation writer, she spends most of her time at home? By using her home address she can keep her applications secret. If she spends a lot of time writing at home she does not have to worry about checking her mailbox in her department.

4. At the beginning of the academic year, new assistant professors are expected to have their dissertations "in hand," that is, defended, revised, and approved.

5. An excellent point, we think.

6. Sandra is in fact quite discreet about her strengths and is clearly at pains not to write anything that might give an impression of "boasting." Mildly then in paragraph 1 she notes that her teaching interests are *parallel.* In 2 she notes that she has had *considerable teaching experience* and later that *on three occasions* she has been involved in a particular type of teaching. In 3 she just mentions that certain experiences *will be valuable,* and in 5 she mentions that some research projects *could very easily involve undergraduates.*

7. The original is once again rather modest. Alternatives a and b are a little stronger; however, alternative a might in fact come off as insincere; c is too strong a claim and may cause offense. b might work the best.

8. Yes, Sandra does not make very much of her research methodology. If she had been applying to a psychology department, she would probably have written quite a lot more.

9. We think Sandra has done well on this in her initial application.

10. You never know with search committees! However, the *who / whom* distinction seems to be made less and less frequently these days.

Note 9 (not answered in e-mail form) (sample response for Task Eleven)

For Position B, we clearly need a stronger orientation toward her research; for C presumably she should emphasize her considerable experience of working with children as her research subjects.

Note 10

Precht, K. 1998. A cross-cultural comparison of letters of recommendation. *English for Specific Purposes* 17:241–65.

Note 11 (sample responses for Task Thirteen)

1. This adds nothing and additionally makes the recipient think that this recommendation is one of those "one size fits all" kinds of letters.

2. Yes, there should be some variety, particularly since the letter writer states that she knows the candidate well.

3. Not very; and is the statement *While assisting Ms. Matthews with her papers* helpful, considering this student is applying to a graduate program?

4. Considering that the intended readership is a graduate applications committee, the letter fails to say very much about Ms. Matthews' academic strengths and interests.

5. The adjectives describe her personal attributes rather than her intellectual ones.

6. The detail in the second paragraph is misplaced since Ms. Matthews is applying for a degree in art history, not for one in art itself.

All in all, this is not a very good letter, and you can certainly do better.

Note 12 (sample responses to Language Focus on recommendations)

We would not mind being described by our recommenders as *articulate, effective, creative, imaginative, confident, efficient, innovative,* and *reasonable.* We would be happy to "pass" on most of the others.

Note 13 (answer key for Task Fourteen)

 1. ??
 2. b
 3. a
 4. b
 5. a
 6. b
 7. ??
 8. a or ??
 9. a
10. a

Note 14 (sample response for Task Fifteen)

We only give one example.

3. Sergei is a very responsible person. To cite just a single example, when we had an accident in the lab last year, it was Sergei who responded first by calling for assistance and administering first aid.

Note 15 (sample responses for Task Sixteen)

1. There is room for disagreement on this tactic. If Melissa turns out to "under-perform" in interviews, then these comments may be helpful to her. On the other hand, if she performs well, these comments may undermine Melissa's chances by suggesting that she behaved "out of character" on her campus visit. One thing is for sure, the letter writer has not considered that Melissa could rise to the occasion and do a great job. There are risks here.

2. Yes, at the end or in a postscript. But keep in mind that since this negative comment is read last it may cloud all the other positive things said earlier.

Note 16 (sample response for Task Seventeen)

We believe that this strategy can be used, but only in truly exceptional cases. One famous professor in the United States is known for saying of nearly all his graduate students that "X is the best student he has ever had." Faculty at other universities who know this tend to disregard his letters.

Note 17 (sample responses for part one of Task Eighteen)

1. Positive   This person is so well qualified that you will be lucky to be able to hire him or her.

   Negative   This person is so lazy that you'll be lucky to get any work out of him or her.

2. Positive   It was a pleasure to have had an opportunity to work with this exceptional individual.

   Negative   I am pleased to say that this person no longer works with me.

3. Positive   I urge you to make this candidate an offer as soon as possible because many others will be wanting to hire this person.

   Negative   Do not waste any time on making this weak candidate an offer.

4. Positive   This candidate is such a good worker that it is hard to believe.

   Negative   This candidate does so little work that it is unbelievable.
   Or:
   This candidate is untruthful.

5. Positive   Without a doubt I fully recommend this candidate.

   Negative   This candidate lacks qualifications or skills.

6. Positive   This is the best person for the job.

   Negative   Hiring nobody would be better than hiring this candidate.

Note 18 (sample response for part two of Task Eighteen)

> To Whom It May Concern
>
> 1. I am writing this letter for Mr. Charles Green,
> 3. who has asked for one. Mr. Green is the most
> 5. difficult of all my past and present colleagues.
> 7. I have often written supportive letters for him,
> 9. because he has put me under pressure to do so.
> 11. I think it is my responsibility to suggest to you
> 13. to pay very serious attention to Charles Green,
> 15. a person unworthy of a senior position with you.
> 17. I believe I have communicated my true opinion.
>
> Honestly yours,
>
> Eileen Over

Our Chinese participants, for example, say that there is a long history of such letters in China, such as those in which the "true story" is contained in the first characters of sentences.

Index

There are many names in this book, especially in sample texts that contain citations. We have indexed only the names of researchers and scholars whose observations on research English or on other relevant discourses have contributed to the conceptualization of this volume.